D1593913

Death,
Property,
and
Lawyers

Thomas L. Shaffer

Death,
Property,
and
Lawyers

A Behavioral Approach

DUNELLEN

© 1970 by the Dunellen Publishing Company, Inc.
145 East 52nd Street
New York, New York 10022

International Standard Book Number 0-8424-0021-4.

Library of Congress Catalogue Card Number 72-132980.

Printed in the United States of America.

for Nancy and
the olive plants

Acknowledgments

Chapter 1 is based in part on my article "The Psychology of Testation," 108 *Trusts and Estates* 11 (1969), which is used with permission of the publisher: Copyright 1969, Fiduciary Publishers, Inc., 132 West 31st St., New York, New York 10001

Chapter 3 contains as an appendix a survey developed by Dr. Edwin S. Shneidman, which is used with his permission.

Chapter 4 is a rewritten version of my article "The Estate Planning Counselor and Values Destroyed by Death," 55 *Iowa Law Review* 376 (1969), which is used with the permission of the publisher and copyright holder.

Chapter 5 is a rewritten version of my article "Will Interviews, Young Family Clients, and the Psychology of Testation," 44 *Notre Dame Lawyer* 345 (1969), which is used with permission of the publisher and copyright holder.

Chapter 6 is a rewritten version of my article "Psychological Autopsies in Judicial Opinions Under Section 2035," 3 *Loyola University of Los Angeles Law Review* 1 (1970), which is used with permission of the publisher and copyright holder.

Chapter 7 is a rewritten version of my article "Undue Influence, Confidential Relationship, and the Psychology of Transference," 45 *Notre Dame Lawyer* 197 (1970), which is used here with permission of the publisher and copyright holder. The chapter contains quotations from *The Psychiatrist and the Dying Patient,* by Dr. K. R. Eissler, Copyright 1955, International Universities Press, Inc., 239 Park Avenue South, New York, New York 10003, which are used with permission of the publisher.

Contents

1 Introduction

Let's talk of graves, of worms, and epitaphs
Make dust our paper and with rainy eyes
Write sorrow on the bosom of the earth.
Let's choose executors and talk of wills. . . .

Richard II

Shakespeare's morbid monarch and a talk of estate planning I heard several years ago illustrate the purpose of this curious book.

King Richard has a fine layman's appreciation for the fact that the will-making experience is a *memento mori* as well as a routine law-office transaction. It is a mood we lawyers overlook, and it might somehow justify a book on psychology by a mountain-grown Hoosier law professor.

The estate-planning expert did not appreciate King Richard's mood either. He made a remark about client investments which has become a motivating irony for me: "Pity the poor fella," he said, "who happens to die at the top of the market."

Lawyers who deal with wills and so forth probably make a mistake when they let themselves be called estate planners. It is a fawning phrase, a piece of flattery for a man who is supposed to feel better when his mortgage and pension plan are called an estate. I agree with Joseph Trachtman that "estate planner" is a poor substitute for the ancient and honorable title "lawyer." There is deeper harm, too, beyond self-delusion—the harm that leaves us obsessed with manipulation and taxes, the professional fixation which diverts our observation

1

from the here-and-now feelings of the men and women who consider death in the law office. We have tended to suppress our own empathic instinct for the confusion and concern involved in "planning estates," and part of the reason, I think, is that we have let ourselves be duped by public relations when we should have been deepening our human relations.

Our clients are not as interested in taxes as we suppose them to be. Or, to put that idea positively, they are more interested in values and identifications in their property which are not taxable, and in the people they love. My empirical disappointment in attempts to impress my clients with lucid prose convinces me that they are even less interested in our draftsmanship or in the hopeless rhetoric a secretary or a magic, fingerless typewriter will compose for their signatures. Our clients' thoughts and emotions are on deeper, more puzzling realities than taxation or legal rhetoric. Maybe they tend, at least in their hidden selves, to something like King Richard's sense of doom. The chance that they might is worth a passing look by our profession, and by psychologists. But aside from a recent study of motivation for life insurance (Briggs)* I have not found even one systematic consideration of the subject in either profession's literature.

Psychology is now, finally, interested in attitudes toward death, but this new thanatology has yet to broaden its concern to the law office. The pioneer work in the field, edited by Dr. Herman Feifel, contains only one or two passing references to wills and law offices. Parallel sociological anthologies, notably Professor Fulton's collection of 1965, show even less concern about law as behaviorally significant. Psychologists and sociologists probably don't know much about wills clients. Practicing lawyers, on the other hand, know a great deal—more than they reflect upon—about will-making, but most lawyers are not sophisticated in psychology. Many lawyers, in fact, avoid introspection and observation about affect in the lives of their clients; they are not only unsophisticated, they are also callous. Lawyers show curiosity about psychology when they need expert testimony in criminal-responsibility, personal-injury, and will-contest cases (and not nearly enough even then), but they otherwise take their psychology, if at all, from around a cracker barrel.

Too many of us "counselors at law" tend to regard wills clients—and

---

*For complete citations to references in the text and in the chapter notes, please consult the Table of References.

I think most wills clients tend to regard themselves—as seekers of black magic, anxious to pay as little as possible for a sheaf of paper they will never read and a funereal ritual they won't understand. These negative thoughts may explain why I find that the psychology of testation is therefore, for the present, something for us law professors. But if it has any value, it should not remain the concern only of law professors. Lawyers should be able to realize that the lawyer-client relationship, in a testamentary context, is an opportunity for human counseling. There is more involved than legal counseling; we will-drafters are dealing with the complexities of love and will and death and ownership. Our learning should reflect more of the wholeness celebrated by Mr. Gerhart, in the *American Bar Association Journal,* years ago:

> The old family doctor knew he was treating a whole man. The legal general practitioner can do the same—treat the whole client, especially in the important family aspects of estate planning. *** If he is living up to the ideals of our great profession, he is, after all, a wise counsellor.

I have organized this book on a tentative classification of the contents of a psychology of testation. There are not separate phenomena in the lives of real people, but I think that these behavioral points of focus are usually present in wills clients and that the legal counseling they seek from us involves these things and the relationships between them.

First, the wills client, like King Richard, is probably thinking about death. My observation is that he is not terribly willing to talk very much about death. His lawyer is even less willing to talk about it; both parties will probably confine the necessary discussion of death to a bare minimum and surround it with euphemism. But death, after all, is the biological center of the professional service involved. The focus of testation is the question of what is to be done with property when its owner no longer needs it; and there are two kinds of men who don't need their property: those who are gone and did not take it with them, and those who expect to leave it behind. The first part of a tentative law-professor's psychology of testation should therefore be an inquiry into attitudes toward death.

Second, the client is thinking about his property. Thoughts about property are tangled and esoteric and may, in turn, have a number of different focuses. Thoughts of property in an acquisitive man, the sort of man Freudians think of as retentive, may center in some idea of wealth. They may involve something as relatively straightforward as an

3

adding machine tape based on the latest *Wall Street Journal.* I have not met many men who stood in such simple relationship to their property, or, to put it most accurately, I doubt that anyone stands in a pure wealth relationship to all of his property.

The wills client may be thinking about his projects, as well as or instead of his wealth. For instance, the client's property focus for the moment may be his family business, which is something more to him than ledger entries or valuations. In either of these situations—but in the second more than the first—the client's property is part of what the metaphysician Martin Heidegger called the *Eigenwelt;* it is an extension of himself and at the same time outside of himself. Property is part of the way he defines himself; it is probably part of the way he will define his death and his attitude toward death. Consider some sort of tangential evidence for that proposition: the creative sociologist Erving Goffman noticed, for example, that it is relatively easy to manage a man who is stripped of all his possessions. When that happens to him, there is less man left behind. This is from Goffman's study of asylums:

> The personal possessions of an individual are an important part of the materials out of which he builds a self, but as an inmate the ease with which he can be managed by staff is likely to increase with the degree to which he is dispossessed. The remarkable efficiency with which a mental hospital ward can adjust to a daily shift in number of resident patients is related to the fact that the comers and leavers do not come or leave with any properties but themselves and do not have any right to choose where they will be located.

Goffman enlarges on the idea by showing how inmates "illegally" develop places to keep what few possessions they accumulate. This is the theory of the "stash," which forms an important part of the way he explains the "secondary adjustment" of people in "total institutions"; the stash is essentially a matter of having property despite the rules against it. The same thought was expressed by Gresham Sykes, a student of prison societies:

> In modern Western culture, material possessions are so large a part of the individual's conception of himself that to be stripped of them is to be attacked at the deepest layers of personality.

One psychological way to explain Goffman's observation and to explain how our clients may feel about their property can be borrowed from

Karl Menninger and Edwin Shneidman, therapists who have been especially concerned with the psychopathology of suicide. It is possible that Goffman's mental patient, cowed by his utter lack of possessions, is already partially dead. Something of his very self has been taken away from him. A similar but milder situation is illustrated by the appropriation of property personality. Dr. Van Den Berg's chatty little book about the bedridden includes the thought that a man who surrenders his street clothes for pajamas and bedsheets has lost something of himself. He feels like the victim of some inhuman invasion. It is like finding out that our possessions are less unique than we thought they were: "We are not really pleased to find another man wearing the same tie; it seems as if we meet an attribute of ourselves which he has unlawfully appropriated."

The third factor in a psychology of testation is the client's attitude toward giving, which I think expresses a relationship between the people he loves and the things—wealth or projects—he owns. This relationship, in the testamentary experience, is temporarily focused on the part of a man's life which comes after his death. One can sometimes usefully regard the property relationship involved in giving as a tangible extension of an attitude toward persons, in which property is partly a symbol and partly a personal extension of (or toward) someone else. I might treat your dog or your automobile or even your child as I would treat you or would like to treat you. The founder of psychoanalysis devoted a book to this phenomenon, and many of his case studies suggest a sort of property personality. Here is an example from a patient, reported in Sigmund Freud's *Psychopathology of Everyday Life:*

'Several years ago there were some misunderstandings between me and my wife. I found her too cold, and though I fully appreciated her excellent qualities, we lived together without evincing any tenderness for each other. One day on her return from a walk she gave me a book which she had bought because she thought it would interest me. I thanked her for this mark of "attention," promised to read the book, put it away, and did not find it again. So months passed, during which I occasionally remembered the lost book, and also tried in vain to find it.

'About six months later my beloved mother, who was not living with us, became ill. My wife left home to nurse her mother-in-law. The patient's condition became serious and gave my wife the opportunity to show the best side of herself. One evening I returned home full of enthusiasm over what my wife had accomplished, and felt very grateful to her. I stepped to my desk and, without definite intention but with a certainty of a somnambulist, I opened a certain drawer, and in the very top of it I found the long missing mislaid book.'

This idea is useful, I think, but it is too modest to regard property as only symbolic of personality. There is more than symbol in the patients and prisoners described by Goffman and Sykes. Property is often involved more deeply in the personality of the human being who owns it, and he in its "personality." I was struck by this possibility when I read recently Nancy Hale's nostalgic recollection of her childhood with eccentric parents. This is the way she felt about being in her father's studio after his death.

> A place just quitted by someone beloved does not merely speak of the person. It is the person. The scent of my father's presence was in the air, and I felt in precisely the same relationship with that air as I had with him.

Houses are like that; they are potent pieces of property personality, a point to which I will return in Chapter 6. Jung's autobiography, *Memories, Dreams, Reflections,* reaches something of a climax when he constructs his eccentric home on Lake Zurich. Even Emily Post, writing on interior decoration, entitled her book *The Personality of a House.*

A more puzzling instance of property personality is suggested in the anthropology of funeral rites, especially in the curious things we human beings do with corpses. Primitive cultures, as well as our own, apparently regard the corpse as part of the dead man's property. Primitive people, and many of us who are more civilized, are also afraid of corpses. The dead body is a potent, fearful thing in which the dead man still resides, in which he is slowly dying, and with which he draws his loved ones close and imprisons them until the process of dying (which ends in decay) is over. This is true not only of houses and corpses but also of a dead man's personal possessions. Goody reports that the LoDagaa of Western Africa will not touch a dead hunter's quiver or a dead housewife's calabash until after the funeral ceremonies, which assimilate the dead man to his ancestors, are over; in that tribe and among non-African primitives, the dead man's most personal possessions are never distributed to near relatives; and they must, through ritual and custom, be freed of his influence before they can be distributed to anyone. Mandelbaum found one American Indian group in which there is no accumulation or inheritance of wealth because no one will accept or use anything which belonged to a dead man. (He noted a modern erosion of principle, a small area of modern compromise which allows the dead man's relatives to trade in his automobile; thus is laid, I suppose, the cornerstone of capitalism: the distinction between property-project and wealth.)

The anthropology of *inter vivos* gifts suggests several other aspects of property personality, most notably the idea that a man's property is part of his person, a part that remains with the property, especially when the property is given away. Goffman reports elaborate gift rituals in American mental hospitals. Mauss found that the Maori refer to the thing given and to the spirit of the thing given; the latter, which is clearly part of the giver himself, creates a bond and an obligation and a presence. It compels an awe and a system of duties not present in bargained-for exchanges or in the acquisition of property from nature:

> To give something is to give a part of oneself. . . . One gives away what is in reality a part of one's nature and substance, while to receive something is to receive a part of someone's spiritual essence. . . . Whatever it is, food, possessions, women, children or ritual, it retains a magical religious hold over the recipient. The thing given is not inert. It is alive and often personified. . . .

As societies become more cosmopolitan and more commercial, this rendition-of-the-person feeling about property transfer has to be either confined or eliminated. It would obviously impede economic growth. Most societies appear to have purged themselves of personal extensions in property sold, but there are some interesting remnants: There has been until recently, and may still be, a provincial French ritual for separating a cow from the spirit of its vendor. Mauss's account of it adds charming anthropological color to every law student's favorite cow case, *Sherwood v. Walker,* celebrated in Dean Prosser's raucous lyric as the Rose of Aberlone.

Giving expresses love or, at least, respect or fealty among the relatively healthy. Among the neurotic, giving may consume love, so that the person who loves must constantly give. The early psychoanalyst Ernest Jones notes that "both from the psychological and physiological bases of love, the greater part of all love-life is modelled on the prototype of giving and receiving," a process which extends even to the type of love in which "people are always making presents, they woo their mate by only one method of making themselves agreeable." We are not all neurotics; however, most of us give, not merely gifts, but with them something of our selves. The psychoanalytic basis for that is the infantile experience of toilet training, which is the person's first experience of property—something both of himself and outside himself and something which he gives in response to or in request for his mother's love. So there is nothing unusually pathological about the milder forms of love as giving. Even psychiatrists, as part of fostering a positive rapport with certain patients, have suggested gifts from doctor to patient. Dr. Karl Eissler, to whom I will return in Chapter 7, has made of gift-giving a therapeutic ritual in dealing with the dying. His patients accept gifts as confirming a "transference" (parental) relationship. He encourages their feelings, which is a way of saying, it seems to me, "Yes, I am willing to be your father, and here is something to prove it, because everyone knows that fathers who love their children give them things."

This relationship with property and with giving, either because of love or because of conventional circumstances which are supposed to suggest love, is capable of a focus on death and on the part of a man that will continue after his death. In Louis Auchincloss' short story "The Ambassador From Wall Street," (in *Powers of Attorney*) a lawyer and his client conceive of the client's real property as a permanence, a perpetuity which will outlive—and through which the client will outlive—everything but nature itself:

> He seemed to hurl an articulate challenge into the astonished face of eternity, shouting that the rights and prerogative of Miss Johanna Shepard were more than transiently enforceable squatter's claim of a withered old maid to a bit of top soil on the Atlantic Coast, that they were, on the contrary, fixed and eternal and had their place—their important place—with the mountains and forests and the tossing sea.

As the story turns out, not only her property but even her giving of it will outlive her. She seems to typify one of Jean-Paul Sartre's metaphysical observations about property:*

> To the extent that I appear to myself as creating objects by the sole relation of appropriation these objects are myself. The totality of my possessions reflects the totality of my being. I am what I have.

---

*Sartre's observations about property appear in *Being and Nothingness* and in two chapters published separately as *Existential Psychoanalysis*.

Owning and giving, and maybe even loving, are not as subject to mortality as breathing is. This is the commonest of human facts in the estate-planning practice. Lawyers who reflect on their will interviews realize how often they encounter property as immortal personality, how often clients make wills as a socially acceptable attempt to frustrate or at least to manipulate the grim reaper. It may help to consider that fact in a bizarre testamentary context, a relatively clinical context. Here is one of the suicide notes analyzed by Shneidman and Farberow (*Genuine and Simulated Suicide Notes*):

> My dearest family: I am terribly sick and it is all my fault. I blame no one but myself. I know it is going to go hard with Tommy and Sister. Please see that Tommy gets a Mickey Mouse Watch for his birthday. Helen I am counting on you to take care of Mother. Please do not follow in my footsteps.
> Mary my darling I know you did everything possible to avoid this, but please forgive me, as I think it was the only way out. God forgive me and help take care of my family.

This man's concern is the use of his property to give an expression of love; the care of his family; the grief of his daughter—all focused on his real and imminent self-destruction, all on the things and the lives which will be in his environment when he is no longer part of it.

These seem to me self-evident points, each of them inviting further research and explication. I was somewhat surprised, therefore, when I found that no one has bothered to consider in print the possibility that wills clients are people, complex people, worthy of behavioral examination in their personal relationships with their lawyers. I have come to share some of E.M. Forster's frustration at how little people seem to be concerned about themselves:

> Man is an odd, sad creature as yet, intent on pilfering the earth, and heedless of the growths within himself. He cannot be bored about psychology. He leaves it to the specialist, which is as if he should leave his dinner to be eaten by a steam-engine. He cannot be bothered to digest his own soul.

I believe that the relationship between client and lawyer, in the testamentary context, is worthy of detailed behavioral study. This book contains some preliminary work on it, with survey and observation research and with encouragement from "death" psychologists and from some of my brothers at the Bar. If there is any validity to my

9

aspiration, the possibilities are fascinating. If lawyers were willing to give behavioral researchers access to the will-preparation conference, for instance, an immense amount of what the social scientists call participant-observation could be fruitfully carried out. If they were willing to cooperate in encouraging clients to expose themselves even more fully to research, surveys, and experiments, new and useful information for both professions would turn up. In other recent death studies, psychologists have used to good effect complex batteries of tests, including story construction from pictures, word completion, skin response, personality inventories of various kinds, sentence completion, and samples of other devices they have developed for finding and measuring the growths within a man.

Most of these devices probably require very specialized control; some few of them may safely be trusted to lawyers, though. In any event, I suspect that the human insights into the relationship which lawyers can bring to the enterprise guarantee to those of us who are interested in it some important place in finally formulating a psychology of testation.

What about the objection that there are only two kinds of estate-planning clients anyway—the rich, who only want to save taxes, and the not-so-rich, whose problems are not worth the time of lawyers because they won't pay their way in fees? Assuming the validity of that simple-minded division of the human race, it seems to me there is an answer at both levels. I don't believe that the rich only want to save taxes; I think that is what some lawyers and estate planners want them to want, for the same reason vacuum-cleaner manufacturers see the human condition in terms of dust and suction. But I have not seen any evidence deserving of serious consideration to prove that the human expectations of the man who has half a million dollars are so easily dismissed. (Estate planners predict the enormity of tax problems and then resolve them in a magnificent spiral of self-fulfilling prophecy, but the spiral doesn't prove anything.) In any event, we lawyers are obviously willing to give the wealthy as much time as the complexity of their problems demands, and we should be willing to consider the possibility that their problems may include anxieties about death, identifications with property, and hang-ups in the family.

Less wealthy clients pose a different problem, in no small part because lawyers tend to neglect their special concerns and interests. I wrote a few years ago a modest article and will form for the young-family client, the person who has, in my eccentric argot, a "non-estate." That article was successful far beyond its intrinsic merit, which convinces me that we have neglected small clients *and* that many of us are willing to make up the oversight. If middle-class clients are deserving of enough professional time to produce humane property arrangements, the legal profession is not ready to retire from the field in favor of mutual fund salesmen. If lawyers are willing to do a humane job for middle-class wills clients (and even for poor ones), but have, despite professional good will, serious problems in finding enough time to do what is required, then we academics and the commercial "estate planning" industry should turn our attention to the human depth of will and trust preparation, and provide our busy brethren in the field with concise, dependable empirical and secondary behavioral information. I hope that this little book can be regarded as at least a contribution and a stimulus in that effort.

The project has some difficulties which readers who go beyond this page will doubtless detect. One difficulty traces to the fact that lawyers turn slowly if at all to behavioral science, and we have a special sort of snobbery about psychology. I have cited Kinsey in discussions of obscene literature, and I have argued in court from text books on psychopathology, but I have not in either situation had the effect that I have with the elusive "case on all fours." Psychologists, on the other hand, have a snobbery of their own, a special sort of liberal bias perhaps, about property. It is ironic that a fairly thorough search of the literature produces nothing empirical on the psychology of ownership, that the best of the present sources are a philosopher (Sartre) and anthropologists who are able to see in Africa and in Pacific Islands what European and American psychology has not yet begun to see in its own culture. One who purports to talk about a psychology of testation has a good deal of inventing to do, and a good deal of scissors and paste-pot welding of law and behavioral science.

What follows is divided into three parts. The first, Chapters 2 and 3, takes up death attitudes in environments familiar to lawyers. Chapter 2 considers the reaction of judges to graphic evidence of death; Chapter 3 reports an attempt to use encounter-group sensitivity training as a research device on death attitudes. I have appended to the third chapter a questionnaire on death attitudes developed by Dr. Edwin Shneidman; this appendix is an invitation to the reader to learn what for me is the first lesson for the dilettante in psychology—that I am my own best resource for learning.

The second part (Chapters 4 and 5) broadens the study to include all of the elements I see in the psychology of testation—death, property, and giving. Chapter 4 suggests client feelings about the effects of death; Chapter 5 reports client interviews (the emotional content of both clients and lawyers) at the points at which death, property, and giving most intensely appear.

Part 3 considers the psychology of testation in the shadow of the courthouse. We lawyers do what we do in a unique counseling context; our product is vindicated not only in the lives of our clients, but also in the arenas of legal sanction. It is therefore important to look at the psychological dimension in judicial administration of death, property, and giving. I have done that, with a good deal of expert help and advice, with reference to will contest (Chapter 6) and a death-taxation concept, the "gift in contemplation of death" (Chapter 7).

The most important dimension in all of this is not litigation or taxes or even property distribution; it is counseling. Our clients, in this context, are testators; they are the living who will be dead, but, because of our efforts, or in spite of our efforts, living somehow even though dead. We have always realized that our professional efforts would have consequences for those who survive our clients. I suggest here that we should realize too the consequences we have on the clients themselves.* This is a counseling objective and it is so important that it is raised repeatedly in these chapters, in every aspect suggested here as relevant to the psychology of testation.

---

*Even that ubiquitous popular counselor-by-mail Ann Landers seems to realize both aspects—to the client and to his survivor—of this relationship (from the *South Bend Tribune*, 26 January 1970, p. 8, col. 1):

> DEAR ANN LANDERS: What can I do with a husband who refuses to make out a will. Albert is 64, in excellent health, and has no physical complaints. Yet, one never knows what tomorrow will bring. Whenever I broach the subject of a will he says, "You have been trying to bury me for the last twenty years. Do you have your next husband picked out."
> Albert is a good man. He stays home with me every night or we go out together. He has always handed over his check and I pay the bills. We have no debts and we own our home free and clear. Please tell me why he is so stubborn about making a will. If he would spend just one hour with a lawyer and get it over with, I would have peace of mind forever.—Forty Years a Wife.
>
> DEAR WIFE: Many people avoid making a will because it requires them to think about death. Ask Albert if he will give you an anniversary present or a birthday gift (whichever comes first) the one hour you need for your peace of mind. Once he does it, he'll be glad he did.

Part 1: Death

2   Death in the Courtroom

Introduction

Death in primitive societies, and in the primitive shadows of our civilized lives, is a violent interloper. Death is not something I do; it is something that happens to me. The anthropologist Robert Hertz reports of people in the primitive societies he has studied that they never see death as natural; "it is always due to the action of spiritual powers, either because the deceased has brought disaster upon himself by violating some taboo, or because an 'enemy' has 'killed' him by means of spells or magical practices." There is a tradition among the Chinese that the death of a father is to be attributed to his eldest son, because of the son's inadequate filial devotion. The Naga defy death spirits—"If we could see you we would kill you with our spears. . . . Where have you fled to? We have no enemy crueler than you, who destroy our friends in our midst."

"Society," Hertz says, "imparts its own character of permanence to the individuals who compose it: because it feels itself immortal and wants to be so, it cannot normally believe that its members, above all those in whom it incarnates itself and with whom it identifies itself, should be fated to die."

Death is presumably seen as an intrusion because it is the most unpleasant of unpleasant subjects—an attitude not confined to people

I am grateful to Mr. James H. Seckinger, of the Colorado Bar, for the many hours of valuable assistance with the report on which this chapter is based; to my colleague Professor Robert E. Rodes, Jr.; and to Judge Creighton R. Coleman.

15

in primitive societies. Ashley Montagu quotes the distinguished scientist and president of Columbia University, Frederick Barnard: "If the final outcome of all the boasted discoveries of modern science is to disclose to men that they are more evanescent than the shadow of the swallow's wing upon the lake . . . I pray, no more science."

"I will live on in my simple ignorance," this great American intellectual said, "as my father did before me; and when I shall at length be sent to my final repose, let me . . . lie down to pleasant, even though they be deceitful, dreams."

Herman Feifel, who is probably this generation's foremost death researcher, found that hospital administrators would not let him conduct either counseling or research projects with dying patients, even though the patients were willing to cooperate. "I was up against . . . a personal position," he concluded, "bolstered by cultural structuring, that death is a dark symbol not to be stirred, even touched—an obscenity to be avoided." He was told that "the one thing you never do is to discuss death with a patient." The result, of course, is that dying people are left alone, frustrated, miserable, without even the consolation of a farewell by loved ones or an expression of concern from professional counselors.

Feifel recognized that his own emotions about death also posed subtle dangers in his work. He saw emotions in himself as well as in the hospital administrators who frustrated him. He might on the one hand become "swamped . . . by his own anxieties about dying" or on the other fall into "overintellectualizing his approach, dissembling behind a facade of pseudorigorousness . . . refusing to observe any but the grossest and least emotionally tinged dimensions of what is happening."

He recognized in himself and in his intractable hospital administrators something that is probably endemic to the whole culture—the feeling that death is a failure, a mischance, an accident. "Fear of death is no longer so much the fear of judgment as it is fear of the infringement on the right to life, liberty, and the pursuit of happiness." The cultural result of this resentment of the inevitable is a mass system of disguises, so that, Feifel says, "we 'exist,' 'cease,' become 'defunct,' 'demised,' or 'pass on'—but rarely die." Realistic death has given way "to the Gothic fantasies of horror films which now seem more acceptable to the public than details of the real thing." Death is "not so much . . . tragedy, but . . . dramatic illusion." Physicians, psychologists—even lawyers—refuse to talk about death or to bring to bear on death their professional competence in counseling and research.

This is the culture which an inquiring legal mind will find when he turns to the most common beginning point for legal inquiry, the courtroom. This is the culture in which I first observed judicial reactions to death, as a reporter for sessions of a judicial conference devoted to real and demonstrative evidence. I assisted at four sessions on demonstrative evidence at the 1967 Indiana Judicial Conference, all of them conducted by Judge Creighton R. Coleman of the 37th Judicial District of Michigan (Calhoun County). Each session was attended by a group of 25 to 35 Indiana trial and appellate judges.

This project involves some consideration of what evidence in court is and of my approach to the conference. My interest there was keyed to the persons involved, rather than to the evidence presented. I am interested less in categories of demonstrative evidence than in judges who see it. This is justified even in "pure" discussion of the law of evidence; in this species of law making the immediate response of a trial judge is almost always the last word on what the law is. Rulings on demonstrative evidence are more closely related to immediate response (I would say "emotional" response, but that adjective has a bad name in a legal system that still pretends to be Aristotelian) than to the intellectual rationalization that characterizes appellate law. This relationship is especially important because rulings on demonstrative evidence are probably as immune from appellate interference as any that a trial judge is likely to make. (Judge Coleman explained that one reason for this narrow review is that the record on demonstrative evidence is almost always limited. The fact is broader than the explanation, though, as he indicated: "Normally an appellate court will be very slow to reverse rulings on demonstrative evidence. You've got all the power there is." Very few appellate judges attended these conferences, but of those who did, only one mentioned a case in which his court had reversed on a demonstrative evidence ruling; that case involved the introduction of the picture of a homicide victim laid out in a casket.)

The trial judges' responses which I reported were seen as reaction to repulsive evidence. (Both real and demonstrative evidence are directed to the senses of the fact-finder, but real evidence is that which has a direct part in the facts, while demonstrative evidence explains or illustrates the facts.) The opportunity for me to gather information of this sort was fortuitous: Judge Coleman's most evocative exhibits were repulsive exhibits.

I was able to observe and compare four kinds of evidence against my impressions of repulsion and judicial reaction to repulsion: (1) evidence of death; (2) evidence of suicide; (3) evidence of a vaguer "indecent" import; and (4) evidence of pain. Across all of these categories I was able to make some observations on the judicial impulse to protect co-adventurers in the judicial process (jurors) from the repulsion felt at all of these kinds of evidence.

In other words, there are two general questions involved in the presentation of repulsive evidence to a trial judge: What repulses him? What does he do about what repulses him? My first hypothesis is that death, suicide, indecency, and pain repulse him. And my second hypothesis is that he tends to react to this revulsion in terms of the accuracy of the evidence, not, as has been generally supposed, in terms of the relative revulsion the evidence has for him; he does protect jurors from the psychic shock of ugly evidence, but he does it under a standard of value to fact-finding, not under a standard of the relative discomfort the evidence causes him.

Treatises and appellate opinions would lead one to suppose that the prejudice probably generated by a given piece of evidence, utterance, or demonstrative device has to be weighed against the probative value an appellate court thinks it had. (The past tense is appropriate because appellate courts always look back at a trial.) In specific reference to repulsive evidence, especially graphic evidence of death, this suggests rulings by trial judges that balance prejudicial effect against probative value. But this *appellate* distinction was not borne out in the attitudes of the 1967 group of trial judges, although they may have talked as if it were. Instead, I think, these trial judges looked at a given piece of evidence in terms of its accuracy. If it accurately portrayed a fact (or if, in the case of real evidence, it was the fact), these judges regarded it as admissible. Furthermore, they regarded it as admissible despite the horror it evoked in them.

I concluded that these trial judges also conceive of their duty in dealing with real and demonstrative evidence as a matter of control. There is a distinction between the trial judge who sees himself as a referee, a peace keeper who settles disputes between suitors (i.e., between the lawyers in his courtroom), and the trial judge who sees himself as a representative of the community with a responsibility to see that the trial is fair, that jurors are protected from psychological harm, and that the record for appeal is adequate. The judge in the first group is interested primarily in the rules of the courtroom battle.* The judge who sees himself as responsible for fairness will, if the occasion demands, act on his own initiative to prevent prejudice (or inaccuracy) or a vague trial record. He will, for instance, consider jurors' reactions to evidence of death as well as his own reaction.

Sources of Repulsion: Death

Judge Coleman brought with him a set of color slides that had been taken in the police morgue in Detroit. He projected these slides for the Indiana judges with little or no advance explanation. The judges' reactions to three of these death evidence cases illustrate my hypothesis on repulsion and accuracy.

In one case (three slides), a young man had been beaten to death by blows on his head with a pistol. The first slide showed his head and shoulders, on a morgue table, and illustrated clearly the location and nature of his wounds. The second and third slides had a less revolting perspective and an additional element: Someone was holding a pistol by the dead man's head to demonstrate how the wounds were made.

The second case was very similar; death had been caused by a blow on the head with a lead pipe. The wounds were on the back of the skull, which had been shaved to make them visible. The first slide showed the wounds. The second slide was taken further back and was somewhat less revolting; it also showed a piece of pipe which was held next to the wounds it supposedly made.

The third case showed no body at all. The victim had been killed by a knife wound that pierced his heart. The slides (three of them) were of an excised portion of the aorta. One showed only a small, pale piece of tissue on a morgue table; the second showed the same tissue with a serrated knife next to it; and the third was an enlarged version of the second.

Judge Coleman posed the same question for all three sets of slides—a case (civil or criminal) in which death and the cause of death were at issue. In terms solely of their rulings, a majority of the judges in each of the groups would have (1) admitted slides from the first and second cases which showed the wounds alone, (2) excluded slides from those two cases which included the pistol or the lead pipe, and (3) admitted all of the slides from the third case.

In the first and second (pistol and lead pipe) cases, the pictures that

---

*A young lawyer with whom I practiced law wrote to a celebrated Indiana circuit judge, asking for a copy of the judge's rules of court. The judge wrote in reply: "This court has always been conducted on the rules promulgated by the late Marquis of Queensbury."

did not show the pistol and pipe were more revolting than the pictures that did—this was because they were taken closer to the bodies and because the presence of the metal object tended to divert attention from the bodies. None of the judges, however, objected to the repulsive exhibits before them, although many of them expressly objected to the attempt at demonstration that was involved in the pictures comparing the wounds with the pistol or pipe. Some of their comments: "Let that come in by testimony . . . this is too theoretical." "The jury's guess is as accurate as the fellow's who posed the photograph. . . . It's unrealistic to pose the pipe." "This enters into the realm of speculation . . . don't know as how I could go along with that." The last judge emphasized that he thought the comparison similar to testimony by a morgue police officer on how the death occurred, which would be excluded because the officer was not present when the wounds were inflicted. One judge thought that, in a criminal case, the comparison would violate the defendant's right to confront and cross-examine his accusers. "You're introducing a separate element, a foreign object," one judge said, although he admitted that he would allow a comparison of the pipe and the picture of the wounded skull by a witness whose competence to testify on the issue was shown. This alternative, another judge at the same session said, would remove the hearsay objection. It did not alter these conclusions to point out, as Judge Coleman did in one session, that the officer who "posed" the weapon was present and testifying when the slide was shown.

The fact that these slides were in color raised a small amount of interesting discussion. At one session, Judge Coleman asked, before he showed any of these slides, whether the judges objected to color photography when black-and-white pictures of the same matter were available. No one said he had general objections to color, although some indicated that they had changed attitudes on that point in the last decade. Furthermore, no one indicated a change of mind after he saw the slides. Some, in fact, said they preferred color pictures. "Blood is red, isn't it?" Judge Coleman said to them. However, each of the groups demonstrated revulsion ("Holy cow!") at graphic color slides.

In the third case, the knife-aorta pictures were not repulsive, but they clearly involved a certain amount of posing. The two most representative comments on these pictures were probably that of a judge who expressed spontaneous admiration for the close detective work the "posed" slides demonstrated and that of a judge who said that the fundamental purpose of trials is to discover truth—"you have to use common sense." All of the judges would have admitted the picture of aortic tissue without the knife; a very clear majority of them would have admitted the aorta and knife; a bare majority of them would have admitted the enlarged picture of the aorta and knife. The general and strong objection against posed pictures that was demonstrated in the skull-wound cases was eroded when the demonstration involved was (1) clearly accurate, and (2) not repulsive.

Can the difference be explained solely in terms of gruesomeness? The aorta slides were not gruesome at all. The lead-pipe slides were very gruesome and the pistol-whipping slides relatively gruesome. But I did not detect the balancing between probative value and gruesomeness that is found in the appellate literature. ("Gruesome" is probably the usual word to describe this sort of evidence, but I prefer "repulsive," which is also better for my purposes than "repellent," because "repulsive" covers the observer's reaction more than it covers a supposed inherent quality in the exhibit.)

I detected instead clear disposition (1) to let the jury see the results of what happened (the skull pictures), (2) to protect them from conjecture as to how it happened—at least from conjecture outside the courtroom (the pistol and lead-pipe pictures), but (3) to expose them to conjecture which was not repulsive and tended to demonstrate clearly its own probative sanction (the aorta and knife pictures).

This is not to say, though, that revulsion is unimportant. The pistol-whipping and lead-pipe demonstration pictures, which these judges would not have shown to jurors, were less accurate than the knife-aorta pictures, but they were also more repulsive than the knife-aorta pictures. (They were more repulsive than the same scenes without demonstration, an interesting comparison, which suggests that one's emotional reaction is reduced when there is some neutral object in an otherwise repulsive picture.) I think it is fair to say that the test of accuracy is applied somewhat more closely where revulsion is involved. In other words, it is possible that a demand for accuracy almost instinctively burst forth when the evidence was repulsive. The test propounded by the law of evidence is applied somewhat differently when graphic death is presented to judges. That generalization is subject to further data, and I have a little.

The aorta slides are an inadequate test because they were relatively less repulsive than the skull slides as well as relatively more accurate. The best test would be a picture as gruesome as the skull slides and as accurate as the aorta slides. Judge Coleman had a possible case for that test: two slides showing the head and shoulders of a young woman who had been fatally shot through the head. One of these slides showed the corpse only; the other showed the corpse with a probe inserted into and out of the fatal wound, demonstrating the path the bullet took. One group would have allowed the second of these slides on the expressed theory that otherwise the party having the burden of proof could not have demonstrated the path of the bullet. (Testimony, though, was available on that point.) Another group, however, would have allowed it only after a testimonial foundation from the person who inserted the probe; otherwise "How can you tell it's not pinned?" The third group agreed that the question was one of the illustrative value of the probe. In the fourth group, one judge said he had allowed a similar picture. This bit of first-hand experience tended to dampen discussion; one other participant, though, said he thought that the picture without the probe proved nothing that testimony could not prove as well. The probe picture, therefore, may demonstrate that a repulsive picture with an accurate demonstration in it is admissible, even though an equally repulsive picture with a less accurate demonstration is not.

Another way to test the hypothesis would be to see if accuracy is less closely guarded where the evidence is not repulsive. Judge Coleman had several exhibits and orally presented several abstract problems, which were relatively bland and involved varying degrees of accuracy:

1. A building collapses and the builder is sued for defective construction. There are offered in evidence (A) samples of the brick and mortar from the defective building and (B) samples from a "good" building not otherwise at issue. Most judges would have overruled objections to the defective material but sustained objections to the "good" material. The articulated reason for the difference was that the second exhibit involved an out-of-court demonstration of the way bricks are properly laid. Some of the judges, however, said they would allow a demonstration to the same effect in the courtroom.

2. In a slip-and-fall accident case, plaintiff's counsel offers exhibits of properly roughened tile to illustrate why the defendant's smooth tile fell below the standard of care. Most judges would not have admitted the tile, absent evidence of a custom in the business community. Judge Coleman mentioned that in a recent case in his court he had not permitted evidence on reflectorized tape on railroad cars nor a showing of Interstate Commerce Commission regulations requiring its use.

3. In a narcotics prosecution, the government offers a spoon and syringe used in taking heroin. Most judges would have permitted the

spoon and syringe the defendant used, but not any sort of model.

4. In a will contest involving mental capacity, a snapshot of the testator taken at about the time of the will execution is offered by the proponent. Most judges would have required a showing of the relevance of physical condition; their discussion suggested that a physical image of the testator might otherwise influence the jurors improperly. (Is this because it might not be accurate on the issue of mental capacity? Or is the judicial caution tied up somehow with a revulsion at bringing the image of the dead testator into the courtroom and thereby disturbing the otherwise comfortable ritual we use to pass around the dead man's property?) In one session, this question evoked a relatively vigorous debate:

> Judge A: "That could be very misleading to a jury." (Murmurs all around.)
>
> Judge B (to Judge A): "What right do you have to substitute your judgement for that of the jury?"
>
> Judge C: "There's no probative value in that." (Murmurs all around.) Judge Coleman then asked whether the judges would allow sound movies of an entire will execution, and the judges replied with renewed unanimity that they would.

5. Judge Coleman presented an interesting contrast between Indiana's little-used rules on jury views and the use of composite pictures and models. The picture involved was used in a rape-murder prosecution. It showed 100 yards of verdant, residential river bank. The victim had been knocked down at the far right edge of the scene, raped at about the center, and murdered at the far left. The picture was a clear, exactly done composite of 12 enlarged exposures. No one at any of the sessions disapproved of it. What is the difference between this picture and the "posed" comparisons of skulls and murder weapons? Which has the greater possibility of error? Which is repulsive? It is interesting to note that some of the judges who approved of this picture would not have allowed the slides showing the probe through the gunshot wound or the knife-aorta slides.

The model, which Judge Coleman described orally, showed a curved section of highway on which a collision occurred. It presented an aerial view, which was inadequate to illustrate the perspective presented to the driver of an automobile on the highway. The model maker had corrected this inadequacy by providing a sort of periscope, into which jurors could look, which simulated the scene as it was presented to the driver. The judges expressed nothing but admiration for this reconstruction and approved of the Michigan trial judge who had admitted it into evidence. One judge recalled that he had allowed a similar model showing automotive acceleration. Judge Coleman remarked to these judges that most questions of accuracy go to weight, not admissibility. Compare the reconstructions involved in the autopsy pictures of the pistol and lead pipe in terms of their accuracy and repulsiveness. The judges who admitted composite photographs and models but disapproved of photographic comparison of weapons and bodies seemed to be referring to degrees of demonstrated accuracy rather than to degrees of revulsion. A judgment on accuracy, rather than a balancing between gruesomeness and probative value, seems to me the best explanation of the "law" as it was developed in these sessions.

The above discussion of the first hypothesis implied that revulsion was less important than accuracy but admitted that revulsion continues to count for something. I suggested that the test of accuracy in real and demonstrative evidence is applied differently when graphic death is presented than it is when some emotionally neutral fact is being proved. What is involved in this revulsion?

The first and most obvious factor in revulsion was a sudden confrontation with death. In only one of the four sessions did Judge Coleman announce to participating judges, before he turned on his projector, what his slides were or where he got them. Three of the groups, in other words, did not know until after one or more slides were shown that they were looking at dead bodies. This circumstance posed an opportunity to observe revulsion at death.

The first slide shown to each group showed the head and shoulders of a middle-aged woman; she was reclining on what was in fact a morgue table, but it could have been viewed as a treatment table in a hospital emergency room. Her eyes were closed, and there was a round black-and-blue mark, about an inch in diameter, near her swollen right eye. The picture, assuming it illustrated a less-than-fatal wound, was not repulsive. The three groups who saw it without first being told that the woman in the picture was dead showed no audible or visible reaction to it. Neither did the group who knew before they saw it that the woman was dead. But the three groups who learned the woman was dead as they looked at her, by Judge Coleman's telling them the picture had been taken in a police morgue, visibly and audibly reacted to this information. The three groups were not revolted at the wound itself, and members of a similar group were not revolted by death when they were prepared for it in advance. Death is obviously a principal source of revulsion to real and demonstrative evidence. This seems to bear out the commonplace observation in psychological literature that death is to our culture what sex was to the Victorians; sadism, gore, and the messier kinds of violence are "naughty" subjects not raised in polite conversation but only raised, and then enjoyably raised, in the worst sort of pulp literature and in whatever provides for the moment a barracks level of male conversation.

Death is a factor that heightens the interest of trial judges in accuracy and causes them to be wary of exposing the evidence involved to the eyes of jurors; the suggestion of death results in a more demanding law of real and demonstrative evidence.

Suicide

Two sets of slides bore interestingly on a second factor in revulsion, a *suicide* factor which is perhaps a refinement of the death factor. These sets of slides were each presented by Judge Coleman as involving a single death. One of them showed the head and shoulders of a young woman who had been hanged. The body showed rope burns, and a gag was still around the head and into the half-open mouth. In the other slide, the young woman's wrist was shown, and on it were several scars made by a knife or razor blade. These scars were, Judge Coleman said, the "hesitation marks" commonly found on the bodies of suicide victims, who often attempt to bleed themselves to death before they choose some more efficient method. (Both sets of slides might be relevant in civil litigation under, for instance, the suicide clause of a life-insurance policy. Both could also be relevant in a criminal prosecution for homicide.) None of the judges would have excluded any of these pictures, assuming their relevance was shown, although all were revolted by them. None would have required black-and-white pictures instead.

It is possible, though, that the judges were more revolted by the fact of suicide than by the fact of more conventional death. It is a bit speculative to reach this result solely on the basis of the hanging and hesitation-marks slides, but a third series somewhat strengthens the conclusion. In this third series, as Judge Coleman put the problem, the body of a middle-aged woman was found, terribly scarred by scalding, in the bathtub of a hotel room. The issue (civil or criminal), as he put it, was whether she was killed or had committed suicide. The judges saw these slides, however, *before* this issue was posed to them. It seemed to me that they were more revolted after the suicide question was posed than they had been when they first saw the scarred body itself. It is possible to conclude from these observations, although the conclusion may not be exactly compelling, that evidence demonstrating suicide is more revolting than violent accidental or homicidal death. In any event, all of the judges would have admitted the picture, and none would have required black-and-white versions of it. "It would help me," one judge said. "I don't know what it tells you for sure, but it might tell you something," another said. And a third: "If it's part of their theory . . . they should be entitled to develop it by evidence."

The eminent "suicidologist" Edwin Shneidman reported the case of a clergyman he knew who had been asked to counsel a young married man shortly after the parishioner had attempted suicide. The clergyman spent four hours in the company of the young man and his wife: they discussed sexual behavior with candor and in detail. But no one of the three, at any time during the four hours, mentioned suicide, even though suicide was, as Dr. Shneidman notes, "the *raison d'etre* of the meeting." Suicide is taboo in our culture in almost all the ways anything can be taboo—the action is taboo, talking about it is taboo, and the thought of it (as these judges indicated) is taboo. It shares in the death taboo—"its dark motivation for immortality, punishment, and reunion, is spun from the same loom," Shneidman says.

Suicide taboos are so strong in occidental cultures that the act occurs rarely even in those persons in whom the culture might almost approve it—among the terminally ill, for example. The taboo has made it almost impossible to draw reliable conclusions from public-health statistics on causes of death. Shneidman instances the midwestern sheriff who reported all suicides without valid holographic note as "self-inflicted violent death." My Indiana judges may have expressed this same implied prejudice in favor of violent accident or homicide.

One judge commented, on the suicide slides. "As a judge, I would let it in; as a lawyer I don't know if I would fool with it." This illustrated the judges' concern for jury revulsion, which another group discussed at some length, in terms of the means a judge might use to lessen the sickening effect of this sort of picture on jurors. Most of the judges in that group agreed that they should try, *even on their own motion,* to prepare jurors for the experience by warning them, or asking if anyone had a weak stomach. Or, as one judge put it: "Suppose a juror refuses to look?", an intriguing question which brings to mind the crew of the *Bounty*, assembled for one of Captain Bligh's floggings. This discussion assumed that greater exposure to the revulsion produced by seeing death reduces the revulsion. (Kasper produced some evidence that the reaction of physicians in the presence of death is suppressed but not reduced.) This instinct for the protection of jurors was an expression of two facts, I thought: (1) Judges are probably more hardened to the revulsion of death in the courtroom than jurors are, or at least judges think that is true. (2) The threshold of revulsion in the average man is not the test in the law of real demonstrative evidence. These judges were willing to attempt to prepare jurors for an unpleasant experience; they were not, however, willing to relieve them of the experience.

Pain

Pain is certainly a primary source of revulsion possibly, as Freud indicated, a stronger source than death itself. (Chapter 4 discusses that possibility under the question of whether fear of pain is one of the distasteful aspects of death.) What was to me the most repulsive picture in Judge Coleman's collection showed a mangled leg. It was taken in the morgue, but it was presented to the judges as having been taken in a hospital emergency room. The picture showed only the mangled leg, which had been virtually severed in a bumper accident. The victim had been apparently pinned against a wall or automobile by an automobile bumper.

Almost everyone found that picture sickening; it was not only bloody and vivid but also spoke eloquently of human pain. In fact, it was on the issue of pain that the judges said they would require a foundation showing some period of consciousness after the injury, although some judges found it relevant on another kind of pain, the more subtle anguish caused the victim when he saw his own mangled limb, whether he felt pain in the injured area or not. ("That's what he had to wake up and see.") One judge said he would have found the picture admissible but added he would probably not have admitted it ten years ago. His updated opinion was apparently like that of one Indiana judge who said, "The jury has a right to draw conclusions. . . . The picture ought to go in, for whatever it's worth." This routine admissibility was, however, accompanied by expressions of distress at the picture: "Man o' man!" "Sure is graphic." "Would increase the damages a little . . . might get a settlement." "Holy smoke!" "You say that's typical (of bumper-accident injuries)?" Two judges in one group were more skeptical. One said he would require a strong showing of necessity before he would admit such a vivid color picture; it may be relevant that his experience on the bench has been exclusively in a criminal court. The other dissenter said the picture would have to tend to "prove something, . . . otherwise the tendency to inflame outweighs probative value."

Revulsion was a minor obstacle to the admission of the bumper-accident picture. An abstract question, put by Judge Coleman, on allowing jurors to see the scars made in accidents or by assaults at issue in a given case drew a clearer response. All the judges would permit jurors to see these scars, subject, apparently, to a limitation posed by "decency." Very few would permit jurors to feel the scars, however, even where their texture is relevant, and that too may have been a matter of decency. This abstract and fairly vague example, coupled with heightened caution and apparent revulsion when a color picture was presented, suggests that graphic demonstrations of pain are a principal source of revulsion—which is to say that they present another circumstance in which the test of accuracy will be applied with heightened care.

An ancillary set of impressions on the pain factor in repulsive evidence was stimulated by Judge Coleman's arsenal or surgical and orthopedic devices. The surgical devices included a skin-grafting knife (a long-scalpel which is used with a metal screen and roller in removing skin for grafting), drill, screw driver, and orthopedic plates and nails (for inserting metal support to fractured limbs), a scalpel, an amputation saw, and an incredibly heavy mallet and chisel which are apparently used in orthopedic surgery. A majority of the judges reacted negatively to these devices. In one group a probably representative judge said he couldn't see any purpose in offering them. He may have been questioning their relevance, although that group's discussion did not otherwise raise questions or relevance. Another said he would admit devices actually inserted in the patient (nails, plates, etc.), but not the tools with which they were inserted. Another group seemed to approve of the devices, even in an automobile personal-injury case. One judge in this group advised his brethren to admit the surgical device "and you let the jury feel it," he said. Another judge in the same session agreed, but indicated practical limits: "I don't think you have to introduce the entire hospital."

Several judges in a third group were worried that the tools, if not marked and admitted into evidence, would not be part of the record on appeal. These judges proved to be more strongly negative than those in the first group. Surgical tools, a member of this group said, are never relevant outside medical malpractice cases. "Doesn't matter how it was done . . . highly prejudicial . . . too remote from the thing that's on trial." Another said he would allow surgical devices only in bench trials. A third said, "I'm not going to permit these demonstrations . . . startling to (jurors) . . . patient sees none of it, feels none of it . . . is oblivious to it."

However, one judge in this group disagreed; he likened the surgeon's procedure to a carpenter's and said that, in any event, oral testimony from the surgeon was as prejudicial as a glimpse of his tools would be. This judge was not only in the minority, but he was even met with what is the most radical procedure an Indiana judge ever suggests—the belief that a demonstration of surgical tools should be stopped by the trial judge on his own motion. A second opponent of liberality agreed: "I would listen very closely to a motion for mistrial." In fact, he said he had once granted a motion for mistrial in a similar situation.

The fourth group was more evenly divided, although it had its voices of emphatic disapproval ("It's inflammatory when they bring in all this equipment") as well as its proponents of liberality (who said, for instance, that the mallet may bear on the patient's post-operative pain).

Orthopedic devices provoked less cautious attitudes, possibly because they are not as crudely suggestive of surgical mayhem. Judge Coleman had in his materials a neck collar and home-traction devices for use on a door (neck traction) and in bed (back traction). Most of the judges said they would have permitted these, both as evidence and as demonstration, on a showing that they were either the same devices the litigant uses or wears, or exactly like them. "If it was used in the treatment of the injury, it would be admissible." Most would allow the devices to be passed to the jury. The main source of dissent on orthopedic devices was the use of them without their being marked as evidence. One judge said he would stop nonevidentiary use of a neck collar on his own motion. "I'd speak up . . . you can contaminate a jury"; another disagreed by stating "that means in Indiana we have no illustrative evidence." Most of the judges indicated they would control the practice of leaving demonstrative or evidentiary devices in the sight of the jury during later or earlier stages of the trial.

One explanation of the difference in attitudes toward surgical and orthopedic devices is that the latter usually involve conscious pain and are therefore usually relevant on damages. Surgical devices, however, are normally used when the patient is unconscious and are therefore irrelevant. On the other hand, not all surgical devices are used under

29

anesthesia, and not all orthopedic devices involve pain. When these distinctions were raised in the discussion, however, the immediate tendency of the trial judges toward suspicion of saws, mallets, drills, and a much calmer reaction to collars and traction devices, remained. An alternative explanation may be that the pain factor is more starkly present to a judge when a surgical device is presented to him than when a traction device is presented. Graphic pain, pain approaching mayhem, is more repulsive than the subtle suggestion of pain raised by orthopedic devices.

"Decency"

Another factor, and one not completely illustrated in these sessions, was that of "decency." Judge Coleman repeatedly mentioned that his exhibits contained nothing indecent. In the cases of the hanged and scalded woman, he mentioned that there were full-body slides which he had excluded from his demonstration because they were not decent. (And, apparently, jurors in his court would not be allowed to see them for the same reason.) In the discussion on exhibiting scars to the jury, one judge said he did not allow witnesses to disrobe in his courtroom because it was indecent; others also indicated that decency would set limits on disrobing in their courts. "Decency," in these examples, apparently means a circuitous treatment of sexual anatomy: It would be worse to exhibit the scalded female body in toto than to see a relatively asexual part of it, and the difference is not due to the increased exposure of scalded tissue. The objection to seeing the body of a hanged woman, with ugly slash marks on her wrists, would be increased, maybe even increased to the point of exclusion, if the picture were also sexually complete.

(Judge Coleman, after reading this paragraph in manuscript, wrote me the following comment: "While I hope that I do have a standard of decency, certainly I have no problem myself in observing slides of fully exposed human bodies. I think that I would allow my jurors to see such pictures if relevant to the case.")

Decency, apparently, is usually suggestive of protection from sexual candor. But it seems also to be used in reference to other facts or images which produce anxiety. For instance, decency, or something like it, seemed to figure in a special revulsion associated with pictures of dead children. Judge Coleman had two sets. In one, a small, fair-haired child of perhaps five had been electrocuted when he touched a high-tension wire. The relevant wound was a small burn, about half an inch in diameter, in the palm of his hand. In the first slide only the hand and arm of the body were shown. It was a fairly clinical exhibit that might have been important in, for instance, illustration of expert medical testimony. No one objected to its admission. The second slide was of the head and face of the dead child and was, of course, more affecting. The judges clearly indicated that, given a choice, they would have excluded the second and admitted the first. Judge Coleman's questions did not, however, give them a choice. Some judges would have admitted both slides ("that'd be worth a lot—that child's head in there"). One judge noted that this was not a case of demonstrative evidence but was real evidence—the thing itself. Some vocal members of another group were opposed to the second slide, but it was not clear to me whether they would have excluded it if it were the only picture offered (or would perhaps have ordered counsel to crop it). A third group found the first picture preferable but would, if pressed, have probably admitted both.

The second case of death in a child, a case for which two slides were offered, showed the body of a ten-year-old child who had been shot through the chest. One slide (frontal) showed the entrance wound, and the second showed the exit wound in the child's back. None of the judges would have excluded either picture, since each had an accuracy value not present in the other, but several judges expressed dismay at the pictures ("Who shot that child?"), which they had not expressed at equally ugly wounds in adult corpses. The graphic confrontation with the death of human beings who seemed far removed from death and toward whom one feels instinctively protective is more revolting than death in an adult. This special revulsion at the death of children, this special feeling of protection of "decency," is a complex thing which is discussed more elaborately in Chapter 4, under the question of whether causing grief is a source of distaste at the idea of death.

Consequences of Revulsion: Control or Protection?

I came away from this experience with Indiana trial judges with the impression that there is a distinction between control, by which I mean the judicial conduct appropriate to a referee, and the ability to respond, by which I mean a chosen duty of responsibility for the sound administration of justice. These trial judges saw their function more as one of control than as one of responsibility. This hypothesis is relevant to attitudes on death in at least one rather involved respect, the instinct to protect jurors. Judges may want to protect jurors from prejudicial influences, from the possibility that jury verdicts will be the product of emotions; that at least is the usual and official explanation for the law of evidence. But they may also, especially in the presence of death, want to protect them from psychologically painful experiences. The latter possibility suggests that judges regard their jurors as coadventurers toward whom human concern is appropriate, as distinguished from remote superior appellate judges who need no concern from the trial bench.

The judges' dialogues on surgical and orthopedic devices may illustrate the distinction, in terms, first, of responsibility for a good appellate record and, second, of responsibility for jurors. (The two points tended to shade into one another in discussion.) In one group, Judge Coleman asked what these trial judges would do if one attorney in a trial were using unmarked, unadmitted surgical devices during a physician's testimony, to a clearly prejudicial degree, and the attorney for the other side did nothing about it:

> Judge A: "If the lawyer for other side doesn't object, you can do anything you want, can't you?"
> Judge Coleman said he thought a trial judge has responsibility for a fair trial and for an adequate trial record.
> Judge B: "If [the lawyers] fail to act, should the trial judge protect appellate justice?"
> Judge C: "The less they [appellate judges] know, the better."
> Judge D: "It [the situation Judge Coleman presented] would not be the basis of error in the appellate court."
> Judge B pointed out that the appellate court can call for exhibits it does not find in the record, and that it has, in his experience, done so.
> Judge E said he thought that if the testimonial record were clear enough and the surgical devices were purely demonstrative, they need not be marked and introduced, and, by implication, that he would not stop the hypothetical demonstration on his own motion.

These dialogues, considering the caution these judges showed toward repulsive pictures, suggest that they are more alert to keep the evidence clear and maybe even as unrepulsive as possible for the jury than they are to keep the record clear for the reviewing court.

Corroboration for the conclusion that juries are more important than appellate courts was available in their discussions of sloppy, illegible blackboard diagrams. Most judges said they tried, on their own motion, to keep the diagrams clear, but very few showed any interest in the occasional suggestion that photographs be made of blackboard diagrams for insertion into the record. Very few, to take another example, thought it particularly important that clear record references be made to exhibits being handled during testimony. Most judges, to take yet another example, would require, on their own motion, that surgical and orthopedic devices be taken out of the jury's sight after they have been presented, but many were not concerned that these devices be offered in evidence and made part of the appellate record.

Making a good appellate record is, in these judges' opinions, the least important part of their task. What about their sense of responsibility for a fair trial, their willingness to reduce prejudice, not in terms of possible appellate review, but in terms of a fair verdict and of protection of jurors? The hypothetical question on misuse of surgical devices suggests they would not interfere with a lawyer on their own motions to prevent prejudice. The small amount of other data available here indicates that they are rarely willing to act at any other time, on their own motions, to prevent prejudice, that control, keeping the peace between the lawyers involved, is the more important factor, and that the course of the trial rests in the hands of the lawyers as long as they act in an orderly manner.

3   Death in the Living Room

My chapter title sounds like an Agatha Christie mystery story, but it is meant to suggest only a discussion of death among sensitive people who talk to one another candidly. It is a change from the relatively formal, heavily controlled atmosphere of the courtroom (Chapter 2) and a preparation for the more limited discussion of death which occurs in the law office (Chapters 4 and 5). The idea to explore death attitudes in this prosaic way came to me from a counseling psychologist who is interested in research, Dr. William R. Coulson of the Center for Studies of the Person in LaJolla, California. Dr. Coulson is a philosopher and clinical psychologist who has been for years heavily involved in the sensitivity-training phase of practical psychology. He is a colleague of Dr. Carl Rogers and has been influenced by Rogerian "client-centered" psychotherapy.

Dr. Coulson suggested that I attempt to use a sensitivity-training group as a research tool. The idea is one he has developed in other contexts, notably research on religious vocations. In an unpublished outline "Notes Toward the Basic Encounter Group as a Research Tool," Dr. Coulson suggested that both of the traditional methods of psychological research—the experimental and the clinical—"study man under limited conditions." Of the first of these he noted that the subject studied is limited by the instructions of the experimenter. In the second, he said, the research subject is limited by pathology. Even recent interest among clinicians in broader implications of psychological health are inadequate, he said, because "any kind of question-and-answer approach, even a sophisticated, 'depth' one, still treats the subject as responder."

Neither of these methods considers man in his health environment, which is a community. Where, Dr. Coulson, asked, might a sort of environmental study of psychological health begin:

"Where would a psychological study begin which would investigate the behavior of men in their creative moments—Skinner inventing his boxes, Freud creating his theories? It could begin . . . in the basic encounter group, a unique contemporary invention designed to set conditions of freedom and safety such that participants help one another to turn on. They help one another become their *own* Freuds and Skinners."

He quoted Rogers' description of the basic encounter group:

"It usually consists of ten to fifteen persons and a facilitator or leader. It is relatively unstructured, providing a climate of maximum freedom for personal expression, exploration of feelings, and inter-personal communication. Emphasis is upon the interactions among the group members, in an atmosphere which encourages each to drop his defenses and facades and thus enables him to relate directly and openly to other members of the group—the basic encounter. Individuals come to know themselves and each other more fully than is possible in the usual social or working relationships; the climate of openness, risk-taking, and honesty generates trust, which enables the person to recognize and change self-defeating attitudes, test out and adopt more innovative and constructive behaviors, and subsequently to relate more adequately and effectively to others in his everyday life situation."

Rogers' more recent work on groups—notably an article he wrote in the December, 1969, *Psychology Today*—suggests that use of the group for research is not as precise as research psychologists insist it should be. "We must," he said, "depend on naturalistic observation," rather than on controlled experimental devices. A second reason for some caution is that the group experience is therapeutic by design; this point was in fact the thesis of Rogers' recent article. It is an experience in which "group members become more spontaneous and flexible, more closely related to their feelings—open to their experience, and closer and more expressively intimate in their interpersonal relationships." (This point may cast some doubt on the distinction Dr. Coulson draws between people in sensitivity groups and patients in psychotherapy.)

With some of these misgivings I proceeded to attempt what Dr. Coulson suggested in the spring of 1968, and, without resolving these misgivings, I report it. It is not a precise and reliable piece of research. On the other hand, it is in some respects superior to heavily controlled questionnaire and observational research, because the subjects here have relaxed their defenses; they have moved toward the psychic state in which analysis explores patients through word association or hypnosis or dream analysis. Another reason I feel this is valuable data is that it suggests major themes which occur in later chapters, some of which resulted from more controlled research and in heavily controlled reports from research journals. But I hope the reader will decide that the most important reason to include a chapter on group-research in attitudes toward death is that the conversation was intrinsically interesting. I will test that possible reaction with an appendix, at the end of this chapter.

Dr. Coulson's suggestion was welcome in 1968 for two reasons. First, I had been frustrated in my efforts to discover in reported psychological-literature data which would relate a man's attitude toward death to his attitude toward his loved ones and his property, this three-way relationship being, I thought, fundamental to what I call the psychology of testation. Secondly, I had begun to use an encounter-group of law students (and the wives of married students) as a means of instruction in legal counselling. (I do little instructing and much participating; I have been assisted by counselling psychologists from the Notre Dame Faculty; Robert T. Grismer and I have elsewhere reported the results of this experience.)

With agreement from all concerned, we of the "legal counselling" group sat down one evening and talked about death. (I will report my conclusions at the end of the chapter, but they are not important enough to limit the creative reaction of the reader. In many ways the reader is able better than I, a participant-observer, to formulate conclusions. The value of my experiment rests more in the conversation itself than in conclusions from it.)

The Discussion

The participants were eight married couples and the husband from a ninth couple. This husband (Herb) and his wife had come together to other sessions of the group, but she was absent from this session. One other member of the group, an unmarried man, was absent, as was the psychologist who directed the group but who attended only about half of its meetings.

All the couples' names have been changed except the Shaffers (identified below as Nancy and Shaffer). All of the men except Shaffer were third-year law students. All of the women had attended college and most of them had graduated.

The couples were George and Martha; James and Dolly; Andrew and Rachel; Frank and Eleanor; Jack and Jackie; Harry and Bess; Cal and Grace. Herb's wife was not present. The group met on April 18, 1968, a significant date in a discussion of death, as the transcript will demonstrate. (The participants' feelings about deaths of John F. Kennedy and Martin Luther King, Jr., recall the observations of Hertz [Chapter 1] on the resentment we feel when an important personage dies.) After a short, halting discussion of funeral customs, especially modern American customs involving commercial funeral directors, this is what happened:

> Shaffer: [The idea behind funeral customs is] to get the dead man put away. Because you're afraid of him. But at the same time you don't really want to put him away because you loved him. And so you've got to resolve that—kind of torn in two directions there.
>
> * * *
>
> George: . . .We forget about a person's bad habits, his liabilities, say, after he's dead. And we seem to have this great concern for him, this great reverence. And the thing is he doesn't really need it.
>
> Shaffer: I suppose I would say that, to me, the reason for that may be that I am afraid of death.
>
> Nancy: I wonder, though, if the deference—I don't know about reverence—the deference, is not out of respect for the people that he was close to, the other people. What you're doing is more for who's left.
>
> James: I think that's it.
>
> Frank: I wonder about that. Take the assassinations of John F. Kennedy and King, for example. It seems like in a social group to say something bad about them is almost taboo.
>
> Jack: . . .the good things that are said about him can be said now because he's no longer a threat. Therefore, you hear Senator Long from Louisiana praising Martin Luther King, because he isn't going to go back to Louisiana and cause trouble. . . .
>
> * * *
>
> Rachel: I think at times we say, "I don't want to be buried, to be laid out there and have people come up and say 'OH, what a good person he was.' " Like you say, Herb: yesterday, you might have had a big fight with this person, and then next day come up and say "Oh, he's such a wonderful person," I mean, certainly I remember yesterday as much as the bad times, as much as . . . you remember the good times. Which I think is hypocrisy, too.

***

Shaffer: Did you say that you were thinking, Rachel, of what the person you had the argument with would say if you were laid out?

Rachel: Um hmm.

Shaffer: You forget the argument.

Rachel: Yeah.

Shaffer: You said it wasn't pleasant to think about that person saying, "What a grand girl she was," when yesterday she had a fight with you.

Rachel: I've heard several people say that, you know. It just seems like whenever you talk about death to someone, perhaps you're talking about being cremated, or whether you would rather . . . be buried . . . they always bring up that subject . . . and people go up and say, "Oh, look at how wonderful she looks. Isn't that beautiful? Doesn't she look so nice?" And then say, "Oh, she's such a wonderful person." And then they say . . . well, yesterday, they probably had a fight with the person.

***

Cal: . . .You're happy for the living at a wedding and you're sad for the living at a funeral. . . .When I go to funerals, I cry more for myself than for the person who's being buried, who's died. The thing that puzzles me about death is what has it meant to me. Because somebody close to me or somebody I love has been taken away. And all of a sudden here's this void and you've got to fill it.

* * *

There's a real problem of life here, not a problem of death.

* * *

Frank: It seems to me that what you're saying is that your feelings have to be one way or the other, rather than a tension between two feelings simultaneously.

* * *

Cal: . . .You say that you're afraid of being dead. Now, I didn't really understand you when you said that. Because it just didn't ring a bell in my experience.

Shaffer: It didn't?

Cal: It didn't. No.

Shaffer: You said a while ago that you were sadder for yourself than for the dead man. I didn't understand that, and I think if I really understood that it might bear on what I was thinking.

Cal: When I say myself, I mean in my situation. The person closest to me—now this is unfortunate: I've known a lot of people die but they really hadn't been very close to me. The person closest to me that has died has been Grace's brother. And that to me, you know—this is something that's living with us constantly today, through Grace's folks. I mean they still feel this very deeply. And . . . you have to stay a whole night with a mother who, a year after she has lost her son, still cries out of self pity, because she's alone now, because this guy was really a fantastic person. And so . . . this person is lonely without him. So much, . . . so much of their whole energy has focused around this growing vital person. And so you feel sadness, you know, through your situation, because it would have been something more with this person. And when the person's gone, you feel that something is missing, someone's missing. And . . . so she cries for herself. And, you know, we cry for ourselves, because somebody important has left.

* * *

Shaffer: You can't have a relationship with him after he's dead.

Cal: It doesn't seem so, because we don't know what the life of the spirit is, we really don't know what that is. I mean, that's the only way I can think to term it. We know what the life of the living is. And we can sense its vitality. But what's this life of the spirit, . . . what's he got to do, what's he got to yearn for? You don't have these feelings. You know, you can communicate with a person who's living because you know, basically, their yearnings and their disappointments. But this life of the spirit, it's supposed to be one of complete fulfillment, so there's no yearnings, there's no anxiety, there's no joy, there's just one big . . . ball of fun, or something. So that there isn't any common bond of experience. So you sense that your communication is cut off.

Shaffer: I think that's what I was maybe getting at. That it's a strange situation and one I can't understand and one therefore I'm a little afraid of.

* * *

Bess: That body lying there, to me that is the farthest thing away from the living being. To me it's just no different than looking at a picture.

Jack: You know, I hate to say this, but I think we're—in all this arguing about where we're going to hold the wake just goes back to what you said: that there's such a taboo on death that nobody's really willing to face it down.

Shaffer: Yeah, I thought this, too, Jack. Nobody's talked about my death.

Cal: . . .I don't want to sound melodramatic, and this is why I didn't bring this up before. King's death has had a real impact on me, and especially in light of the fact that, the night before he died, he talked about his own death. And that thing, that just terrified me, and—I don't know if I can express this—but you said that what is another person's death, that another person's death threatens me. The only way I can see another person's death threatening me is because I am faced with the fact that I am going to die. And, for some strange reason—I don't have the slightest hope of articulating why, but—whether it's environment or what, culture—but I want to have lived a life worth living, or . . . like King said, I'd rather die at 38 and have had a life where I fought for something. You know, life isn't worth living unless what I die for is worth dying for. That's what accounts for the dramatic, and frontiersman, and all that. But it really had an impact on me. It means that I've got to decide to do something with my life that will not make me afraid of death. Like King said, "I've just . . . I've forgotten about death because the thought of death hampered me in my daily living. So I had to accept the possibility that any minute I could die and the important thing was for me to live as I should right now." So at the same time he was constantly conscious of death, but disregarding it. And, I'm wondering, is that possible? I mean, that seems to me to be great. To be so tied up in something that . . . you are willing to die. Now, can every person do that? I'm wondering if they can. It seems to me that's the type of—that in confronting death, I think about the kind of life I want to live. Precisely! Because once that leaden box is there, I don't know what they're going through, I don't know if there's anything there or not. I mean, is it just a shell of flesh or what? I don't know. And I have come to the conclusion that I can't know, no matter how many times I see it. So the only thing important about death to me is that I—I'm not sorry when it comes, in terms of the quality of the life, not the years of the life, I've lived.

* * *

Frank: I think what King was saying is that there's something more important than living. . . . I think just about everybody feels that way. For example, take anybody that has kids. Now, if they were put in the situation where if they didn't choose death, their child would die, I can't imagine too many parents not making the choice instinctively. "I'll die." That seems to me to be about the same thing King's talking about. You're doing a specific sort of thing. You see something is more important than life.

Cal: In other words, you're confronted, though, in that situation, with a life and death issue. . . .

Herb: You don't see the way you live as a life and death issue?

Cal: Oh, I do, . . . in my fantasies and things like that, but it's hard to be constantly aware of the fact that . . .

Frank: I think, Cal, it's probably hard to be aware of the threat of death. For somebody like King the issue is probably focused because he knows that his life is always threatened. But most people don't live day in and day out like that.

Cal: . . . [W]hat I mean, it seemed to me, that . . . I'm just wondering if an understanding of the thought of death in terms of the fact that it terminates life makes a real difference, if we're constantly aware of it. . . . Is it somehow placed in your value system, so that you're making decisions all the time in this vein, in the fact that this is part of life that could be terminated . . . ? It seems to me that people want to, that this isn't in the value system. . . .

Nancy: It is or it isn't?

Cal: It isn't, in a way.

* * *

Shaffer: I think most of us look on . . . I think I probably look on my own death as a catastrophe, as a misfortune.

Cal: Why? Because you haven't done what you wish you'd done, or what? You see, that point . . .

Shaffer: I'm sure, when the time comes, I won't have. No.

Frank: I tell you, Cal, I tried an experiment one time, to get up in the morning and to try to pretend that you're going to die that night. No, seriously, try to make it as real as possible. You'd be surprised what you can get done in a day.

***

Bess: I think that would be the worst thing in the world: to know when you're going to die. Oh, that scares me to death. I never think of death. I just think of it. I think of it in the terms of, well, "When I go I'm going to go." Like if I took an airplane ride, I think, well, "If I'm supposed to die, I'll die, and if I'm not I won't." It doesn't matter if the plane crashes or anything. But the thought of knowing I was going to die scares me to death. I don't know how I would accept that.

Nancy: Would you want the doctor to keep it from you?

Bess: Yes, I would want him to. But yet it would really bug me knowing that I didn't know the truth. . . . I would want to know the truth, I would want to know the truth, but at the same time it would really frighten me. . . .

Eleanor: Well, I think I'm like you, I'm afraid too—just the thought of it—I mean, I've had a baby and everything, you know, my teeth drilled and all that. But every time I think of it I get scared, and that's . . . I don't think of death. I mean even, just tonight, [a law student working on a clinical estate-planning project] was drawing up my will, and he asked me what I wanted—well, just very nonchalantly. It didn't even click until I came here and you said what we were going to talk about tonight, and I thought "What did I go through already?" you know, and it never—I never even thought of myself dying. Here I was writing my will and telling him where I wanted things to go and putting up trusts and whatever, and it never occurred to me that I really might die.

Shaffer: It's a little like Rachel's thinking about what people say when they look at her laid out in the funeral parlor.

Eleanor: I think, I know I probably steer away from it. I don't like to think about it. I don't know why. I think because I'm afraid—because you don't know if you've lived right, you know, you're going to go to heaven or hell, too, you know. . . .

42

Bess: Now, that isn't what bothers me. I never think about that either, about going to heaven or hell, I just think, "Well, if I live the way I think I should live, I can't do any better." And I never think whether I'm going to go to heaven or hell. I never think of that either.

* * *

Nancy: You know this story about they asked St. Francis and he said, "Well, if I knew I was going to die at the end of the day, I'd just finish hoeing my garden."

Bess: Yeah. I don't think I could go out and do great things, you know. I think I would just go right on scrubbing floors.

Herb: That's a great thing.

Nancy: Would you call your mother or something like that?

Bess: Yeah, I think I would. . . .

Rachel: You know it's really strange, in the kind of work I did [X-ray Technician], we just had come across two young boys, ages like 20 and 22 years old, who had terminal cancer. They knew they would die within such—you know, within a six-month period of time. And very strange to say, inwardly I'd love to, I would really like to know what they're thinking. But outwardly they are the most happy people I've seen. You know, they really . . . you know, it's really strange. And I thought "My God, they're doing to die. . . . How can they be so happy?"

Bess: I kind of think, too, that once you accept the initial shock that you're going to die I think that you have to overcome it. From the people I have known who have found out they had cancer, I think they really inwardly still have an inner hope that maybe they will survive it. I don't know, I don't think anybody ever gives up the hope of living.

Rachel: I think that outwardly they have this appearance for the people around them. So that they won't be so depressed. . . . They're thinking more of their parents, and they're thinking that, "Well, if I act real happy then they won't, feel quite so bad about it, where if I run around feeling very depressed, they're going to feel more depressed."

* * *

Eleanor: Well, if you knew you were going to die, would you go on doing what you're doing, or would you . . . I don't think I would change my life. You would do things that you enjoy doing. Stay home and do what I've always done.

George: You would, Eleanor, you say?

Shaffer: Would you talk to Frank about it?

Eleanor: If I knew I was going to die, would he know? You mean, and talk. I don't know. I think he would make me all confused. Really. This is a terr . . . but I think he would. I would wonder if I was doing the right thing, whereas if I just did it, I would feel like I would be doing the right thing. But if I asked him I think that I wouldn't know. I mean . . .

James: He must be a great consolation for you.
[Laughter]
Frank: This is a true educational experience. . . .
Eleanor: . . .I work more on an emotional plane than Frank does, and I think he thinks things out whereas I feel things, I . . . you know . . . I really feel bad about this lots of times because lots of times people think I'm pretty dumb. But I guess I just can't work the way he does, or I just haven't tried. You know, just not trying. But, I don't know if I really would.

* * *

Eleanor: . . .if you knew you were going to die, and you went out and did something you wanted to do all your life—and I don't know what, I can't think of anything right now, but this would just impress on your mind the reason why you're doing it. And I don't think that's why I would stay home. Or, you know, your daily life, your routine, would get you so that you wouldn't think about what was going to happen next.

Frank: You know, Jack, a lot of people say they are afraid of a painful death—you know, of physical pain. And I've often thought, just like this idea of astonishment that you mentioned, that you would be so astonished you would never feel pain. I don't think very many people would. If they were conscious enough to feel anything. You know, "My God, it's really happening."

George: Yeah. Has anyone here ever been very close to death? And experienced that feeling? Well, the astonishment I—I was very close once and I was astonished. I was very astonished. I said to myself, "My God, it's really happening."

Eleanor: I guess you're right because I really thought I was going to die, and it was so ridiculous because I was on a plane that was landing, only I didn't know it was landing. It was an unscheduled stop, and I really thought I was going to die. But I thought: I can't believe it, you know, just like that. I guess I wasn't afraid of the plane crashing, I was just afraid of what was going to happen after that. I didn't think about—you know—burning or anything.

Nancy: Was yours a certainty? Was it a—

George: Pretty close, yeah. I—at least I thought it was. And the people who were with me thought it was, too. And I was astonished, I was very surprised that this was it. And it came into my mind, you know, the fact that they say, just before you die, you sort of live your whole life. Everything just passes before your eyes. I was aware of that, when this was happening, I was aware of the fact. I was thinking this was supposed to happen and I made it happen as a result. I started thinking about my family and things, you know. And it was really surprising, but it was certainly astonishing. I was so surprised that this was going to happen today.

James: How old were you, George?

George: Oh, I was old. I was in college. I was around a junior I think. I was definitely aware of what was going on. And, one thing I wanted to say before is . . . Eleanor, this is when you were talking you said that you would just live your life the way you've always lived it, if you had the knowledge that you were going to die in the very near future. Well, what I find very bothersome is that I won't do things because I fear death. There's so many things I want to do, you know, like sky dive and things like this. I would love to do this, but I have too much of a fear of death to do it. And I think if I knew that my death was certain, if my death were certain, I would I think, I would do a lot of things that I wouldn't normally do because . . .

Eleanor: Well, that to you is living then I guess maybe you're. . . .

Cal: My immediate reaction to that is that . . . if I knew I was going to die in a month, I certainly wouldn't go sky diving tomorrow. . . .

Martha: If you only had a month to live . . .

Herb: You'd try to preserve it?

Cal: I don't know. Yeah. That's the thing that really puzzles me. . . . One word that's been thrown out a lot is I would do the things I enjoy. That's something that in a way doesn't have very much meaning for me. Because I really don't know what I enjoy. What is enjoyment? Is it sitting around having a few beers? Or is it doing what I'm supposed to be doing? Like, in big terms . . . being a good student or something like that? You know, when I'm studying, I wish I could go have a beer, and when I'm having a beer, I say "My God, I should be studying." *** Listen, it comes down again to the total question, I guess, as Herb calls it . . . what is it? You know, when we talk about enjoying life? For me, death means establishing what life is . . . again. . . . In line with what you're saying, or what you're striving at, striving towards, . . . what does life really mean to us? I mean (to Shaffer) what are you actually driving at in this?

* * *

Shaffer: Nothing. I think that's the beauty of this way of talking about it. You just sit down with people you're close to and talk about a subject personally. And I don't think you can bring hypotheses into it. If you bring—it doesn't seem to me it will work if you come in with some ideas that you want to confirm.

* * *

Cal: [When I was in a hospital, with a serious allergic reaction, and nearly died:] It wasn't anything. I was very conscious of thinking of nothing, and conscious of the fact that I was thinking of nothing. And I didn't care and I didn't have any energy to think one way or another. I was just, I was just there. And I felt the possibility, I felt something going out of me. You know, I felt I was losing energy and then they put the adrenalin in me, and then life started coming back. But it was just sort of . . . I was just conscious of losing contact and then it was coming back, sort of like—There was no—I wasn't upset or anything.

Bess: You know, Cal, you say this. Because I had an experience when I was, you know, I was completely out of it; everything was black; and when I came back, the thought came to me that I could die so easily and I never would have known it. Now this really scared me because I always thought that I wanted to be aware that I was dying anyway, instead of like people say, who just slough away. I thought, is this really—of course, I suppose you would awaken, you know. I don't know what happens. But this really scared me, because I thought, "Gee, I could have died."

Herb: Really isn't the point of that that you're dying right now? And I'm dying, and everyone in here is dying right now. [Uneasy laughter]

James: You're saying that someday you're going to die.

Herb: No, you're dying right now.

George: There is a constant disintegration of cells.

Bess: No, I . . .

James: That happens when you're 27 years old, doesn't it, George?

George: Yeah, when you reach 25 . . .

James: I've got, I'm still going on . . .

Nancy: Listen, I'm almost 35 and I feel like I'm living more every day. I know all this theory, this biological . . .

Herb: No, I don't mean it that way. I mean biopsychological, in the way that Plato meant it, that philosophy is preparation for death.

Nancy: I don't know. I feel like I live more every day. Well, there's maybe a few days' regression. But every day life is fuller. I always feel like today—when I'm just thinking about myself and my immediate circle and my own family—I think this is the best moment that ever was. And this is the best day. Of course, if, all of a sudden, I think people are dying in Vietnam, and somebody's crashing over on (highway) 31, and all that sort of thing, well then, right away then I have some perspective. It's sort of a matter of economics I think. Death's sort of like the air in this room; it isn't valuable, but if it were the only air in the world it would be valuable. And I think maybe . . . older people must feel that about death, when they see other people, all their friends, dying year after year after year. But I think even at almost 35 you're still young enough to feel that—Cal, like about Grace's brother, death doesn't come close to—you're still not thinking you're going to die like that, right away, are you Cal? I don't think, when somebody dies, it's a threat to my life. I think once you get to the place, though, where other people's deaths do make you think about your own death—and maybe you are able to think that way—then I suppose everybody . . .

Jack: You know, that point—in one of the books you have some psychologist did a study of the bomb victims at Hiroshima—he was there right after. He said people were just . . . were dying, you know, just right and left, but you could walk down the street, and those who were alive were totally impervious to it, or seemingly totally impervious to it, and it seemed to me mainly because they saw their own death there, and wouldn't recognize it.

Shaffer: They anesthetized themselves. . . . That experience I've had personally. When the first news of King's death came over I was really pretty offhanded about it. And when I read—and I felt guilty later about being so offhanded about it. . . . You know, "too bad."

Eleanor: That's just exactly the way I felt.

Shaffer: That was the sort of reaction I had: "too bad." And I do that when I read the papers, sometimes. I'll see the headline, Four Youths Killed on the Toll Road," and I'll look through the names to see if it's anybody I know. And it hardly ever is. And I say: "Well, too bad." I think maybe that's that kind of reaction, magnified a million times, of course, when you have people laying all over the streets, as those people had, but . . .

James: I want to ask Dolly something I think it's—When we get a paper from [home] and all she does is—the first thing she likes to do is to see who died.

Dolly: Well. I really don't know why. I imagine it's because a lot of my friends, a lot of family friends, are older people. I don't know why I do that.

* * *

James: Most of the people who I've known who have died it's been great: my grandmothers and my grandfather who I think i was very close to, and lived with them for a number of years, and another one who did a heck of a lot for me. When—you know, it was worse the last couple of years of their lives . . . and some of the saddest moments were their last years and their death was a relief for me, and for them too. I didn't get a chance to see them as much, and I knew they missed me, and I felt maybe guilty about not missing them as much as they missed me, and I saw them dying, and I saw my grandfather fighting his life away. I saw him failing, and so their deaths were certainly deaths of grace. The only tragic things that have really, emotionally brought me up, I suspect, were Kennedy's and King's.

Rachel: I felt that the people that had died, my grand-parents. . . . And we could see them going, and it's a blessing when they go, you know because . . . they suffer so much the last few times and now their suffering is over. But, when I was 18 years old, my best girl friend all of a sudden just—I had been out with her the night before, and the next night they called me at midnight to tell me they just took her to the hospital, and she had spinal meningitis and she was going to die. And, you know, just tremendous shock. I was with her almost every night for two weeks when she was in a, you know, complete coma. And she never regained consciousness. And, when she died, now it really took a part of me because we were such close friends. And it really, really hit me strong. You know, every little ailment I've had after that I thought I was going to die for sure. But that, you know, when it's someone your own age. . . .

James: I think you get taught about death by how you experience it. I think my own reaction to death is based upon the people I've seen die. And that's why I think I'm a little less concerned about it. I often wonder how I'm going to react when somebody who's really too young to die, or maybe my own mother and father, go.

Nancy: I wonder if, when you get older, if you begin to think more about death. Now you are all young and full of promise and you all have a lot of ideas. . . .

* * *

[W]hen you get to be a certain age, then you begin to say—to look around and say, "Maybe I'm not going to be as successful as I was going to be," or "maybe I'm not going to be able to do these things that I had in mind," or "maybe I'm not going to be able to . . . to have time to fulfill all these things." Maybe that's when death begins to be more frightening than it is when you just feel like you're pretty sure of licking things, at least long enough.

Eleanor: I don't know. I don't feel these things.

Cal: Do you think that there's a difference between—Like most of the women who were talking said they would continue doing the things that they knew they were going to do, the ones who have been, well, actually mothers I guess . . . their role is defined. Maybe this is my trouble: I don't see my life as having begun yet. You know, I'm still—up until this point, everything has sort of been planned out for me. . . .

* * *

Frank: [George was] saying, he won't sky dive because he's afraid of dying, but if you know it's going to happen anyway . . . [That is, if you know you're going to die.]

George: Yes. . . .

Frank: What difference does it make what anybody says about you, thinks about you, because you're not going to live long enough to worry about it?

Jack: You'd have the total freedom.

* * *

Andrew: I can't quite understand the fearing of death. The fear of death is . . . [Fear of] the circumstances. . . . . But as far as the fear of death is concerned, when you mention sky diving . . . things like that that would be your real thrill. I don't think it's the fear of death that holds you back; it's the fear of bodily injury. [Murmurs of agreement.] As far as fear of death is concerned, I can't see fearing death itself.

Shaffer: Can you imagine yourself sky diving and feel a little tension about it?

Andrew: Not about death, no.

Shaffer: No, no tension about sky diving?

Andrew: I feel a little tension about it, but . . .

Shaffer: Don't explain it, just . . .

Andrew: What I'm worried about is getting a broken leg or something.

Shaffer: Suppose you're taking something that, if it went wrong, you wouldn't have to worry about a broken leg. I should think sky diving is pretty close.

Andrew: I think there would be less fear there. I'd fear something like that less than something, compared to . . . where I'd either be successful or I'd be bodily maimed or . . .

Shaffer: That's what I wondered.

Harry: I think death is always up here. And that you make your decision and take your chance . . . and you're never really certain and you're not deciding to die, but you can come close to it. And what George would like to do . . . there's a lot of things George would like to do that would bring that death dipping toward him but he doesn't want to do it unless he's certain of death. . . .

Shaffer: George, you're saying you would go sky diving if you only had a month to live?

George: Right, I would. There's so many things I want to do now, but my only reluctance is death, I think, more than injury. I would do them. I would do them. I mean I really want to do these things, but I just have a lot . . . I am very reluctant to do them for fear of death.

James: Why do you fear death, George?

Eleanor: It would be over. I'd fear injury because I'd be in pain for a certain amount of time, but if I were, you know, facing death, I don't know, I can't really say, because, you know, I'm not. I don't feel like . . .

George: I just don't think of injury. I don't care about a broken leg, a broken leg, or a fractured skull, or concussions, or broken arms. That doesn't bother me that much. Losing my life is what bothers me.

Eleanor: That's what I mean . . .

George: I would sky dive. If I knew the only thing that could happen to me as the result of a sky-diving mishap would be a broken bone, I wouldn't even hesitate. I would go sky diving.

* * *

Andrew: Well, why do you say dying?

George: Well, my God, I think we all admit a fear of death. I just don't want to die because I don't want to deprive my wife and my children, or I don't want to miss things that may be pretty enjoyable to me in the near future.

Martha: I think it's the risk, instead of the things where you say, well, you wouldn't do this because the chances would be that you would snuff out your life. But then—I mean, I have a fatalistic view, like this—I mean, I could do it, sky diving or not. I wouldn't sky dive because I would be scared to death. It wouldn't be because I . . . you know, I wouldn't think that the day I went sky diving I was going to die. If I didn't die then, if I was supposed to die, I would die walking across the street or something. And that's why I can't really understand this, because I have a little more fatalistic view. I think if I'm going to die, I'm going to die anyway, and sky diving isn't what I would be afraid of dying of. And I would be afraid of bodily injury. I would mind.

George: Well, you know everyone knows they're going to die sometime. It's just a matter of how soon. I mean, you say you have a fatalistic attitude. You know that I'm going to die sometime, it could very well happen falling, going down the stairs. . . .

Martha: Yeah, but you can't make it happen.

George: Going down stairs, the chances of dying by going down stairs or taking an automobile drive, I don't think are as great as they are sky diving.

Martha: You see you don't understand my point. My point is that I feel that there is a previously determined time when you're going to die, and you're going to die then no matter what you're doing. And so your sky diving is not that bad.

* * *

George: I don't think we have really accepted death. We may have accepted the fact that people die, but, the fact that—I don't know, if we have accepted death—I don't know if it's that unreasonable. To accept death is something other than accepting the fact that people die. . . .

Andrew: There is only one alternative to accepting it and that's thinking you're going to be immortal. There's only one alternative.

George: The alternative is not to accept it. You know, it's either to accept the fact of death or not to accept it. I accept the fact that all people are going to die, but I don't accept the notion of death itself, I reject that, I don't even . . . I don't say, "Well, some day I'm going to die, and, well, it doesn't really bother me."

Herb: Well, then you're really divorced from reality. You said there were all kinds of things you would like to do, but you wouldn't do them because you're afraid, of all things, of depriving your family or something. Well, what kind of life can you live on that basis? What kind of life except eat and sleep? Is that worth living for? I mean, if you're not doing any of the things that you said you'd really like to do? That seems to me to be a . . .

* * *

Jack: You know, I think this fatalistic attitude, too, of "When my number's up, it'll be up, doesn't matter when it is," is even less of an acceptance of it. Because to some extent it will excuse such a risk, and . . . well, maybe it's good for somebody who . . . You always hear the story of the guys who are in Vietnam, or wherever it happened to be, really trying to accommodate themselves to the whole idea of risking their lives by the number system. And it seems to me that you're trying to . . . you are even less in an acceptance of death, you're trying to do away with the uncertainty of it, too.

Eleanor: . . .it's someone else.

Martha: What you do is . . . It isn't an issue for you, then. Because you feel that there's nothing you can do to stop it, and you just live your life, and when it happens it happens, and you don't—you can't put it off—and you wouldn't want to, and you just do your thing and that's it.

* * *

George: You see, I don't accept that because I can't picture suicide in that notion. In other words, if there were a knife lying here, I picked it up and stuck it in myself, I would be living if I hadn't done that. I would have died otherwise. In other words, my time wasn't up.

* * *

James: What do you think of a prisoner who, you know, last meal. . . .Everytime I see it, everytime I read about somebody going to jail, like in "In Cold Blood" or something like that, I think it's the most cruel thing, because I identify with the situation. And some jackass asked this guy what he wanted for his last meal, and he can have anything he wants. How could you be capable of going all the way and having huge . . . I don't know what it is. It seems to me to be somebody really laughing in the face of death. I talk about being rather glib about death, and I wouldn't be able to touch a thing. . . . When I read about these things, it always disturbs me.

* * *

Cal: Has anybody here—I don't know, this gets awful personal, but—Has anybody here ever thought of suicide, or known somebody who tried to commit suicide?

Frank: I've thought of it. I wasn't ready to die.

Jack: I think everybody has thought of suicide, whether they thought of it as a practical matter is another thing.

Cal: I mean as a practical matter.

51

Nancy: You mean, thought of. . . . carrying it out?

Shaffer: If I've thought of it, I've got it buried, because I can only remember thinking of it in an abstract sort of way. . . .

* * *

I think when I fantasy it, it is in terms of showing somebody. Punishing somebody.

Eleanor: I've thought of it that way and I've also thought of it as a—as I was feeling in college. There's this really beautiful tragic situation, you know. I remember writing a paper on it. And really when I think of it now I really feel like an idiot. But at the time I really thought this was the thing, you know, and I wrote this paper about drowning in a river and it was just so, I don't know, the flowery words, and just so, almost romantic. . . .

* * *

Bess: I can't imagine anybody committing suicide for a reason like that, unless they are insane. I think if a normal person would commit suicide, it's because he has lost all hope—in living. There was a time when maybe I really had suicidal tendencies. There was a time when I really thought: Why am I living? Because I really had no hope for tomorrow, I had no hope that tomorrow's going to be any better than today. And I just felt like I was lost because nobody really cared, and I was just lost in a whirlwind.

Frank: Don't you think it's really an act of rebellion?

Bess: No, I didn't think of it. I didn't think about any repercussions of it, of it as an act of rebellion. I just felt that I wish I was going to die tomorrow, because I had nothing to live for for tomorrow.

Frank: A sort of escape.

Bess: Yeah.

Nancy: Yeah.

Martha: I think anyone that does that is really in a vacuum. You're just there. Isolated. And you're just . . . that's it, I mean, you're not thinking of other people or tomorrow or anything.

* * *

Frank: It seems to me that something that's as . . . or as meaningful as death . . . to do the act that takes your life . . . it doesn't seem to me you're deprived of your will at that moment.

Martha: No, I'm just saying that they can't live with life. They can't accept it at this time . . .

Frank: All right, that they can't accept it, and . . .

Martha: I will not.

Frank: I will not, yeah.

Martha: I don't know if it's that much. I think your can't is your will, you know. The fact that you can't do it, you are unable to do it, that is your will right there. And your will is unable to force you to do anything other. . . .

Bess: You don't even want to will it. I don't think you're even . . .

Frank: Well, put it this way; I refuse to face the fear, I refuse to face the inability.

Eleanor: And the final act of my will will be to will my own death.

Frank: I'll get out of this situation.

* * *

Bess: Is this discussion bothering anybody? It bothers me. I can't . . .

Shaffer: The suicide does?

Bess: Not just the suicide, but just all this we are talking about: death . . . about what you were talking about before, the guy who killed . . . about the last meal before execution. . . . That just gives me butterflies. Really it does. You know, I think a lot of times in these discussions when people are talking about things that doesn't seem to bother any of you, and I'm just churning inside.

* * *

Martha: To answer your question: No.

Bess: Really? Like tonight when you talked about death?

Martha: Maybe it's because I feel like it's part of an experi . . . I mean, we're here sort of to talk about death, this is it now . . .

Eleanor: It doesn't touch me. It just doesn't bother, doesn't touch me. I just can't feel it.

Herb: It touches me. It touched me coming out here . . . across the bridge. . . . I was rolling up the windows because I knew that if the car fell in the river. . . .

James: Yeah [then] you would be saved, you wouldn't die.

Herb: I mean it's always with you. It was with me on Shaffers' gravel road, because wouldn't it be absurd if this Volkswagen rolled over in the gravel, and there he was, "several people, with a case of beer, on their way to the party, found him."

Jack: That's the point that bothers me, Herb, is that, you know, you live your life and then it ends in something so stupid.

Herb: That's what I meant about the tragic absurdity of it. The point is that if you realize it's going to be tragically absurd, however you go, your life can be more meaningful.

James: I think I would rather go in this way. I can think of nothing better than to get run over by guys going to a party. Cancer and this type of stuff, that is much worse to me than the absurd.

Martha: That's you, see, that's you. I can see that.

Shaffer: I think I sort of look at it as a pretty ridiculous thing to happen. When I think of it personally. It seemed to me that what Cal was talking about, about King, demonstrates a good deal of courage. It seems to me that's courage by definition, to say that what I'm doing involves this risk, and I'm going to do it anyway because this is more important.

53

James: . . .What really krocks me about King's death is the very absurdity of it. It's the wild thing, you know, with our whole lives, the whole country and the whole environment, and that's the way things are and it's so ridiculous. So stupid.

Herb: And that's the wisdom of the Book of Job. Like, I'm standing out there in the yard hoeing tulips or something and my little kid's out there running around in the driveway, and I know that if he goes ten feet in the other direction he could be annihilated before I could bat an eyelash. But what can you do? You have to live in the face of this. . . .

* * *

Shaffer: I suppose you look around and say, "There's a lot of things that might happen, that more or less fall; but this, this is just plain stupid."

Frank: Death is a contradiction. Let me put it another way. I've talked before about death being comical; I guess I'm alone in this, but I can see death being really funny, in a comic sense.

James: I think I'm with you a little bit there. And it seems to me that he's scared by it.

Frank: You made the statement when we started out that when somebody else dies, that threatens you. That didn't come through to me at all. . . .

Eleanor: It's sort of a relief. I mean, the first time I ever thought about death and it's kind of in a comical context. . . . When I was in high school and my father came in every morning and he woke me up, and it was always I had to get up before ten minutes. . . . I'm lying in bed and I'm thinking, "I have to get up," and then I'm thinking, "Wouldn't it be nice just to be dead." And you could just sleep and sleep and be just non-being, absolutely nothing. . . . And I thought, "Gee, that would be really great." And, of course, I got up. But it's to me as though life is rough, it's really tough. You've got terrible responsibility, and we've got to think every minute, and you've got lots to do, and when somebody dies, you know, you say, they just put down their hoe. . . .

* * *

Harry: I'd like to go back to what Professor Shaffer said, that we've been talking about death being a threat to us and Andrew was one—and myself—who said it wasn't a threat . . . and then you said that it's stupid, and this conveyed an idea that it's a mistake, that it's a mistake in the natural order. And I think if you would think it's a mistake, then it would be a threat to you, just as any kind of a mistake would be a threat. And those of us that have accepted it as the natural order, then it's not a threat.

* * *

James: If somebody drinks too much, and comes across the center lane and hits me, it's a mistake, it happened, but it's a common thing, but it's not really, I don't think, it's just too common to be outside the natural order.

* * *

Martha: But I mean that's why I think this is a mistake, and I can see what you're talking about. Everyone thinks their death is a huge mistake, you know, I mean, because everyone's ego makes them, you know, like someone said, I think Prof. Shaffer said, he thought his death . . . he'd look on it as a big catastrophe. I think that's it. Your ego . . . you want to go out in a flash of glory, and maybe what people fear is dying like an animal or something.

Eleanor: The type of dying, the way you die.

Frank: Oh, I understood Prof. Shaffer as saying that—to say that no matter how he died, he'd consider it absurd.

Martha: Right, but that's ego, I think.

Shaffer: Well, I didn't see myself as a martyr.

Eleanor: But if you did, would you think that way?

Shaffer: Yeah, well that—no, probably not.

Eleanor: Would you be afraid of death that way?

Shaffer: Frank touched me a great deal. If you're put in a situation where somebody says he's going to kill his kid or you, he said I'd rather you'd kill me. That was very touching, and I wouldn't see that as stupid, no.

Eleanor: Then—well, that's what I wanted to say: Is that your fear of death or is it the manner of death?

Shaffer: Well, any death I can conceive of as likely to happen to me is stupid.

Frank: It seems to me that the corollary to that is that you think you should be immortal.

Shaffer: Yeah.

Harry: There's different kinds of deaths.

Shaffer: But—sure, I think I am.

[Laughter]

James: Do you think of old age much? Have you ever been around real old people? When their eyesight starts to go and their hearing starts to go?

Shaffer: Just a very little, not as you did.

James: Yeah. Maybe . . .

Harry: It's hell, it's really bad news.

Shaffer: Well, I can say that of people in general.

[Laughter]

Andrew: You won't admit it for yourself.

Frank: Perhaps you can go even further and say you don't even think you're going to get old.

Martha: I don't think anyone really thinks they are.

Eleanor: No, I can't think . . .

Martha: I don't think you can really picture yourself older. You know it's going to happen, but you don't expect the reality of your own old death, your own old age. Have you? Can you see? Do you really think it's going to happen?

James: Have you been around old people?

Martha: No, but I still can't—because I only see them when they're only old. I've never seen someone grow—you know—terrifically old, when you knew them when they were young and vital . . . I mean, I don't know what's going to happen. . . .

* * *

Jack: You know this business about acceptance. I don't think that old age is any more accepted than death is. For instance, if you're saying that death is accepted, why are we sitting here smoking cigarettes? It's almost a profession, holding that thing in your hand, that you're never going to die. And yet . . . for every cigarette you smoke, it's five minutes off your life.

* * *

Bess: Death really is completely divorced then from [Martin Luther King's] whole life, isn't it?

James: Yeah. I remember hearing that, who it was that killed Kennedy, and I remember being very angry, very disturbed at who killed Kennedy. Even his wife said, you know, it was too bad that he had died by some silly man coming by. . . .

James: "Some silly communist," that's the way Manchester quoted her.

Dolly: Instead of dying for a cause, like civil rights.

Harry: What does this mean? I don't understand what this means.

Frank: It's much nicer to die for a cause—

* * *

George: Death has nothing to do with the cause for which he lived. For Martin Luther King it did. I'm talking now, I'm talking about this situation, James, I think that's the big difference. In fact, we feel that if an individual's death has some relationship to the cause for which he lived, then that death was more meaningful. And that's why Martin Luther King's death would not be meaningful had he died in an automobile accident.

Martha: Not to him, not to him.

Eleanor: Yeah. Well.

Shaffer: I wonder about that.

Andrew: Yeah, I think if King had died in a plane crash the only difference would be that there wouldn't have been so many riots.

Herb: Hammarskjöld . . .there's the same sort of thing. Anyone who knew Hammarskjöld's life knows that his life is at least as significant as King's. . . .

* * *

Conclusions

I would like to present two preliminary and personal thoughts about conclusions: First, I am tentative about conclusions because they may cause you, my reader, to neglect the opportunity you have to draw your own conclusions. If that seems to you to be likeiy, I hope you will pass over my thoughts until you have formed thoughts of your own, at which time you may decide my conclusions are not personally important to you. The main value of this chapter is likely to be your personal reaction; if my conclusions will interfere with that personal reaction, I hope you will not even read them.

Second, I have appended to this chapter a research instrument developed by Dr. Edwin Shneidman, which is designed to ferret out your personal experience and attitudes toward your own death. That experience is far more important to reading the remainder of this book than are my conclusions for this chapter. I encourage you to test yourself—if at all—before you read what I have to say about my sensitivity-group experiment. This thought is centrally important because, if this book is of any value to you it will be in encouraging you to feel what clients feel in the testamentary situation. You need empathy, feelings of your own, to bring that off.

With these reservations, I see several interesting research points—many of them verified and extended in different ways in the chapters which follow—in the candid, human way my students and their wives talked with my wife and me about death. Here are some of what seem to me to be the major themes:

Death attitudes are different for different people. The main dividing line, as one might expect in a group of young people, is between the old and the young. The young person tended here to regard death as an intrusion; perhaps that is the way he regards death for himself. In the old, though, he thinks that death is more a matter of life being "rounded with a sleep." Death for the old is "natural," ("deaths of grace"), but death for the young is either a catastrophe or inexplicable fate. There are here both attitudes toward death and attitudes toward attitudes.

Attitudes toward death are ambivalent. My predicate adjective is a trite word these days, a word that comes into our language from chemistry via psychoanalysis. Frank put it in a not-trite way when he indicated that his feelings toward death were "a tension between two feelings simultaneously." To some extent, my students and their wives took positive attitudes toward death; they saw it as almost desirable. It can even be yearned for, as restful. It validates acts of heroism and unselfishness; these acts give meaning to death—so that Martin Luther King, Jr., and Dag Hammarskjöld cannot be said to have died absurdly—

but, implicit in these feelings, death also gives meaning to great deeds, if only because the doer of the deeds is removed and defined by death, and his deeds live on without him.

Death is also romantic; it has a lure about it—so much so that a mentally healthy young person who is being candid will admit that he has thought about suicide positively. This may be more notable among women than among men, but it seems to be present in both sexes. First-hand experience with facing death was not as unpleasant as we might think. It was unusual, somewhat frightening, but not psychologically painful. ("You would be so astonished you would never feel pain.") Finally, death may be an escape—from a hard life in the young, from physical burdens and disabilities in the old.

Death is frightening because it is uncertain, because it will sever important relationships—especially relationships which involve an obligation—and because it will cause experience to cease.

The loss of loved ones to death is a cruel separation, after which the loved one is distant but still significant. Attitudes toward the death of another person are relevant here, if only because death in the other (as Sartre would put it) is the only experience of death that we have. Our young friends thought of the death of loved ones in terms of its effect on themselves and in terms of its effect on living people who were even closer to the dead man. ("All of a sudden, here's this void.") These deaths were sorrowful because of separation but almost inspiring, nonetheless, in those whose deaths could be associated with courage.

It would be desirable to seize death. In some of what these young people said there was, as a group-leader I know would have put it, a note of hostility. Death is resented, perhaps because it cannot be controlled. It would be desirable to take death in hand, to put a date and a place on it. One who thinks of death as a consequence of fate was even seen as in an advantageous position, because fate deprives death of its cruel uncertainty. This suggests—although I admit here to going beyond my students—that planning is one way to cope with death; if we cannot abolish death, we can at least plan to frustrate it by removing the worst consequences of its surprise.

Even though this setting, as Dr. Coulson predicted, tended to relax defenses to death attitudes, defenses were an important part of the reactions to death. The most obvious defense is denial: My death is not likely ("it never really occurred to me"); the only way I could die is to be run over by an automobile or have an accident while, say, sky diving. I don't want to think about death; discussion of death, even in a safe, trusting environment, is fearful. ("Every time I think about death I get scared.") I am surprised and dismayed when I realize what I have been saying or thinking. Death inhibits me from doing the things I would like to do, and makes the things I do less enjoyable. ("They're going to die. How can they be so happy.")

Religious solutions to the problems of death are only a minor consolation, if any at all. So far as I know, all of the participants were practicing Christians, but there was almost no discussion of religious solutions to death. What discussion there was seemed balanced between consolation and thoughts of judgment which made the prospect of death more, rather than less, frightening. I draw a negative inference from this about the value of religious faith in coping with the anxieties caused by death.

Death is faced by making life meaningful. Our young women thought of their children, of their homes, and of their relationships within the family in terms of St. Francis and his garden. They felt that their lives were meaningful and that continuing to live them is the best way to adjust to thoughts of death. The young men thought of death in terms of meaningful lives, too, but their reactions suggested more ambitious and daring meanings—a life, for instance, modeled on Martin Luther King, Jr. They expressed impatience for an end to their nearly 20 years of education, so that they could begin to make the social contributions this model implies. The somewhat older members of the group, my wife and I, were perhaps a shade more realistic, and she a shade more optimistic, than our companions.

Appendix to Chapter 3: The
Shneidman Attitude to Death Survey

What follows is a research device and pedagogical exercise developed by the renowned "suicidologist" Edwin N. Shneidman, while he was teaching at Harvard in 1969. It is included here with his permission. It was used in the course called "Social Relations 155"; it is inserted here to provide the reader an opportunity for personal exploration of some of the attitudes discussed by my sensitivity group. Dr. Shneidman's new book, *Youth on Death,* develops many of the themes suggested here. (I have eliminated from the questionnaire items of ethnographic information, which would be appropriate if I were using it for research.)

1. Compose a brief autobiography, describe yourself briefly, emphasizing those personality features or characteristics that distinguish you from other people.

2. Circle *one* number in each scale.

On a nine-point scale, how would you rate your lethality—the probability of you killing yourself at this moment?

1	2	3	4	5	6	7	8	9
LOW				MEDIUM				HIGH

How would you rate your lethality generally over the past few years?

1	2	3	4	5	6	7	8	9
LOW				MEDIUM				HIGH

How would you rate your present physical health?

1	2	3	4	5	6	7	8	9
EXCELLENT				MEDIUM				POOR

How do you rate your present over-all mental health?

1	2	3	4	5	6	7	8	9
EXCELLENT				MEDIUM				POOR

Rate your present perturbation—how equanimious or how disturbed you are.

1	2	3	4	5	6	7	8	9
LOW				MEDIUM				HIGH

At present, how *depressed* are you?

1	2	3	4	5	6	7	8	9
NOT AT ALL				MEDIUM			EXTREMELY	

3. Feelings:

A. (Check one). Generally, I have been feeling:

____On Top of the world
____Swell
____Cheerful
____On the whole all right
____About like the average person
____Just fair
____Kind of low
____Pretty lousy
____Down and out
____Wished I were dead

B. (Check one). Generally, I have been feeling:
___ That I was bursting with energy
___ More than average energy
___ Not too much pep, but I can keep going
___ Don't have much energy
___ Tired
___ Completely worn out

C. (Check one). Generally, I have been feeling:
___ Full of enthusiasm
___ Everything's fine
___ The future doesn't look too bad
___ Can't complain
___ Sort of discouraged
___ Uncertain about the future
___ Insecure
___ Dissatisfied with everything
___ Can't stand much more
___ No hope

D. (Check one). Generally, I have been feeling:
___ Never felt better in my life
___ Felt good
___ Pretty good
___ A little down, but mostly good
___ Fair to middling
___ As good as could be expected
___ Just about able to keep going
___ Rotten
___ Just plain miserable
___ Couldn't feel any worse

Circle whether you Strongly Agree (SA), Agree (A), Don't Know (?), Disagree (D), or Strongly Disagree (SD) with each of the following statements.

A. In many instances, married couples should be encouraged to use birth control devices.   SA   A ? D   SD

B. Mercy-killing, assuming proper precautions are taken, will benefit people on the whole.   SA   A ? D   SD

C. Preventing conception by mechanical birth control devices is as wrong or almost as wrong as taking a human life after birth.   SA   A   ?   D   SD

D. Laws which provide the death penalty for crimes are morally wrong.   SA   A   ?   D   SD

E. Although my definition of God may differ from that of others, I believe there is a God.   SA   A   ?   D   SD

F. Physical or mental illness, no matter how severe or hopeless, should never be the basis for taking the life of the person involved.   SA   A   ?   D   SD

G. Killing during war is just as indefensible as any other sort of killing.   SA   A   ?   D   SD

H. As unfortunate as it is, killing during wartime may be justifiable.   SA   A   ?   D   SD

I. The possibility that God exists today seems very unlikely.   SA   A   ?   D   SD

J. If a mother's life is seriously endangered forced abortion of the fetus may be necessary.   SA   A   ?   D   SD

K. Life after death seems improbable.   SA   A   ?   D   SD

L. I find the prospect of my eventual death disturbing.   SA   A   ?   D   SD

M. There is some sort of existence after our present life ends.   SA   A   ?   D   SD

N. Forced abortion of the fetus is wrong, regardless of the health of the

mother or the social conditions in-
volved.   SA   A   ?   D   SD

O. In the long run, appropriate use of
   the death penalty for crimes will
   benefit society.   SA   A   ?   D   SD

P. I don't think I am really afraid of
   death.   SA   A   ?   D   SD

Q. The killing of animals in scientific
   experiments is never justified, no
   matter what the goal.   SA   A   ?   D   SD

5. A. Rank-order (from 1 to 12) the following in terms of how they
        have influenced your present attitudes toward death.
        ___ death of a relative
        ___ death of a friend
        ___ death of an animal
        ___ religious upbringing
        ___ specific reading (what?)
        ___ films
        ___ television and radio
        ___ conversation
        ___ ritual (funerals for example)
        ___ drug experience
        ___ mystical experience
        ___ other (explain)

    B. Describe in detail the impact of the three factors you chose as
        most influential in Question 4.

6. Discuss your religious affiliations. (How religious are you? Depth
    and contents of your beliefs.) What role has religion played in the
    development of your attitudes toward death?

7. What does death mean to you; that is, how do you conceptualize
    your own death?

8. What were your childhood conceptions of death and dead people?

63

9. Describe your first contact or brush with death. (Your earliest memory or recollection of death.) What were your feelings and reactions? What "remnants" of this experience are in you today?

10. Discuss the ways in which death was talked about in your family. Was it more or less taboo than, for instance, discussion of sex, finances, etc.?

11. Discuss your beliefs about an after-life. Do you wish you could have a greater belief in an after-life?

12. (Check one). How would you describe yourself at present?
___ A death seeker
___ A death initiator
___ A death ignorer
___ A death darer
___ A death chancer
___ A death capitulator
___ A death experimenter
___ A death welcomer
___ A death acceptor
___ A death postponer
___ A death disdainer
___ A death fearer
___ A death threatener
Please explain your choice.

13. People are more afraid of death at certain times of their lives than at others. After that period in life when you think people are most afraid of death, write the number 1; after that period which takes second place in this respect, write the number 2; until finally you write the number 8 after that period when you think people are least afraid of death.

Up to 12 years ___   40 to 49 years ___
13 to 19 years ___   50 to 59 years ___
20 to 29 years ___   60 to 69 years ___
30 to 39 years ___   70 years and over ___

14. Rank these statements about the consequences of your own death on a 1–7 scale, with 1 indicating the least distasteful and 7 indicating the worst or most distasteful.

___ I could no longer have any experiences.

___ I am uncertain as to what might happen to my body after death.

___ I am uncertain as to what might happen to me if there is a life after death.

___ I could no longer care for my dependents.

___ My death would cause grief to my relatives and friends.

___ All my plans and projects would come to an end.

___ The process of dying might be painful.

15. Check those statements (one or more) which apply to your own thoughts about death:

    ___ It will be wonderful

    ___ It holds the promise of a new and better life.

    ___ All my troubles will be over.

    ___ I don't think about it.

    ___ I have nothing to do with the subject.

    ___ I feel fine and have no reason to think about it.

    ___ It's the end of everything.

    ___ Terror overcomes me.

    ___ I dread the thought of it.

16. At what age do you think you would like to die?

17. At what age do you believe that, in fact, you will die?

18. How often do you think about death?

    ___ Very rarely

    ___ Rarely

    ___ Occasionally

    ___ Frequently

    ___ Very frequently

19. What are your smoking habits?

    ___ Never smoked

    ___ Light smoker

    ___ Moderate smoker

    ___ Heavy smoker

    ___ Ex-smoker

20. If it were entirely up to you, what would you have done with your

body after you die? (Buried, cremated, donated to medical school or science, etc. Indifferent.) Why do you make these choices?

21. Has the recent history of organ transplantation affected in any way your attitudes toward death? Explain.

22. Would you be willing to donate your heart for a transplantation (after your death)? To whom? Under what circumstances? How would you feel having your heart beat in another person?

23. Would you be willing to donate one of your kidneys for a transplantation? To whom? Under what circumstances? What about other organs or body products (such as blood transfusion, corneas, semen bank, artificial insemination)? What organs would you prefer to keep to yourself and die with you?

24. Draw a picture of death in any way you wish.

25. Describe what you would prefer your own funeral to be like.

26. Write your own obituary, with, as is customary, a brief biographical account.

27. If you were told that you had a terminal disease and a limited time to live, how would you spend your time until you died? What things would you especially want to do?

28. What books that you have read have had a significant effect upon your attitudes toward death? What effect did they have?

29. Do you intend to leave a will? What special conditions would you put in it? Why?

30. Have any of your attitudes toward death ever been affected by a drug experience? A mystical experience? Indicate details.

31. At any time in your life have you really wanted to die? Why? Describe your feelings and reactions.

32. If or when you are married, would you prefer to outlive your

spouse or would you prefer that your spouse outlive you? Discuss your reasons.

33. In what ways has the possibility of massive human destruction by nuclear war influenced or colored your present attitudes toward death?

34. Are your thoughts or experiences of death ever connected with erotic or sexual situations? Explain.

35. How would you like to be remembered after your death? (In what ways and by whom?) How much does this matter to you?

36. What is your concept of immortality? Discuss.

37. If a patient is going to die soon, should the doctor tell him? Would you want to be told? Would you like your nearest relatives or friends to be told? Discuss your reasons.

38. Are you inclined to entertain thoughts of being killed or dying of a specific disease or in a certain way? How?

39. Under what circumstances would you be willing to actually sacrifice your own life?

40. What do you think of autopsies? Under what circumstances would you approve of one being performed on your body?

41. Describe your own personal moods that make you think of death, (for example, ecstasy, sexuality, success, failure, depression, etc.)

42. Describe what would be an "appropriate" *date* for you (and in what way it would be "appropriate").

43. Have you ever taken another human life or come close to killing someone? What were your emotional reactions to it? What were the circumstances? What are your present feelings?

44. Relate in detail any experience you have had with the death of a loved one.

45. Have you ever suffered great pain? Great despair? Explain. How has it influenced your attitudes toward death?

46. Describe any near-death (or close to death) experience you have had.

47. Have you ever felt extremely hopeless? Describe the situation and circumstances. Did anything happen to sustain your sense of hope? What? How has it affected your attitudes toward death?

48. Can you ever imagine yourself committing suicide? Under what circumstances? At what age? With what method? (Please be as specific as possible.)

49. Have you ever attempted suicide? Describe the circumstances. What were, as you remember them, your motives or reasons? What happened? What were the sequelae?

50. Have you ever contemplated suicide? Explain.

51. Write the suicide note that you would write if you were going to kill yourself. Please indicate to whom the note would be addressed.

52. Do you believe that suicide should always be prevented? Explain.

53. Would you be afraid to die? Under what circumstances would you not be afraid to die?

Part 2: Death, Property, and Giving

4 Values Destroyed by Death

> To be of assistance to you I will put aside myself—the self of ordinary interaction—and enter into your world of perception as completely as I am able. I will become, in a sense, another self for you—an alter ego of your own attitudes and feelings—a safe opportunity for you to discern yourself more clearly, to experience yourself more truly and deeply, to choose more significantly.
>
> *—Carl R. Rogers*

Lawyers who advise clients and draft documents in the "estate planning" practice are counselors in more than the traditional legal sense. They are also counselors in the therapeutic or developmental sense. They live with their clients an experience which results in change and in choice. They are companions in another man's world. They ought to be among those professionals addressed by Dr. Rogers and by Dr. Leona Tyler, another teacher of counselors:

> The counselor who grounds his efforts in a developmental theory of human possibilities can approach any of the tasks that may confront him with a feeling that he knows what it is that he is trying to accomplish. He can deal with clients who have problems and those who do not, clients who are anxious and

I am grateful for the helpful suggestions given me by my friend Eugene Thomas; by my colleague Professor Robert E. Rodes, Jr.; by James M. Corcoran, Jr., of the Evanston, Illinois Bar; and by Drs. Herman Feifel, William Coulson, Edwin S. Shneidman, and Robert S. Redmount.

those who appear serene and confident. He can formulate a reasonable objective for counseling in the case of a person of limited intelligence . . . or for a person of many gifts and un-limited opportunities. He is equally comfortable with the counseling that is "therapy" and the counseling that is not.

Lawyers show little concern about the therapeutic counseling that goes on in an "estate planning" client's experience. Counseling litera-ture which is available for the legal profession is not focused on the psychology of testation. The legal-counseling or "human relations" literature is helpful because it gives lawyers some understanding of the way people react to law and to law offices, but it falls short of information or guidance, or inspiration, on the narrower and more specific aspects of planning for one's death with property.

Clients in "estate planning" are invited into a relation with property which is probably new to them and which may be unsettling. Death is a part of this confrontation, and death is an unpleasant fact to modern man. With death as his focus, the client experiences property as a part of his person which is immortal. Confrontation with property as immortal is carried out in a context of giving in the client's life, maybe even giving *of* his life, because property is a personal part of his life. Death in this atmosphere is no less inevitable than it is anywhere else; it is here being planned for, however, which is both encouraging and traumatic. Planning for death is encouraging because modern man is attracted to the idea of plans which will organize his future life for him, but traumatic because it involves planning for death and personal death is a thought modern man will do almost anything to avoid. The evidence for these generalizations is developed below.

The testamentary experience is death-confronting, novel, and taboo-defying. For that reason it is probably much more vivid in the mind and heart of the client than lawyers who go through the experience every day suppose it to be. Taboo-defying experiences usually tend to be vivid. People going through them tend to be upset. People who are able to go through their upsetting experiences in the company of a competent, comfortable, accepting professional, how-ever, come out more aware of their lives, more reconciled to what is real in their lives, and better able to make choices and to develop. The question here is not whether the lawyer is a counselor in this relationship, he cannot avoid being a counselor. The question is whether the lawyer realizes what he is doing, is able to accept what it involves for himself and for his client, and has the wisdom and courage to be a helpful companion.

I believe that the client who receives the professional legal service he seeks in this "estate planning" relationship will leave the law office having faced death realistically, and having faced his property and his loved ones in the context of his own death. It seems to me that the "estate planning" experience is one way the client can be helped in his personal reconciliation to death, a reconciliation which comes about partly because he is encouraged to be realistic about death, and partly because he reflects on the fact that his property gives him a limited, temporary immortality. "You can't take it with you," is a maxim of the law of property as well as a *memento mori.* The maxim has in it a consoling corollary, a promise of influence after death, which is the psychological center of "estate planning."

Most lawyers would like to know more about how clients feel in law-office encounters with death, property, and giving. The immediate source of experience and information should be psychology, research psychology as well as therapeutic psychology. However, psychology has not concerned itself with the substance of the law; what is usually called "law and psychology" as an interdisciplinary area of study is confined to border areas, such as insanity as a criminal defense, testamentary capacity, civil commitment to mental institutions. The task of developing psychological models which reach the substance of law itself, and the dynamics of lawyer-client relationships, is one psychologists have not taken up. It is left to reflective lawyers and law professors to find psychological models and apply them to our professional lives. This chapter is an attempt to do this, on the question of "estate planning" clients and their attitudes toward death.

There has been a substantial amount of recent psychological scholarship on attitudes toward death; it is a new area in that science, but an area which has taken on remarkable impetus in the last decade. The names of Shneidman, Feifel, Fulton, Farberow, and Lifton suggest some sources for the psychologically curious. Almost none of their research has examined the psychology of will preparation, which I call the psychology of testation; but some of the data is closely enough related to testation to justify a bold layman's attempt to relate it to the law office. This chapter discusses one relevant example of the new data, a research project on "values destroyed by death," and offers some conjecture, some modest field testing, and some comparisons with other psychological studies and with the life of lawyers. The latter part of the chapter suggests a few devices for legal-psychological research in the psychology of testation and some parallels between therapeutic counseling and testamentary counseling.

The Diggory-Rothman Model

In 1961, James C. Diggory and Doreen Z. Rothman, a teaching psychologist and a clinical psychologist, published the results of a study applying a simple death-attitude, sentence-completion test to 563 casually selected respondents.[1] My present venture is an attempt to compare the Diggory-Rothman test and its results with some of the factors that are involved in the death-property-giving relationship and with my own empirical test. The purpose of this effort is to determine whether death attitudes in testation have characteristics of their own.[2]

Diggory and Rothman asked several hundred people the following question:

> Here are seven consequences of death. Would you please indicate the one that seems to you worst, or most distasteful.
> A. I could no longer have any experiences.
> B. I am uncertain as to what might happen to me if there is a life after death.
> C. I am afraid of what might happen to my body after death.
> D. I could no longer care for my dependents.
> E. My death would cause grief to my relatives and friends.
> F. All my plans and projects would come to an end.
> G. The process of dying might be painful.

These seven possibilities, labeled "values destroyed by death" in their project, may not exhaust all of the reasons for death anxiety, but they are at least a respectable attempt in that direction. My present interest is to inquire how each of these values relates to the feelings of a client preparing for the post-mortem disposition of his property-personality.

At several points in the article I will compare the Diggory-Rothman findings and other psychological findings with some observations I made using the Diggory-Rothman questionnaire on an audience which had gathered to hear me talk about "estate planning." I also make some additional comparisons with data gathered during will interviews conducted by my students in a clinical drafting and planning project, and reported in the following chapter.

Application of the Diggory-Rothman Model to Wills Clients

Cessation of Experiences

The first question is whether wills clients are likely to be concerned about the fact that death will end their experiences, and if they are, whether wills clients differ from a random group of men on the street. In the Diggory-Rothman results, a significant number of casually selected respondents chose this "A" answer. Their response in this first category was higher than their "E" (grief), "F" (projects), and "G" (fear of pain) answers and was especially high among single-divorced persons. It tended to be higher in the highest of three economic subgroups than in the two lower subgroups. Protestants responded to "A" more than Catholics did, and Jews more than Protestants. It was the first choice among persons who listed their religion as "other" or "none."

My impression is that this level of response to death as the cessation of experience would not be maintained where the subject speaks in reference to the preparation of wills. Wills clients probably tend to focus more on care for dependents, or on cessation of projects, or even on bodily deterioration, than they would on cessation of experience. Diggory and Rothman suggest this. They analyze "A" (experience) and "F" (project), for example, as concomitant.

The testamentary device would perhaps appear to clients as a method to *prolong experience* through continuation of projects, provision of support, or maintenance of a bodily surrogate in the form of a monument or perpetually cared-for-gravesite.[3] The wills client, because his confrontation with death involves also a consideration of his property, may tend to regard his property as representing and, in effect, immortalizing him. "The possessed object as possessed is a continuous creation," Sartre says. "If I turn away from it, it does not thereby cease to exist; if I go away, it *represents* me in my desk, in my room, in *this* place, in the world." The thought that property is personality may not occur as readily to a person who is unexpectedly asked what he dislikes about death. My test of this hypothesis indicates virtually no response to the "A" answer, in comparison with a heavy response to the "D," "F," and "G" answers. One of 32 in my group chose the "A" answer, but that person, in disregard of instructions, also chose another answer ("D").

Some reports in infantile formation of death attitudes suggest that the survival of environment, including property, is one of the ways in which the idea of personal termination becomes bearable. Dr. Lifton's observations of survivors of Hiroshima turn centrally on a distinction between feelings about personal survival and feelings about survival of the environment. Hug-Hellmuth reports on an Austrian child who has just begun to think of his own death. "When all people are dead," he asked his mother, "will the earth be removed, and will the architects tear down the houses 'till there is just grass again . . .?" This is a desolate way to look at death. Presumably adults accommodate themselves to death by thinking that the houses, *our* houses, will not be torn down. The thought of property surviving one's death makes the idea of death itself more bearable. The wills client, who is thinking about his property in a death context, also takes a view of his own death which is property related. On the other hand, the man who is stripped of property is likely to be more desolate about death than the man who has no possessions. Chapter 1 cites Goffman, who made that point about patients in mental hospitals. Here, in another poignant example, is part of a picture-story response from a schizophrenic, suicidal patient of Dr. Shneidman's; the patient has been describing how the picture-figure he drew in a projective test plans to jump from a bridge:

> He walks over, still feeling his liquor, still full of self-pity, now he's up ready to jump off. Says, "Gee whiz, this is quite a drop," and his mind answers him, "Yes, it is." And he has quite a battle with himself. Says he's got to stop now, I've invested money in this, I've given away my cigarettes, spent my last money for drink and all that.

It may be possible to say that a person who is stripped of property is partially dead, that his act of stripping away property is itself a form of what Menninger would call "focal suicide," of Shneidman's concept "partial death." It may be like Isaac B. Singer's *Magician of Lublin,* who walled himself away from his possessions into a tiny prayer cell in his back yard. The idea is occasionally suggested in estate-tax cases involving "gifts in contemplation of death" (in Chapter 6).

Another part of the idea of property as accommodation to death is the thought that property is power.[4] That may explain why the schizophrenic patient thought his character, who had given away all of his property, might as well jump. That is why, as Jung said, the process of sloughing away "the whole phantasmagoria of earthly existence [is] an extremely painful process."

One of the things a wills client learns is that death will not rob him of power. In death, as Dr. Wahl observed, the client may see himself as possessing "powers, qualities, and advantages not possessed in the living state." In the realm of power, Dr. Fisher notes, death may be a "last step forward." For this reason, psychologists who conclude that preparation of wills increases fear of death may be wrong. Data obtained from my will-interview study indicate that will-preparation actually reduces fear of death and has a constructive or even therapeutic effect on death anxiety.[5] Shneidman quotes the following passage from *Moby Dick* which seems to illustrate precisely this point:

> It may seem strange that of all men sailors should be tinkering at their last wills and testaments. . . . After the ceremony was concluded upon the present occasion, I felt all the easier; a stone was rolled away from my heart. Besides, all the days I should now live would be as good as the days that Lazarus lived. . . . I survived myself. . . .

There are, of course, other possible explanations for the apparent fact that wills clients find death less related to cessation of experience than other research subjects. It may be, as the *Moby Dick* quotation also suggests, that the testamentary context has the effect of postponing the prospect of death into an indefinite future. This possibility was confirmed in my will-interviews. Other evidence indicates that patients who are aware that they are terminally ill have more difficulty accommodating themselves to a pathetic last illness than they have accommodating themselves to death, because, in the Glaser-Strauss finding, they "think of the time of dying as farther away than indicated by the warning they have received." In fact, detailed, mundane, and totally illogical plans for the future are a means of escaping or perhaps repressing death anxiety. Eissler reports that a dying patient of his gained apparent distraction from her plight by planning a malpractice suit against her physician. Feifel's evidence indicates that property-planning is one of the ways psychological relief comes about. He found that seriously ill people want to know when they are going to die, "in order to 'Settle my affairs,' and to 'Make various financial and family arrangements.' " Of course those subjects were expressing opinions from some relative safety. Where death is more imminent, it is possible that persons lose their accustomed concern with property and substitute for it either a somatic indifference or a frantic and defensive attachment to mundane concerns. Florence Joseph reported on a dying patient who seemed to have been almost withdrawn from planning, but lovers of Tolstoy may recall that the death-ridden Ivan Ilyitch spent his lonely hours in rearranging furniture.

Psychological evidence, some research, and some speculation combine to suggest that the testamentary experience is a relatively hopeful confrontation with death. Property is part of personality, and personality is involved with property in the life of a wills client. His seeing death in relation to property and the survival of property-personality robs death of some of its stark power.

Life After Death

Diggory and Rothman found few respondents who related their death to a fear about eternity. Their level of "B" responses (the worst or most distasteful consequence of death is that I am uncertain as to what might happen to me if there is a life after death) fell between "4" and "5" on a scale ranging from "1" (very high response) to "7" (lowest response). The only subgroup in their study which chose "B" at a significantly higher level were Roman Catholics whom they found to rate about "3." My test of the Diggory-Rothman conclusions on wills clients produces about the same result on anxiety toward eternity.

Three of 34 answers (two if duplications are eliminated) chose "B"; all three were women, two married, one a recent widow. One had two children, one had three children, and one had none. One was in my younger subgroup (under 49), the others in the older (over 65) subgroup; one was a recent widow and all three had lost at least one parent (two had lost both parents). Their testamentary interest was evenly divided—one had an informational reason, one had a reason related to death consequences, and one gave no reason.

Assuming the validity of the general Diggory-Rothman conclusion—that this "B" value was not a principal factor in death anxiety—I question the validity of their lesser conclusion that Catholics find it more imposing than other religious groups. The question may be worth some passing concern, if only because there appears to be some common opinion that religious conviction has an effect on death attitudes. Surveys more heavily controlled than the Diggory-Rothman study, and some carefully conducted experimental research, leave the relation between death attitudes and religious belief in some doubt. Anthony's classic study of formation of attitudes toward death in childhood suggests that anxiety toward death can be kept at a minimum, except in extreme circumstances, when the person takes a position settling the question of death, but she also found that agnostic children have compensating psychic activity to provide security for death anxiety. Alexander and Adlerstein, using detailed psychological testing, found that religiously-oriented male college students are more willing to talk about death, but concluded that the differences are less related to variance in doctrine than to the security which results from having settled the question. Christ reported that the geriatric-psychiatric patient shows no correlation between religion and fear of death. Jeffers, Nichols, and Eisdorfer used more sophisticated devices on older subjects, and found some correlation between religious belief and willingness to answer negatively the question "Are you afraid to die?", but they also found equal correlation between fear of death and low intelligence quotients or limited Rorschach responses.

Kastenbaum, on the other hand, found that religiously oriented adolescents are more willing to talk about death, although Fulton indicates that the fact of willingness to discuss death may or may not demonstrate less fear of death. Swenson, finally, using an essay-writing scheme, associated religion-related differences more with intensity of religious activity than with doctrine.

Dissolution of Body

Diggory and Rothman report the "C" response (the worst or most distasteful consequence of death is that I am afraid of what might happen to my body after death) as the least significant "value destroyed by death." This low level of response was uniformly maintained among their subgroups and is in accordance with the results of my test of their conclusions on will subjects. Only two of the respondents, less than 7 percent, chose the "C" answer. Both were in the middle age group, one was in the middle, and one in the upper wealth-estimate group; one was married with children, and one single; each of them had lost both parents. Most of us appear to be relatively unconcerned about what will happen to our bodies after death, even though we usually are concerned about what happens to our property. Perhaps the reason for this is that our property continues to live while our bodies do not.

The so-called Harlequin Complex is an element in attitudes toward the body and death which is not suggested by these survey results but which deserves mention. Harlequin is a mythical conception of death as a dark lover. The relatively universal tradition out of which he comes is a wedding in poetry of Thanatos and Eros (which conceives of Thanatos as erotic). McClelland, the principal scholar of the complex, raises his question this way:

> In view of the widespread fear of death, it is surprising to come across a person, usually a woman, who not only does not fear death but actually appears to be looking forward to it with a sense of excitement. The possibility both thrills and attracts her,

at the same time that it frightens her. Yet often the thrill seems as strong as the fear, in much the same way that it is for a person who is about to make a ski jump or a very high dive. Such reactions do exist, particularly among women, and they are a challenge to the psychologist interested in how people actually react, as opposed to how they are supposed to react according to philosophy, religion, or psychoanalysis.

He gives literary examples which range from Homer to traveling players in the Middle Ages, Romeo and Juliet, and Zilboorg's *History of Medical Psychology*—along with several clinical examples. One factor involved in the Harlequin Complex as it relates to the present inquiry into the psychology of testation is that, in McClelland's formulation of it, the death-lover is not unattractive and therefore might not be a relevant consideration in questions relating to the distasteful consequences of death. Another factor is that the logic of the complex is a sort of psychosemantic logic in which the body is conceived of as surviving, at least throughout Harlequin's seduction. Diggory and Rothman found that women choose the "C" answer more than men do, which tends to suggest Harlequin's presence because "women value themselves more in terms of their physical attractiveness." A final possibility is that the Harlequin Complex may introduce some ambivalence into anxiety concerning pain.

Dependents

My general impression is that wills clients find the "D" answer (the worst or most distasteful consequence of death is that I could no longer care for my dependents) more compelling than any other. This comes from empirical analysis of will interviews, and from my observation that clients show greatest concern about death when it is focused on the members of their families. Property and considerations of support tend to give death a special focus in the client's mind. I would, therefore, expect wills clients to respond more heavily to "D" than the Diggory-Rothman respondents did. This impression was confirmed in my test of wills clients. I found 46 percent of them chose the "D" answer (33 percent of the men and 56 percent of the women; with somewhat higher choices of "D" among younger subjects).[6] The Diggory-Rothman scale put the "D" response at "4"—which is in the middle of the scale ranging from "1" to "7". They found this response higher in subgroups under age 39 and highest in age groups between 40 and 55. It ranked especially high among men, Protestants, lower income groups, and among married and single-divorced respondents.

Freud laid the basis for an economic theory of the family in *Civilization and Its Discontents.* Freud's theory is that as soon as it became an advantage for man to have a fellow worker around it became an advantage to have the fellow worker under the same roof—partly for sexual reasons in the male and partly for support reasons in the female and her children. Family and family-support are therefore linked at a fairly radical point in Freudian theory, a theory which appears to be borne out by the Diggory-Rothman finding that support is the most common death-concern among men. Additional evidence is found in Goody's anthropological distinction between rights of inheritance in communal (family) property and acquired property as well as in other anthropological indications that the family is legally and economically a unit, a res,[7] and in the following relatively unlikely source:

Stouffer's study *Communism, Conformity and Civil Liberties,* attempted, in part, to determine whether there was a national anxiety-neurosis about communism, but much of the anxiety he found (whether neurotic or not) concerned family support. Stouffer asked 4,930 people what they worried about most. Forty-three percent of the answers fell into what he called a personal-family-business category, of which responses he gave 27 examples. My analysis of these examples is that 13 expressed direct concern about family support and most of the other 14 expressed support-related concern about employment or business. Twenty-four percent of his answers expressed concern about health. Thirty percent expressed concern about "other personal problems"; he gives 20 examples, of which 13 are, in my judgment, family-supported-related and four self-support-related. Eight percent of his respondents expressed concern about world affairs; he gives 11 exemplar responses, each reflecting concern about what will happen to family members if a war begins. Only one percent of his respondents mentioned communism.

The maintenance of a support relationship is therefore of crucial human concern from all three points of view—psychological, anthropological and attitudinal. Loss of that support relation would obviously diminish the range and quality of the human life which lost it. To draw a firm distinction between property disposition and provision of support, as at least one psychological researcher (Burton) does, seems naive. Maintaining the support relationship after death is a principal way in which the lawyer's testamentary services promise reconciliation with unavoidable death.

This effect by lawyers is apparently related to our concentrating the client's attention on what Shneidman calls his "post self." In reference to the life and literature of Herman Melville, Shneidman relates the post-self directly to the part of the family most directly involved in support—children:

> The self or ego relates to the core of one's active functioning, his cognitive and emotional masterings and maneuvers in the present life; the *post-self*, on the other hand, refers to the ways in which one might live on, survive, or have some measure of impact or influence after the event of his own physical death—for example, through one's children. . . .

There are two sides to this point. First, as a behavioral observation: The indefinite provision of support, support which will continue even after the provider is dead, is a step toward immortality. Second, the provision of support is a moral imperative. Moral breadwinners provide for their dependents, and it is therefore immoral for them to refuse to do so, or to neglect their support duties. *And* this moral imperative is applicable even after the breadwinner is dead. One of the things he should do for his family is make present provision for their support in the event of his death. A practical, "how-to" article for life insurance salesmen, written by a psychologist (Briggs), outlines a method for exploiting this moral imperative:

> The prospect buys because he will feel guilty—and thus uncomfortable—if he doesn't buy. No one knows how much life insurance is sold on the basis of arousing feelings of guilt in the prospect's mind, but it must be a considerable percentage.
>   It would appear that life insurance is a product that is particularly suited for the guilt arousal type of approach. This is true because life insurance is presumably bought partly or wholly for the family's protection.

The emotional content of the moment of sale is more inspiring than the salesman's manipulation of guilt alone would suggest. To the prospect, the emotional content is also a means to *present* security because of the feeling that whatever is right about this moment is not going to change. After I presented some of the data in this chapter to an estate-planning council, a veteran life-insurance underwriter told me that he finds the following story very effective on potential customers: Several years after a valued client of his died the underwriter met the dead man's son on the street. In the course of their conversation, the son said, "I wish I had known my father better. You know, after eleven years he's still sending us money."

The wills client's confrontation with death in the context of support is therefore a principal means to his finding comfort in the testamentary experience. This comfort is engendered by his satisfaction in having performed a moral duty and by the less tangible feeling that he has done something which will stabilize the future and rob death of its ability to threaten him with his own hungry children.

Grief to Others

The concern wills clients show for dependent support may be misleading. It may suggest that the testamentary context *creates* concern about loved ones. I doubt that the experience *creates* anxiety, but it may be that the property relationship involved in testamentary planning shifts existing anxiety toward concern for support. Possibly this concern is shifted away from rather than toward concern at causing grief. In any event, it appears to me that casually selected research subjects are more concerned about causing grief than about support, and that wills clients are more concerned about support than about causing grief. The Diggory-Rothman response to "E" (the worst or more distasteful consequence of death is that my death would cause grief to my relatives and friends) was the highest in their survey. The "E" response was highest in all age groups under 40, women, Protestants, Catholics, upper and middle economic subgroups, and single (not divorced or widowed) persons. My test of the Diggory-Rothman results on wills clients indicates a much lower level of response on "E" and a much higher response on "D".[8] Support is perhaps a dominant testamentary motive, even though outside the testamentary context, support concern may not dominate as much as one would think.[9]

Concern at causing grief resembles concern for support in all respects except one: It does not involve property and material security. At the simplest level, a concern at causing grief is sensitivity to pain in someone who is loved. Lester's study of suicidal adolescents, for instance, indicates that a principal deterrent to suicide is concern for friends. A chivalrous academic might expect to find sensitivity more often in women. Feldman and Hersen found evidence of this. The corollary of their findings was supported sociologically by Stouffer's discovery that men are more concerned with money than women are.[10]

Is it possible that these alternatives, such as concern for pain in women, and concern for property in men, are more alike than they seem? There may be some recondite consequences suggested in the "D" and "E" answers which would suggest that the same emotions are involved in choosing a "D" (property) answer in a testamentary context that are involved in choosing an "E" (concern for pain) answer in a more hypothetical context.

Anthony found that, to children, the most frightening consequence of death was separation, especially separation from their mothers, and that a child's death fantasies often involve his mother's death disguised as his own. If mothers are able to sense this sort of complex anxiety in their children—and much of Anthony's data came to her from the observations of mothers—it is possible that the "E" response will occur in mothers who are concerned at causing psychic disturbance to their children. This plausible anxiety in a parent does not seem to contrast significantly with the anxiety a parent feels at the possibility of his children being without material support. In fact, the first form, the "D" form, may be something that is characteristic of fathers, and the "E" form something that is characteristic of mothers. The two things might therefore simply be specific parental applications of the dolorous process of burdening others by one's death and dying.[11]

The differences between women and men in this respect can probably be exaggerated. In both sexes, classical psychological theory relates anxiety at causing pain to relationships with the parent, a subject which becomes immediately complicated by the theory of generation reversal. Even old people might feel anxiety at causing grief in others, in their children, for instance, because older persons according to Freud, Jones, and Reik, tend to maintain their children as parent-figures. (See Chapter 7, Part 2.) It is demonstrable that parents rely for emotional support on their children and that parental attitudes toward children are not as majestic as the stereotypes suggest. (Bloch, Silber, and Perry found a "dissociative-demanding response" from parents, toward their children, after the Vicksburg tornado.) Finally, a *younger* subject's anxiety at causing pain to his parents may be readily explained without alluding to complex theories.

It is possible also that causing grief is, in the subject's mind, a pleasant result of death. Tom Sawyer, attending his own funeral, had that experience, illustrating a form of psychosemantic logic. Hocking and Shneidman and Farberow develop the theory. The dynamics of this sort of logic are an important emotional factor in studies of suicide and are doubtless also relevant to attitudes toward normal death. Singer's novel, *The Magician of Lublin,* provides an example, when the principal character contemplates with some ambivalence the devastating effect his death will have on his wife:

She would not live through the shock. Yasha knew she would wither and flicker out like a candle. More than once he had seen a person die of heartbreak simply because they no longer had any reason to stay alive.

At a less pleasant level, concern at the grief caused by one's death may be a disguise for real apprehension at growing old, ill, and dependent and for a concomitant resentment of those who appear to be young and well and likely to live on. Ivan Ilyitch looked upon his solicitous wife, "brimming with life," in his sickroom: "He hated her with all the strength of his soul, and her touch made him suffer an actual paroxysm of hatred for her." Ivan did not live much longer, but he lived long enough to feel guilt for feelings like that.[12]

A final factor that may be involved in "E" answers, and that would differentiate them from "D" answers, is a simple disgust at the conventional engines of mourning. There is a vast difference between grief and conventional pretense to grief. One of Hug-Hellmuth's child-subjects, for instance, reported to her sister that their grandmother was dead. "Why aren't we sad?" she asked. Her sister replied, "Wait a bit, as soon as the black dresses come, we'll be sad." If that exchange had been foreseen by the grandmother, she might have found it unpleasant. There is a universal human aspiration for a dignified death which is somehow timely and welcome and even to human growth as death approaches. It is possible that conventional grief is seen as inimical to that aspiration. In James Baldwin's novel, *Tell Me How Long the Train's Been Gone,* the principal character, an actor, has a heart attack on the stage and is thought to be dying; his concern as he is carried to the ambulance is that he may not be himself when he dies:

> I had not showered, I had not removed my makeup, I had not got my own face back. The face I was wearing itched and burned, I wanted to take it off. My hair was still full of cream I used to make it grey. . . . No one would recognize me where I was going; I would be lost. "Oh, Pete," I muttered, I moaned, and I could not keep the tears from falling. "Please wash my face."

Some of these explanations for the choice of "E" answers are emotionally similar to explanations for the choice of "D" answers. Diggory's and Rothman's conclusions contrast goal-striving answers ("A," "D," and "F") with answers which suggest passive effects of death ("C," "G," and "E"). It seems to me, however, that concern for grief in others might in some circumstances be as goal-striving and as dependent-related as concern for supporting one's family. This latter thought suggests that distinction between support concern and grief concern is hard to maintain, especially in the testamentary context.

End to Projects

Wills clients are more concerned about providing support than they are at causing grief. This is true even though their emphasis might be reversed if they were asked about death in the absence of a testamentary environment. One might expect a similar reversal of emphasis when concern at causing grief is compared with concern at having to leave work undone. This does not appear to be the case, however, in the Diggory-Rothman study. Their respondents chose the "F" answer (the worst or most distasteful consequence of my death is that all my plans and projects would come to an end) more often than any other except the "E" (causing grief) answer. Their response to "F" was notably high among subgroups of teenagers, people between the ages of 25 and 39, people expressing no religious belief, and people in the middle economic class. It was the highest from single-widowed respondents. My results with wills clients were similar, although the overall choice of "F" by my audience was lower than theirs.[13]

A client's projects may be regarded as the material manifestation of his life, because a man is what he does. In a Sartrean sense, "If I create a picture, a drama, a melody, it is in order that I may be at the origin of a concrete existence." This can certainly be true, on a vaster scale, of entire human lives. Lifton's study of the atomic-bomb survivors (especially in the *Daedalus* article) led him to conclude that there is a

> sense of immortality through one's creative works or human influences—one's writing, art, thought, inventions, or lasting products of any kind that have an effect upon other human beings. Certainly this form of immortality has particular importance for intellectuals conscious of participating in the general flow of human creativity, but applies in some measure to all human beings in their unconscious perceptions of the legacy they leave for others.

Lifton illustrates the point with the Japanese movie *Ikuru*. The movie, which resembles in its human dynamics Tolstoy's story, *The Death of Ivan Ilyitch*, deals with a man who achieves immortality through his last great project—the construction of a park for children.

A man's projects may seem to be property-related in the sense that property is wealth as well as project. In this sense attachment to property is, at least superficially, at cross purposes with death.[14] Man without possessions is either inconceivable or miserable. Possessions are both a part of personality, and a means of immortality.

It seems to me that property as project and property as property are psychologically similar, so that a man's projects tend to define his life, and when they are finished he may be nearly ready to say that his life is complete. In a "composite tape" from the American Academy of Psycho-Therapists, containing more than 300 psycho-therapy sessions, the patient, a young wife and mother, begins at last to accept herself and her role as constructive and worthwhile. She expresses the security this realization gives her by saying "I have been good for something; now I can die." This lady expressed the mood of my point: Projects, which always involve *some* project-property, are a way to turn life into an individual performance. It is in this sense that Brendan Gill is right when he says "art's greatest office is to outwit death"; this is why Ivan Ilyitch temporarily escaped the tyranny of imminent death by moving furniture around. I suspect that even wealthier clients tend to look upon their investments, their businesses, and their family possessions more as projects than as digits in computing wealth.

Fear of Pain

Do people as wills clients express more or less fear of pain in death than people outside the testamentary context? Diggory and Rothman reported a relatively high incidence of "G" answers (the worst or most distasteful consequence of death is that the process of dying might be painful). They rated this at "3" on their "1" to "7" scale and noted that the "G" response was especially high in the 20-24 age subgroup, among women, among Catholics and Jews, among the upper and lower wealth levels (but not the middle level), and among unmarried-engaged people. My test of their results on wills clients yielded a much lower response to "G." Three of my respondents chose this answer. All were women; one did not list her age, one was in the younger group, and one in the middle. One had recently lost her father; two had lost both parents; one had lost neither parent; and one had lost a child. Two had large families of children.

Fulton's conclusions from a rather straightforward attitudinal survey were that more people express fear of the act of dying than of death itself. This distinction is elsewhere difficult to detect, however, and may be even difficult to maintain. I assume this difficulty explains why

Diggory and Rothman put the "G" response in a survey of death attitudes. It would seem, superficially, that fear of pain is an illegitimate "consequence of death," because dead people apparently feel no pain. Furthermore, pain as a peril of existence has two significant qualities death does not have: it is more or less avoidable and it is something most people have experienced. The reason for leaving a fear-of-pain response in the survey is probably that the distinction between death and pain, however easy to maintain verbally, is psychologically difficult. This difficulty seems to persist generally, even though a few cases of exceptional suffering, actual or prospective, may suggest that fear of pain is more intensive than fear of death.

The identification of death and pain is consistent with Freudian theory. Freud held that death cannot be analyzed from experience and concluded that death was not a promising subject for psychological research. Death anxiety in Freudian analysis is often the persistence of infantile castration anxiety, in other words, anxiety at bodily mutilation. (Jung talks of it as a fear of being devoured.) Infantile anxiety is of course the parent of adult anxiety. ("In our innermost soul we are still children and we remain so throughout life," Ferenczi said.) Concern for bodily integrity and freedom from pain and concern for death are therefore theoretically inseparable, and that, too, defends including a pain question on a death questionnaire.

These two elements may even be physiologically significant. A substantial body of clinical literature is presently being developed which indicates that the body tissues signal their own end by foreseeing death, even in cases involving accidents and, as Weisman and Hackett have found, devastating disease. Jung relates a number of such premonitions in his own life and in the lives of those close to him. Somewhat similar are findings on the needs of persons who are in fact dying, whether or not they consciously know it or admit it.[15] Further support for the relation between death and one's adjustment to his body is found in Rhudick and Dibner's demonstration that health is a more crucial concern for the old than for the young, and Alexander, Colley, and Adlerstein's findings that death concern is higher among the unhealthy.

A third observation about concern for pain as a part of death attitudes is that our society tends to regard age and illness in the same way it regards death. Age and illness are often painful. Even when they are anesthetic, they share with pain an involvement in the deterioration of the body. To a substantial extent these states of existence share, in our social attitudes, some of the horror of death; it is therefore probably relevant to consider them as part of death and to conclude that the anxiety they inspire is related to and maybe even part of death anxiety.[16]

These are seven ways in which wills clients experience death anxiety in the testamentary experience. Some of them (for example, provision of support for loved ones and continuation of life projects) are especially significant in the practice of "estate planning." Lawyers who understand these anxieties are able to help their clients leave the law office realistically consoled by the discovery that law provides ways to feed one's children, to continue one's business, and to rob death of some of its ability to frighten the living.

Beyond the Diggory-Rothman Model

Parental Death, Child Death, Recent Death

Diggory and Rothman assembled ethnographic data from a wide variety of subgroups, but apparently did not determine which of their subjects had recently experienced a death in the family, or which had children. My replication of their study indicates that people who have lost both parents tend to show less concern about dependent support than people who have one or both parents living, that people who have children tend to be more concerned about dependent support than about abandoning their projects, and that the response of childless people differs from the response of parents in other respects. Where the respondent had experienced a recent parental death, my results indicated a peculiarly high level of concern for dependent support and for the continuation of projects.[17] Unfortunately, I was unable to determine whether people who have experienced the death of a child react to the Diggory-Rothman question in a peculiar way.

Consideration of the recent-death aspect of the psychology of testation is especially important, because a death in the family is often what motivates clients to consult lawyers for wills. Death in the family has a momentous effect on most human lives. The classical theoretical explanation of this is probably contained in Jung's paper *The Significance of the Father in the Destiny of the Individual,* in which he analyzes four cases of parental death which caused serious neurosis. An archetype which is central in Jungian analysis is of the father who embodies both a demon and a god, and whose death, as he shows, has profound effects in the life of the child.

89

There is a good deal of empirical corroboration for this theory in recent studies. In the Bloch-Silber-Perry study of the after-effects of the 1953 Vicksburg tornado, for instance, it was found that serious psychological effects from having seen *friends* mauled or killed in the storm were virtually nil, but that serious effects from having seen the same things happen to members of one's family were common. Eleven of 12 children studied in the latter category were seriously disturbed, as compared with no significant disturbance in those who saw friends injured or killed. Other studies, reported in Fulton's anthology, have demonstrated that grief reactions often take the form of seriously anti-social action, including juvenile delinquency, suicide, and radical behavior in which the actor himself virtually dies. This behavior will not necessarily follow immediately on the family death. It may be delayed for months, for years, or for a lifetime. Delay seems especially likely where the death involved is of the patient's mother. Stern, Williams and Prados even affirmed a strong personal relationship remaining between mother and child for years after the mother's death. Among the milder and more common effects of parental death are a heightened concern about one's own death and heightened dependence on the surviving parent or on parent figures.

Anthropology also presents some interesting corroboration. Goody reports that among the LoDagaa of Western Africa the death of a child under the age at which he begins to walk and talk is not considered the death of a person. This practice is a curious result of high infant mortality and of the fact that the community's emotional and psychological energy cannot be stretched far enough to cover all infantile deaths. The solution is to reclassify the deceased infant as not a human being. Hertz reported like behavior among Pacific Island cultures, and Blauner reported like behavior during certain periods in French history. Where social custom will not guarantee against radical grief behavior, custom may have to compromise. Among the LoDagaa, for instance, it is customary to restrain mourners at funerals, so that they will not mutilate themselves or commit ·suicide. This follows an elaborate hierarchical structure in which the strength of the material with which one is tied relates directly to the closeness of his relationship to the decedent. This would not, theoretically, be necessary at the brief, simple "funerals" of dead infants, but the custom is to restrain mothers in that situation and, as Goody demonstrates, often with good reason.

All of this indicates that a key question in the will interview is whether the client has recently experienced death in his family. If he has, or if some remote death in the family still exerts an influence over his life, his death anxieties will tend to be stronger, probably less rational, and more focused on human relationships. These feelings can usually be brought out in the will interview if the lawyer is patient and understanding. If they are brought out, and brought to bear on the client's testamentary decisions, the anxiety they cause will be reduced. This is an important aspect of the system of legal counseling which is suggested more fully below.

Testamentary Interest

It was interesting to ask wills clients why they sought the testamentary services of a lawyer. I thought that the answers to this inquiry might demonstrate whether the testamentary motive correlates with values destroyed by death and whether the Diggory-Rothman approach is useful for research in the psychology of testation. Their replies indicate a tentative answer to each of my reasons for asking the question.

Approximately half of my audience said they were interested in wills for reasons of general information—e.g., "general interest" or "to know legal matters pertaining to them." The remaining half expressed interests which seemed to relate to the consequences of death outlined in the Diggory-Rothman question. These answers are not so numerous that they cannot be quoted here.

> To stop a family fight.
> I have two sons and I would like to protect their future, should I die before they are able to care for themselves.
> For my own benefit.
> To be sure of an equitable distribution of my property.
> So I'll know more about what to do for ourselves.
> Disposal of my estate.
> Might leave house and land to children.
> Would like to avoid having my estate probated; also, no misunderstanding among the children.
> To avoid probate.
> To help my husband.
> Have had good intention toward making a will and as yet have not done so. Maybe this is the shock I need.
> Interested in disposal of things and property accumulated.
> To see that my possessions are disposed of the way I will it.
> To leave money where it will be used well.
> Because I do not know anything about them and they are necessary.
> To protect ourselves and children.

Exactly half of the respondents used answers to the will-interest question which seem to indicate an attitude toward the consequences of death. Six of these do not appear to correlate with answers chosen in the death-consequences part of the questionnaire. Two explanations may be given for this. First, the respondent may be using this question to add another answer. Duplication and oral comments from persons filling out the questionnaire indicate that many people experienced difficulty isolating a single attitude toward death, preferring instead to choose two or three.

Another explanation arises from the obvious fact that the wills-interest question asks for more information than the death-consequence question. Interest in testation involves more than the fact of death; it also involves a man's relationship to his property and his attitude toward giving it away. Several of the answers to my question exhibit a property-related concern, but relatively few exhibit a family concern. In cases where the wills-interest answer seems to tend more toward concern for property, the respondent may be related to his property in a personal way, i.e., the respondent views the property as an extension of himself. He is interested in a will, therefore, because he wants to extend himself through his property past his own death. Why else a concern for *himself* in connection with a will ("for my own benefit" or "to see that my possessions are disposed of the way I will it")? Thus, the Diggory-Rothman test is not entirely adequate if will-interest is the subject of inquiry, because more is involved than a value destroyed by death. What may be involved instead is a way of preserving an ownership value from the ravages of death.

Prospects for Research and Counseling

Research

Lawyers know very little about wills clients and about the dynamics of their relationships with lawyers. Available research information is not directed to this professional situation. Useful information which is available is hidden in an incredible variety of technical psychological journals. Researchers in the legal profession have done little of significance about counseling psychology and literally nothing about counseling in the testamentary context. What then are the prospects for gathering helpful information for lawyers on the human content in "estate planning"?

Feifel has categorized the human phenomena involved into "verbally-expressed attitudes toward death, fantasy notions, and below-the-level-of-awareness ideas." The first of these appears to be fully available to legal researchers and the second and third are promising for interdisciplinary cooperation with behavioral scientists.

Much of the significant research on verbally-expressed death attitudes has been basically observational. Lifton's important work on the A-Bomb victims is probably the most recent example. Hug-Hellmuth's small, classical observation of a single child's growing awareness of death is another. Even Anthony's work on the orthopsychology of death, which involves story completion testing and intelligence evaluation, is fundamentally a matter of gathering information compiled by the mothers of the children who were research subjects.

Some research on the human content in estate planning would therefore involve observational projects. Previous studies such as Fox's work in the experimental ward of a hospital and Glaser and Strauss's study of death in a general hospital suggest that some of the observational research might become very elaborate. There are opportunities for less elaborate studies, however. The continued relevance of smaller studies as a research tool is demonstrated by the Feldman-Hersen study of nightmares, the Bloch-Silber-Perry interviews following the Vicksburg tornado, and the sensitive generalization from particular cases which is evidenced by Barry's studies on grief reaction. Regardless of the degree of elaborateness of the research study which is conducted, part of what the lawyer will learn may involve nothing more than opening his eyes to an awareness of the human content which is involved in the counseling context. I discovered this with respect to will interviews of young family clients (Chapter 5).

Although behavioral scientists could benefit from collaboration with lawyers, survey research of a more technical nature might arguably be left to them. For instance, Feifel's second and third categories, which involve analysis of fantasies and extraction of reactions below the level of consciousness, call for more technical proficiency than a legal researcher is likely to possess. The lawyer's role in this sort of research is best limited to collaboration and especially to the encouragement of psychological researchers to interest themselves in legal relationships such as the relationship between a man and his property. The promise of such an inter-disciplinary approach based on collaboration is exciting.

A final avenue of research consists of examining existing information in secondary literature and in data which has been compiled for other purposes. The Viennese school of psychiatry developed a classical example of this type of research in its work on war neuroses. Enough research has been done recently with probate records to suggest their value as a tool for modern legal-psychological research on testation. Shneidman and Farberow's work with suicide notes suggests a project in this area. They used notes left by successful suicides which were on file with public authorities in Los Angeles. They "matched" these real notes with pseudo notes written by living people chosen to resemble the suicides. Could a similar comparison be done with wills? Suppose, for example, that a legal researcher compiled a random selection of wills from a representative set of probate records, matched the testators with living persons who resembled them, and conducted in-depth testamentary interviews of the living subjects. Would the comparison between testamentary results be useful in measuring the result of careful counseling in the testamentary context? Shneidman's work on death certification focuses on what he refers to as the psychological autopsy. It has been developed as part of an effort to put human content and scientific objectivity into death certification. Shneidman demonstrated this device by showing in detail how he would investigate the death of Captain Ahab. If Herman Melville can provide a suitable subject for the psychological autopsy, imagine what somethng as common to lawyers as appellate judicial opinions might provide for the psychology of testation (See Chapters 6 and 7).[18]

Research suggested by this discussion depends on lawyers being receptive to psychological insight. Intellectual curiosity among lawyers would uncover a great deal of information in the presently inadequate psychological literature. At present the literature of law and psychology is exhausted in considerations of litigation. With help from psychological literature, lawyers could not only become more aware of useful information around them, but also more communicative about it. The opportunity for legal research in this area, and for stimulation of inter-disciplinary research through collaboration with research psychologists, is a literally untouched opportunity for new information and new guidance for the entries we make into the lives of our clients.[19]

Counseling

Counseling wills clients is a matter of human empathy for a man who is being forced to confront his own death. There is little literature available concerning the testamentary counseling relationship itself. Valuable analogy may be found, however, in Carl Rogers' description of successful, client-centered counseling (in Porter's book on therapeutic counseling):

1. The individual comes for help.
2. The helping situation is usually defined.
3. The counselor encourages free expression of feeling in regard to the problem.
4. The counselor accepts, recognizes, and clarifies these negative feelings.
5. When the individual's negative feelings have been quite fully expressed, they are followed by the faint and tentative expressions of the positive impulses which make for growth.
6. The counselor accepts and recognizes the positive feelings which are expressed, in the same manner in which he has accepted and recognized the negative feeling. In this type of situation, insight and self-understanding come bubbling through spontaneously.
7. This insight, this understanding of the self and acceptance of the self is the next important aspect of the whole process. It provides the basis on which the individual can go ahead to new levels of integration.
8. Intermingled with this process of insight—is a process of clarification of possible decisions, possible courses of action.
9. Then comes one of the fascinating aspects of such therapy, the initiation of minute, but highly significant positive actions.

These are only the first nine of 12 steps described by Rogers. The purpose of the three remaining steps, which I would not claim for a wills lawyer, is to lead the client to a final state of "integrated positive action" and a relaxation of dependence on the counselor. It is quite enough for lawyers to aspire to the "minute but highly significant" moment when the client finds relief in seizing the future through his property. This future includes his own death, of course, but I believe that one way the client reconciles himself to death is by making death a part of his life. This is accomplished when the client plans for death's consequences to his property-personality and to his family.

Testamentary application of the first five steps in Rogers' scheme is a matter of the client's expressing the real reasons he wants to make a will. My study of will-interviews indicates that these reasons will probably be negative. An illustrative, but not exhaustive, listing of the client's feelings is presented below. The accompanying quoted language illustrating these feelings is from my tape-recorded young-family client interviews and from the answers to my questions discussed above, on why people came to hear me talk about wills.

1. He is aware that he might die suddenly. (Young-family client: "What if something happens, supposing, now, when we're going home, there. You know, something happened now.")

2. He is aware that his children might be orphaned. (Young-family client: "It's so—kind of a sad discussion to think who would take care of them. . . .") (Member of audience said he was interested in wills because "I have two sons and I would like to protect their future should I die before they are able to care for themselves.")

3. He is aware that he has liabilities, or projects that must be carried on, and he hopes that supporting persons will carry them on. (Young-family client: Q. "Do you have insurance on your land contract?" A. "No, because I'm sure, if anything happens to us, that her folks will take care of it.")

4. He is afraid that the delays of the law will complicate the support of his family. (Young-family client: "There's a possibility that, if I would just turn over everything to Hanna's parents, that money would be a long time in making that step. . . . It would be tied up for some time.")

5. He is aware that property which is especially significant to him will somehow survive his death. (Young-family client: ". . . as long as the jewelry and the paintings and the art objects go to my daughter. Or my son. The rest of it—I don't care.") (Members of my wills audience said they were interested in wills "for my own benefit" or "to help my husband.")

6. He is aware that his death will sever the expression of his love for his children. (Young-family client: "What would happen to the children immediately? Who would take care of them? Would the state throw them into an orphanage?")

7. He senses that the survival of his property-personality alone will not prevent the family strife that he feels he could prevent if *he* were there. (Members of my wills audience said they were interested in wills in order "to stop a family fight," or "to be sure of an equitable distribution of my property," or "to leave money where it will be used well," or so that there would be "no misunderstanding among the children.")

8. He fears that the mysterious machinery of probate will do harm *to him* unless he plans for it. Probate may be a part of the mystery of death, and planning may be seen as a way to penetrate the mystery. (Members of my wills audience said they were interested in wills "so I'll know more about what to do for ourselves" or "becasue [I] would like

to avoid having my estate probated" or "because I do not know anything about them and they are necessary" or "to protect ourselves and children.")

Testamentary counseling is a matter of helping the client to accept, recognize, and clarify these negative feelings. My observation of will interviews in my own practice, in my students' work, and in the practice of other lawyers, is that this critical beginning is evaded as long as possible and occurs very late in the typical will interview. I have also observed, however, that the interview does not become genuine or meaningful until the reasons for the will are expressed. Therefore, at the very least, lawyers should refuse to aid and abet the process of evasion. Ideally lawyers should act positively toward guiding the client to an early and frank realization of the fact that his death is involved in testamentary counseling. I believe that both of these objectives can be accomplished by the reflective system of counseling that Rogers suggests—which is fundamentally a matter of listening closely and empathically to what the client says and of exhibiting to him that what he says and feels is understood.

Once the reasons are expressed, the session often becomes positive. The client can begin to feel and express what he hopes to gain from the lawyer's services. This corresponds to Rogers' fifth, sixth and seventh steps. I have found that young-family clients eventually come to a realization that their small wealth must be applied for minor children, if both parents should die while they have minor children. In addition, the young-family clients come to realize that the surrogate parents they chose must have broad discretion. As a result, the clients come to emphasize in their judgment the support of their children over less realistic objectives such as college education. This is a dogma in planning property settlement—that first things must come first. The moment in which a client understands this sort of priority and focuses his reasoning around it is suggestive of what Rogers experiences when his psychotherapy patient's "insight and self-understanding come bubbling through." Here is an example from a young-client interview:

> If you are going to put into the terms of the trust that . . . the last four thousand dollars . . . must be given to each one for their college education. . . . [That] may bind the trustee in a way that is not very good for things you can't foresee now. [Better to] allow the person who has the property to use it more or less as you would, you know, as things come up, he has a chance to do things more or less as if he were their parents. . . .

Another client in that project ended the interview by thanking the students who helped him; he expressed with some satisfaction the decision that he wanted to revoke his present will which set up rigid guardianships for minor children and make a new one. It is important to notice that the clients themselves should arrive at these realizations and these decisions. This can be accomplished when their counsellors are patient, accepting, and gentle. I believe that this kind of lawyer-client relationship produces a positive experience for clients. It is, to paraphrase Rogers, one of the fascinating aspects of being a lawyer.

Conclusion

There are two ways in which consideration of the preceding discussion might be helpful to the practicing attorney. One is that behavioral information should help lawyers to realize how their clients feel, especially about death and the values that death will destroy. Psychology presents a significant amount of information on the subject and promises to develop more as the decade-old effort to explore death as psychologically significant continues in the hospitals and laboratories commanded by that science. The other source of value, less tangible than the first, is a matter of a counseling attitude, an openness, which is more affective than systematic.

Although most lawyers do not realize the influence they exert on clients, the realities and values of the client's situation are heavily influenced by the verbal and non-verbal reactions of the lawyer to what the client says. "The selection of value and facts should then largely dictate the conceptual and idea framework that helps to set the direction for both problem and solution," according to Dr. Redmount (*Connecticut Law Review,* 1969). "The counselor needs logical skills and he needs to develop an experimental mode of inquiry if he is to perceive and organize the realities and possibilities in a party's situation most effectively."

This suggests a number of attitudes in testamentary counseling. One is an "experimental mode of inquiry," which is a search for feelings and attitudes as well as for information. It cannot be fulfilled with a fill-in-the-blanks system of will interviews, and lawyers who insist on operating their wills practice as if they were taking driver-license applications should get into another line of work.

The "experimental mode of inquiry" also excludes narrow value systems which reflect what the lawyer thinks the client should do with his property. At the very least, an openness to the client's own feelings and values about property and family requires that the lawyer realize that he communicates his values and attitudes to the client, whether he wants to or not. It may be that a life-estate trust for the client's wife is, in the lawyer's opinion, a poor idea. But the value of the idea should be tested against the way the client feels about his wife, about—for instance—her remarriage after his death, and about her ability to plan for and support their children. It should not be based on a moral absolute which represents the lawyer's own feelings and values. Redmount continues:

> Poor legal counseling, with the adumbrated view of facts and highly parochial, legalistic conceptions of experience, may be particularly ill-suited to preventive means of dealing with experience. Failures of perception and a restricted range of information and understanding may make the prediction of other than very narrow issues quite hazardous and unreliable. The lawyer who is not "counseling-oriented" has the opportunity and perhaps the disposition to be more effective in highly identified matters that require correction. He is less likely to handle well somewhat unidentified matters that require future planning.

Affectively significant counseling equipment is not altogether the result of attitudes, nor is it altogether the result of study and preparation. Both sensitivity and information seem to be required, and, although this is not the place for a comprehensive discussion of the process of making counselors from lawyers, it may be helpful to suggest two avenues to more skillful counseling.

One is study. The literature of counseling, suggested in the introduction of this article, and in Professor Freeman's excellent casebook is readily available to lawyers. Other "helping professions" (medicine, nursing, social work) have been aware of it, and have been systematically developing their own versions for decades. The legal profession has, meanwhile, neglected its ancient claim to the title "counselor." That neglect should be redressed in law-school curricula and in the professional reading of those in the practicing profession.

The other avenue is an affective openness, a candor, that is probably inconsistent with the image of lawyers as tough-minded, relevance-centered, masters of order. If, for example, the "estate planning" lawyer thinks it a poor idea to set up support trusts for wives, and an even poorer idea to attempt to restrict a widow's ability to remarry, rapport would probably be advanced by his candid admission of his feelings and some expression of an honest interest in his client's

reaction to them. The Jungian therapist Marvin Spiegelman expresses
the idea:

> I find that the best interpretations come out of what is actually
> transpiring in the relationship, where both are in the grip of the
> same complex, which seems to travel back and forth. The
> implication of the foregoing is that the relationship itself is
> central and that the desired objectivity, individuality and under-
> standing come out of the actual experience, rather than out of
> some presumed knowledge or objectivity (intellectual or feeling)
> in the analyst.

If the lawyer expresses his negative feelings obliquely (by, say, making
faces or shaking his head), the client perceives an obstacle between him
and his counselor that he cannot deal with. Candor, and sympathetic
interest, are what Rogers was talking about when his ideal counselor
said to the client that he wanted "to enter into your world of
perception as completely as I am able . . . become in a sense, another
self for you . . . an alter ego of your own attitudes and feelings . . . "
That is a sound and lofty aspiration for the "counselor at law."

Reading Suggestions

This is the first of four chapters which will turn on some fairly complex
psychological theories. Some of these theories are traditional, but many
of them depend on recent research and clinical information and are
therefore not likely to be found in traditional psychological sources. A
few notes on the reading I have found helpful may be useful. (Complete
bibliographical information on these sources is in the table at the end of
this book.)

Lawyers and law students might usefully begin by considering their
own attitudes toward death, personally as well as in their professional
selves. Feifel's paper, *Physicians Consider Death,* is analogously useful
for that purpose; the questionnaire appended to Chapter 2 of this book
might also help. Literary reading often contains insights that are almost
beyond the reach of science; I find Tolstoy's stories on death,
particularly those gathered in the volume *Three Deaths,* very helpful;
there is also some artistic material, graphic and literary, in Feifel's
anthology, *The Meaning of Death.* Shneidman's articles on *Moby Dick*
and on Herman Melville are fascinating as a thanatologist's loving
examination of difficult literary material. The Feifel anthology, Fulton's *Death and Identity,* and Shneidman and Farberow's *Clues to*

Suicide all contain articles on this subject. More intensely to the point is Glaser's and Strauss' *Awareness of Dying* and Fox's *Experiment Perilous,* which tells of interpersonal relationships in the experimental ward of a large hospital. I found especially affecting Florence Joseph's story of her countertransference with a dying young lady, Eissler's *The Psychiatrist and the Dying Patient,* and the Zinker and Fink study.

It might then be useful to consider how more "normal" people feel about death. The three anthologies mentioned above are all useful for that, particularly Feifel's, which has also the advantage of being the pioneering work in the field for American psychology. The Diggory and Rothman report will lay useful background for this chapter, but is a relatively terse piece for us lay readers. Robert J. Lifton's work, which has now been gathered into the volume *Death in Life,* is an almost unique exploration of death attitudes in people who have been through a traumatic death-confronting experience (the Hiroshima bombing).

It is, finally, always helpful for lawyers to read in apposite anthropology. The Hertz and Mauss books which I cite in this chapter are relatively hard to find; Goody's *Death, Property and the Ancestors,* is, however, fully available and very useful.

Notes

1. Diggory and Rothman, *Values Destroyed by Death,* 63, *Journal of Abnormal and Social Psychology* 205 (1961), in *Death and Identity* 152 ed. R. Fulton (1965).

2. With this objective in mind, my empirical test was designed to ask a number of ethnographic questions not found in the Diggory-Rothman study. The additional questions were pointed toward family and economic data, recent deaths in the family, and the reasons for the subject's interest in wills.

3. See Sheridan, *Power to Appoint for a Non-Charitable Purpose: A Duologue or Endacott's Ghost.*

4. An illustration of this thought is the development of the trust in 19th Century American law. See Friedman, *The Dynastic Trust.*

5. Death anxiety is almost universal, so that one can speak of reducing it as a general goal of enlightened humanism. See S. Freud, S. Ferenczi, K. Abraham, G. Simmel, and E. Jones; Southard; Golding, Atwood and Goodman; Teicher.

6. Sixteen (14 omitting duplication)—the most numerous group (46 percent omitting duplication)—chose consequence "D". Two of these

were men (representing 33 percent of the men answering). Eight were in the young age group (under 49)—of a total of 11 in that group. Seven were between the ages of 50 and 65; one was older than 65. This answer was chosen by three of the six people who had experienced recent deaths of relatives and by two of the three who had recently lost a spouse. Of the total who had both parents living (five), two chose this answer. Two of the persons who chose this answer were childless—out of a total of six childless persons who answered the questionnaire. Eight of the 16 "D" answers listed their testamentary interest as general information; six had testamentary interest related to death consequences; and two did not indicate what their testamentary interest was. Of these 16 respondents, five estimated their wealth as upper middle class, seven chose middle class, and three chose lower middle class.

7. M. Mauss, *The Gift; Forms and Functions of Exchange in Archaic Societies* 48 (I. Cunnison transl. 1954). Applications of this concept to mourning rites are worked out by Goody, and by Hertz.

8. Three persons chose answer "E" (the worst or most distasteful consequence of death is that my death would cause grief to my relatives and friends). All of these were in the middle age group; all were women; all were married and had children. Two of them had lost both parents; one had lost her mother recently. The third had lost her mother but not recently. Two of the three estimated their wealth as middle class; one chose lower middle class. One possessed a consequence-related testamentary interest, one an informational interest, and one did not indicate her interest.

9. Shneidman and Farberow, *Genuine and Simulated Suicide Notes, Appendix, Clues to Suicide.* Shneidman and Farberow, as a part of their study of suicide, selected 33 notes left by successful suicides and matched the persons who wrote them with live subjects chosen for their similarity in sex, religion, economic status, and so on. They asked these matched respondents to prepare suicide notes. This produced 33 "real" notes and 33 "pseudo" notes. Although it was no part of their study, it is interesting, and mildly contradictory of my suggestion, to examine those notes for a testamentary context—to ask, in other words, whether people who are really facing death are more concerned with testamentary disposition than people who are only pretending that they face death. Of the total of 66 notes in the study, 15 attempt to make some testamentary disposition; 12 of these 15 (80 percent) are genuine. Sixteen notes express concern for dependent support, but of those only seven (44 percent) are genuine. To state it most accurately: In a group of people made up equally of those who are facing death and those who are pretending to face death: (1) those who express testamentary concern are, four times out of five, those who really face death; and (2) of those who express support concern (24 percent), less than half are really facing death. There is, in other words, more to the testamentary context than support. There is element of prolonged mortal-

102

ity, perhaps, which is broader than material obligation. There is room, for example, for an expression of concern at causing grief.

However, the Shneidman-Farberow study was made on subjects who faced or pretended to face death. Wills clients undoubtedly confront death in some way, but I think it too strong to say that they *face* death. The comparison of moods and moments that testamentary consideration of suicide notes presents may mislead, because we are talking about clients in a law office who expect to survive their experience with a lawyer. It is probably still correct to conclude, generally, that the values presented by the "D" answer (support concern) loom larger in a testamentary context than the values represented by the "E" answer (grief concern).

10. *But cf.* Rhudick and Dibner.

11. Burton reports the results of questioning an experimental group of psychiatrists, and a control group of ministers, as follows: Would as many people miss me if I were to die today as I would miss if they were to die today? Nearly 20 percent of the psychiatrists (and one of the ministers) thought that more people would miss them than they would miss. About 6 percent of the psychiatrists (16 percent of the ministers) had the opposite opinion; 47 percent of the psychiatrists (32 percent of the ministers) thought they would be missed about as much. as they would miss. Regardless of what those results say about the effects of religious practice on humility, they say something on death anxiety among physicians. See Feifel, *Physicians Consider Death.*

12. It is interesting to compare that frequently-identified syndrome with the situation where everyone in the environment is ill or dying, and therefore relatively willing to participate in mutual support. R. Fox, *Experiment Perilous: Physicians and Patients Facing the Unknown* (1959), is a remarkable, book-length study of the experimental ward of a hospital, in which all patients were seriously ill and many were terminal. Zinker and Fink, *The Possibility of Psychological Growth in a Dying Person,* applies this principle to support and therapy from family and hospital staff. An early example of the effects of mutually supportive behavior in death-anxiety situations is reported in Southard's work on war neuroses.

13. Four of my 34 answers were "E". Two of these were in the middle age group; two were in the older group. Two were men and two women. This represented a disproportionately high number of male answers, but the male sample was very small. None of them had experienced recent death; two of the four had lost one or both parents; none had lost a spouse; two of the four were childless. Two considered themselves upper middle class, one middle and one lower. Two had consequence-related testamentary interest and two had informational testamentary interest.

14. Here is E.M. Forster making, through a character in *Howard's End*, the point that if we didn't have death we would have to invent it:

> "Miss Schlegel, the real thing's money and all the rest is a dream."
> "You're still wrong. You've forgotten Death. [Leonard could not understand:] If we lived forever what you say would be true. But we have to die, we have to leave life presently. Injustice and greed would be the real thing if we lived forever. I love Death—not morbidly, but because He explains. He shows me the emptiness of Money. Death and Money are the eternal foes. Not Death and Life. Never mind what lies behind Death, Mr. Bast, but be sure that the poet and the musician and the tramp will be happier in it than the man who has never learnt to say 'I am I.'"

15. Zinker and Fink found, for instance that a dying person's need for safety and physical security tends to grow and that his need for self-esteem tends to diminish. Florence Joseph's touching clinical analysis of a dying cancer patient shows many of the same conclusions in a more personal context and illustrates, too, that her patient was aware of her death and planned for it, even though she never discussed it and possibly never consciously admitted it.

16. Fulton, *The Sacred and the Secular: Attitudes of the American Public Toward Death, Funerals, and Funeral Directors*, in *Death and Identity*:

> When we reflect upon the fact that some of the aged in this country are no longer welcome in the homes of their children and are no longer secure in the belief that with age comes respect, we can appreciate why they would uproot themselves from their families, friends, and their established place in the local community and flee in unprecedented numbers to retirement cities and other locales on the Pacific Coast which are literally as well as figuratively on the edge of American society. By denying their children or other relatives the opportunity to give them the gift of the funeral at their deaths, they give vent to their hostility and resentment toward a society that has rejected them.

17. Here is a table on parental death:

		One Parent Dead	Both Parents Dead	One Parent Recently*
A	(3%)	10%	0	0
B	(9%)	10%	12%	0
C	(6%)	0	12%	0
D	(46%)	60%	41%	67%
E	(9%)	10%	12%	33%
F	(12%)	10%	6%	0
G	(9%)	0	12%	0

*Within past three years.

18. See, for example, Dunham, *The Method, Process and Frequency of Wealth Transmission at Death*. Consider the psychological autopsy suggested by a claim my students and I discovered in the probate records of the Elkhart County, Indiana, circuit court: An agreed claim for $185 to one Margaret Yoder for:

> . . .carrying six or seven buckets of coal a day from basement to heating stove, emptying commonettes, digging paths in snow in winter, keeping lights filled, making beds, carrying water in, doing the shopping, moping [sic] and washing of windows, checking on decedent two or three times a day and other similar services.

19. Kalven, *The Quest for the Middle Range: Empirical Inquiry and Legal Policy, in Law In a Changing America:*

> Does not the failure of law and social science to mix more zestfully require some explanation from the social science side too? Why has not the law as phenomena seemed of sufficient interest in the social scientist to move him to put *his own* questions to it and to study it not as law but as part of his study of society?

5   Will Interviews

The psychology of testation—the human content in will interviewing and consequent "estate planning"—is a mixture of attitudes toward death, attitudes toward property, and attitudes toward giving.[1] This chapter is an attempt to examine this human content in five specific lawyer-client settings. The clients are young married couples with small children; they are people to whom death would seem remote, whose property is skimpy and largely devoted to dependent support, and whose attitudes toward giving are likely to be narrowly focused on members of their immediate families.

My opportunity to be a participant-observer in these professional relationships came about this way: I teach Property III-IV at the University of Notre Dame Law School, an eight-hour "package" covering material traditionally taught in courses on wills, trusts, future interests, fiduciary administration, and federal estate and gift taxation. In the 1967-1968 academic year my students and I spent about a third of our time and effort in clinical projects. In the fall semester the projects involved analysis and planning of "large" estates (i.e., those with tax problems). In the spring semester it involved planning for young-family clients, and drafting for both kinds of clients.

In the early part of the spring semester, the eight clinical groups— each from six to ten students—worked with live clients. Each set of clients was a young couple who had two young children and a modest accumulation of wealth. The project involved (1) interviews; (2) planning sessions among the "lawyers" involved; (3) drafting, each lawyer doing his own; (4) criticism and revision of the drafts; and (5) execution of the instruments and advice on ancillary transfers and life-insurance arrangements.

The client interviews followed about a semester of four hours a week of formal instruction in property settlement. Three of four classes dealt with young clients and included a movie on "solution oriented" interviewing and some independent study of my law review article "Non-estate Planning," on young-family wills clients.[2] I attended and participated in all of the interviews except one, and that one was tape recorded for me. I have given the couples names drawn clumsily from the novels of C.P. Snow:

A. Mr. and Mrs. Lewis (Margaret) Eliot, who have two young daughters. Mr. Eliot is a white-collar worker in industry; Mrs. Eliot is a teacher. They are close to and have confidence in Mrs. Eliot's brother and his wife, Mr. and Mrs. Charles (Mary) Austin. Mr. Austin was one of the lawyers in the interview.

B. Mr. and Mrs. Kurt (Hanna) Puchwein, who have two pre-school age children, a boy and a girl. Mr. Puchwein is a public-school teacher, on leave and in a graduate program. They have confidence in Mr. and Mrs. Puchwein's parents, Dr. and Mrs. Leonard (Ruth) March.

C. Mr. and Mrs. Vernon (Muriel) Royce, who have two young children. Mr. Royce is a teacher and part-time insurance agent. They have some confidence in Mrs. Royce's brother, John Cottery, and his wife, Rachel.

D. Mr. and Mrs. Francis (Katharine) Getliffe, who have two young daughters. Mr. Getliffe, is an independent small businessman. They have a good deal of confidence in Mrs. Getliffe's brother and his wife, Mr. and Mrs. Charles (Ann) Simon. Mr. Simon was one of the lawyers in the interview.

E. Mr. and Mrs. Roger (Caro) Quaife, who have two young children. Mr. Quaife is a graduate student who plans a professional career; Mrs. Quaife is a teacher on a part-time basis and in the summer. They have confidence in a number of relatives and friends.

This chapter will be structured in terms of four inquiries: (I) Is the will interview a confrontation with the idea of one's own death? (II) If it is, does the confrontation seem to involve a denial (or evasion) of the idea? (III-A) Does Does the client's attitude toward his property suggest that somehow his personality is involved in what he owns? (III-B) If his personality seems to be involved, does property-ownership relate to the client's attitude toward his death? (IV) Does the experience of making informed choices about property disposition appear to have a therapeutic effect on clients?

Confronting Death

Each client in these interviews confronted the idea of his own death. Of course, as Tolstoy said, "If a man has learned to think, no matter what he may think about, he is always thinking of his own death." But I mean here a confrontation more necessarily advertent than that.

One of the immediately remarkable features I noticed was that this confrontation tended to occur at the same point in each interview. This surprised me because the lawyers involved had no formal instruction—and, I believe, no uniform informal instruction—on the order that will preparation interviews should take. In each case serious "what if. . . ." talk about the client's death was the *last* subject taken up by the lawyers. In each case the lawyers inquired first into family arrangements, and into assets second. After this information was thoroughly laid out—usually for an hour or more—the subject of death awkwardly surfaced.

Christ found patients willing to discuss their deaths, but hospital staff, relatives and friends reluctant to raise the topic. Most (fifty-four of sixty-two) said they had never discussed their deaths with anyone; one patient reported that members of his family put him off by saying, "Why do you have to talk about such a morbid topic? You should be grateful to be alive." This may suggest the analogue that my lawyers were at least partially responsible for the delay in discussing death in these interviews.

Even references to the death of persons other than the clients or their children, which often preceded discussion of the clients' deaths, were made haltingly and dealt with, I thought, hurriedly. Here is an example from the Getliffe interview (Mrs. Katharine Getliffe's brother, Simon, is one of the lawyers):

> Lawyer: [speaking of the value of her father-in-law's house] Would you like to live there?
> Katharine: Oh, I live six blocks away. . . . I wouldn't want to inherit it, if that's what you mean.
> Lawyer: That's what I mean. [Laughter]
> Simon: Hey, wait a minute here. Don't be so in a hurry.
> * * *

Lawyer: [to Francis] Is there any realistic expectancy of an inheritance?

* * *

Francis: Well, my parents are old, but—

* * *

Katharine: [interrupting] —they never—
Francis: We know that eventually they will—
Lawyer: Would it be substantial?
Francis: At what point would you say it's substantial?

* * *

Simon: Well, my dad leaves everything to my mother. When she dies, everything goes to Katharine and me. But I doubt there would be very little left. I hope that—you know—you hope your parents spend everything, at least we do. . . .
Katharine: Spend it all.
Simon: At least we do.

When the clients' death was directly confronted, it was in circumstances which suggested serious, advertent consideration of the idea. (This has been the experience, reported by Glaser and Strauss, Fox, and Eissler, in treating the seriously ill.) The most potent example of that, and the most intense portion of almost every interview, occurred relatively late in each interview when these women were asked what they wanted done with their children if both parents died while the children were minors. Here is the Getliffe interview during a discussion of guardians (for physical care):

Lawyer: . . . . You'd want to make sure they were in a position to care for them—they had the time and interest.
Katharine: Well, the interest is where the difficulty is.
Lawyer: Oh, sure, I think—
Katharine: I mean we've gone through—discussed this—and it's so—kind of a sad discussion to think who would take care of your children if you were—weren't there to take care of them. And no one can—of course—take care of them as well as you can.
I mean—[The interview was relatively jolly up until this last exchange. I thought it then became much quieter, more, somber, and more sensitive.]

* * *

Lawyer A: Well, now do we want to go on and figure out—what if this goes on and—What happens if Katharine is not alive and the two children aren't alive—uh, do we want to go on . . . ?
Lawyer B: . . .Do you expect to have more children?
Francis: We hope to.
Katharine: We never thought beyond our children.

Lawyer A: I know. That's just it.

Francis: Yeah. Say we all got killed. What would happen in that case?

[In the discussion following the clients were unable to decide what they wanted to happen to their property in this situation.]

Katharine: What would happen if we didn't have a will and we—we both were in an accident—both killed, what would happen to the children immediately? Who would take care of them? Would the state throw them into an orphanage?

Here, in a fairly extended example, is similar information from the Eliot interview:

Lawyer: Well, what would be your idea as far as a trust is concerned?

Lewis: We would want the kids to have an education. The thing is, if something would happen to me—the way we're set up now, we plan on both of us living that long, with our stock program, we're—planning on all the money to go . . . for their education. By that time, I'm sure our savings . . . will pan out. Now, if anything—if something does happen to me, when the insurance policies go to her, well—what do you suggest about that? I haven't thought about it.

[These last few words with impatience in his voice—not a normal thing for him in this interview.]

Margaret: For example, there is this thing about the house. I figure, you know, with the insurance coming to me, I can plan—in another five years—plan on at least ten thousand a year.

* * *

[A discussion of their financial situation followed. It seemed to me to come with relief on all sides. Then:]

Lewis: . . . This is a good time to talk about wills, you know, because if something happened to both of us, what would happen? This is more or less why we thought of a will this way.

Margaret: When we talked to Charlie about it originally—

Lewis: A couple of years ago—We'd like someone to look after them, instead of going to court and having—having a guardian assigned for the children, we'd sort of appoint someone.

Lawyer: How about if both of you should die?

Lewis: This is . . .

Margaret: [interrupting] This would be our major concern.

[One of the lawyers then abruptly changed the subject, and busied himself in removing the Eliot children, who were present, from the room.]

Lawyer A: . . . We should settle—If you both were to have a simultaneous, or nearly simultaneous—problem—or accident—uh, death, yes.

111

Lawyer B: Should they both die.

Lawyer A: Yes. Right.

[One of the lawyers then changed the subject.]

* * *

Lawyer A: [After a pause] Are we ready?

Lawyer B: Yes, if simultaneous—if something were to happen simultaneously, or if, we will say, or if, you were to die, and then five years later she were to die—if, uh—that also. . . . If something—let's say within six months of each other, if something were to happen, what would be your hopes?

Margaret: Well—you know—the primary thing here is what would happen to the kids. And we want Charles and Mary to be—whatever you call it.

* * *

Lawyer: I have one thing on this trustee's discretion. Do you want Charles to have discretion to—uh, say something did happen in the next few years, something when the kids are still under, say, ten, do you want him to have discretion then to use the money for their interest, too?

Lewis: Yes, this is what I'm saying—that's what I'm thinking of. What if something happens, supposing, now, when we're going home, there. You know, something happened now. And the kids are only six and four, we would still want him to use the money—you know. . . .

As these excerpts indicate, Lewis and Margaret placed considerable reliance on Charles and Mary Austin; they, it seemed to me, took relief from the thought that the Austins would look after their children. One of the lawyers affected them, visibly and audibly, when he asked them who would look after the children if the Austins were also dead. The response seemed fairly typical of these interviews. The Eliots had great difficulty in coping with the question—difficulty involving hushed conversation, thoughtful pauses, and a false start or two. An early and prevalent content in death anxiety is the fear of separation. Researchers on death attitudes in children trace the fear of death-separation to childhood fear that the mother will die. Hug-Hellmuth reported that "Of the whole idea of death, visibly by far the most unbearable to him [the child being observed] was the thought of a child being separated from his mother. . . ." I have tried, in Chapter 7, to account for this reaction in the parent in terms of the Freudian theory of generation-reversal. A more direct growth, proceeding not from the parental status of the parent, but from the fears he had as a child, is traced by Wahl, and by Volkart and Michael. The empirical fact is that separation is such a potent part of the death anxiety that one must differentiate psychologically between death envisioned more or less individually, when environment and supporting persons will not die, and death in general disasters, when the environment is destroyed, and supporting persons die with it.

The lawyers experienced a similar effect at two other points in this part of the Eliot interview. The first was on the question of trust remainders—who should get the property if one of their daughters died, while the trust was in effect, leaving a husband and children of her own. The second question was also awkward to the lawyer who asked it:

> Lawyer: If, Lew, something should happen to the children between now and—you know—and while you were both still alive, and following both your deaths, do you have any—what are your thoughts on who you would like your estate to go to then?

The Eliots spent a long time on that question and found themselves unable to answer it at this interview. It was settled later, by correspondence with the lawyers.

Compare the Royce interview:

> Lawyer: [during a discussion of life insurance] It sounds like your plans for buying this term insurance would indicate that you have given some thought to what—you know, to what the family situation will be in the event of your death. In the event of the death of both of you at the same time, have you ever given any thought to how the children will be taken care of? Or by whom you would like them to be taken care of? [There was a long pause here, followed by a couple of false starts.]
> Lawyer: Who are they close to? Friends? Relatives?
> Muriel: . . . give them to my mom and dad. . . .
> Lawyer: Do you think they could take care of them? [Vernon and Muriel then discussed several possibilities.]
> * * *
> Lawyer: One decision you are undoubtedly going to have to make, and talk to people about, is in case of a common disaster.
> Muriel: I think [Rachel Cottery] would probably be most likely. . . . Well, you know, she has children. . . . I think that would probably be best.
> Lawyer: How would she feel about it?
> Muriel: I don't think she'd mind at all. I will talk to her before you put it down. . . .

One of the lawyers then suggested that this guardian, who had children of her own, be empowered to use trust funds for her own children. The other lawyers attempted to explain reasons for this, but the clients reacted to their explanation with continuing silence. Maybe this indicated that Muriel (Mrs. Royce) had not thought of her children as being in *another* family. It was important to her to think that her children would be taken care of by a trusted relative, but she did not think of the relative as having other children. That thought somehow broke her confidence in the survival of a supporting person, possibly because it forced her to think of the guardian as existing for some purpose other than the care of Muriel's children. It seems to me that this phase of Muriel's interview is psychologically similar to Katharine Getliffe's wondering about her children being thrown into an orphanage. Eissler suggests from a clinical analysis that this sort of attachment in a psychotic patient may grow so strong that a mother who thinks she is dying may kill her children to prevent their being left without care. In the case Eissler reports, the patient located a person to care for her children and thereby avoided what he, as her psychiatrist, feared; she then, however, made of the surrogate mother both a mirror image of herself and a figure for transference. The experience led Eissler to conclude that the plight of those who know they are dying would be eased "by pre-mourning, so to speak" in which the patients "divorced themselves from their love objects." He believes, though, that "the ego cannot achieve this under ordinary circumstances." Here is another "supporting-persons" example, from the Eliot interview:

> Lawyer: Do you have insurance on your land contract?
> Lewis: No, because I'm sure, if anything happens to us, that her folks [who hold it] will take care of it.

And, from the Puchwein interview:

> Lawyer: I think we've probably reached the point where we'd be interested in having you tell us how you would probably like your property to be divided—as far as the children, and that—
> Kurt: We anticipated this question . . . so we asked Dr. and Mrs. March if they would take the younger child; you know, they have already agreed to take [the older], and they said they would take [the younger].
> Hanna: We'd probably want it drawn up pretty much the same as [the will] before, only including [the younger child]. I don't think there's much else. . . .
>   * * *
> Kurt: [speaking of expectation of inheritance from his father] . . . He's not a millionaire or anything. . . . I don't know

how much he has. Let's just say I don't expect anything.

Hanna: Nobody does.

Kurt: No, nobody does. My mom doesn't even . . .

* * *

Lawyer: I didn't study your [present] will too carefully. In the event you and your wife are not here, and your children do go to the guardians, what happens to your estate—your property and your insurance proceeds?

Kurt: [explaining that he made his father beneficiary of one large life insurance policy] . . . so that, if anything should happen to Hanna and I, the money would go to him. [Kurt then explained he had a similar arrangement on an even larger policy on which Dr. March was beneficiary. He added that he would leave all of his property to Dr. and Mrs. March to take care of the Puchwein children.]

Kurt: Yes, that would be my intention.

Hanna: Well, they would be—

Kurt: [Abruptly] No, they—they can handle it.

I interpret the exchange to mean that Hanna does not have as much confidence in giving her parents unrestricted ownership of their property as Kurt does. This begins to break the security provided by the thought of supporting persons. This concern again came up later in the interview:

Kurt: Another important thing that we've touched upon, but still doesn't ring clear with me, is that if—if Hanna and I die, and then Hanna's parents follow a short time thereafter, say two years, when the kids are still only twelve and eleven—something like that—and my sister gets them, there's a possibility that, if I would just turn everything over to Hanna's parents, that money would be a long time in making that step from their death to my sister. It would be tied up for some time.

The lawyers were affected by these discussions almost as much as the clients were. When Katharine Getliffe asked about her children being placed in an orphanage, for instance, the lawyers, with haste and even confusion, assured her that such an event would not happen. But none of the lawyers knew what would happen instead. Their collective advice on the matter amounted to an assurance that members of Francis's and Katharine's families would care for the children while—and until—the Probate Court worked out guardianships, and that the guardians, when appointed, would be members of their families. In other words, the lawyers invited these clients to rely on the survival of supporting persons. This done, one of the lawyers changed the subject:

> Lawyer: Okay, well, let's start talking about the more possible situation of you not dying until a much older age—
> Katharine: Good.
> Lawyer: —and—you look very healthy to me, both of you. And, say some of your children will be past maturity . . . and some will be under twenty-one. . . .

The Quaife interview, finally, presented the death confrontation in a child-care, supporting-persons context very clearly and concisely:

> Lawyer: If anything happened to both of you, and your children didn't—survive you—there would be a guardian or something?
> Caro: Yeah, um hum. As it stands now, probably my parents. My mother is working presently, but will not be after this summer. But it should be so—
> Lawyer: And alternatively perhaps your sister?
> Caro: No, no. Parents.
> [Pause.]
> Caro: And so they could split it up, so they'd be with my parents part of the year and with Roger's parents part of the year—whatever they wanted. . . .

These are examples of parents reacting to the suggestions that (a) they might predecease their children, and (b) even the persons designated to be substitute parents might die—or be occupied with other concerns—before the children became adults. There were, of course, many other mentions of death in the interviews, but many of those could have been conventional. They may not have involved a clear consideration of the possibility of death. The child-care discussions demonstrate convention much less. In the course of these discussions every client considered his own death as the event which would leave his children orphaned and subject even to contingencies threatening alternative means of care for them. It is all but impossible to guess at the consequences this sort of confrontation has on property-settlement decisions, but the attitude one takes toward his own death is central in the attitude he takes toward his life—so much so that many psychologists conclude that death anxiety is the basis of all anxiety.

Evasion and Denial of Death

Man is the only animal that contemplates death, and also the only animal that shows any sign of doubt of its finality. This does not mean that he doubts it as a future fact. He accepts his own death, with that of others, as inevitable, plans for it, provides for the time when he shall be out of the picture. Yet, not less today than formerly, he confronts this fact with a certain incredulity regarding the scope of its destruction.

—Hocking

These clients and lawyers (and I should emphasize that I am reporting on the conduct of lawyers as well as the conduct of clients) evaded and tended to deny the reality of the clients' deaths. This was to be expected. Golding, Atwood, and Goodman, using a variety of testing devices (including galvanic skin response measurement and time-delay, and word-response tests), concluded that "normal" people resist the idea of death and, as a principal defense mechanism, tend to react to it in a rigid, dogmatic way. There is even some suggestion in the empirical literature that a more cordial attitude toward death is a symptom of suicidal pathology.

This evasion and denial among my lawyers and clients was most noticeable in verbal fumbling and awkward pauses, especially among the lawyers, when the dynamics of the interview had reached the stage where mention of personal death was almost unavoidable. In the Eliot interview, for instance, the moment came when the final, belabored information about assets was completed. The group fell silent. One of the lawyers then haltingly suggested death:

> Lawyer: Should we start looking now at what your intentions will be in the—uh—on the property? If something were to happen . . . what are your—uh—your thoughts?
>
> Lewis: Well, if something were to happen to me, all the property would pass, then, to Margaret. That's the way we would have it set up . . . [If both spouses were dead?] I'll have to think about this now. Would it be important at this point to set up, like a trust type thing for the children, as far as moneywise, or does it make any difference?

In the Quaife interview, and in others, examination of the beneficiary designations of life insurance policies afforded a relatively smooth, euphemistic way to raise the subject:

> Lawyer: I take it that you would want your will to read the same as these life insurance policies—you know, like, if anything happens to you, it's your wife, and then your children, and then your parents, or—

Roger: Yeah, generally, right.
[Pause; the mood became quieter, more somber. This change in atmosphere is quite noticeable even on the tape.]
Lawyer: Do you have any concern in this regard for your brothers and—
Caro: Just personal effects I think.
Lawyer: Is there some specific—anything specific—anything specific that you want to give anybody? Paintings, books, and so forth?
Caro: No, nothing like that. If something happens to both of us, it would be all for my [sic] children. Jewelry and things like that. If something happened to all of us—Oh, then, I think, to my mother, if she chose anything that she wanted.

In several groups, mention of death was sustained for a few minutes and then someone, usually one of the lawyers, changed the subject. (In the Eliot interview, one of the lawyers busied himself with removing the Eliot children from the room, and this provided a break in the train of the discussion which lasted for several minutes.) Here is an example, from the Getliffe interview (beginning during a discussion of Katharine's parents):

Lawyer: I guess this brings us to a good question—I mean, why do you need a will?
Katharine: I mean I can see, in a case where we have little children, and we're all involved, but with my parents—I mean. Well, I never even think about it [that is, for them].
Simon: . . . Now *they* [the Getliffes] need a will because of two minor children.
[One of the lawyers then changed the subject and began talking again about inheritance from parents. This went on for a while, until another lawyer brought the subject back on course abruptly. He took the bull by the horns.]
Lawyer: The next thing would—uh—be to—uh—start asking what you want done with your estate should one of you die and then should both of you die at the same time, should your children die with you—all of these differing steps we'll probably have to go through one by one. And the starting point would probably be, in the case of your [Francis's] death, say our next step will be—
Francis: Well, if I were to die, I would assume she could take care of everything, that it would then go to her.
Lawyer: Everything?
Francis: Yeah.
Lawyer: You feel that she has sufficient experience in background and handling money that she could handle it on her own without, say, another person helping her out in the business

matters?

Francis: [to Katharine] Well, what would you say? [To lawyers] I think so. We work together so much that—

Simon: Well, it seems that if you had two kids to take care of—I mean, you're going to be running the business and. . . .

Katharine: Well . . . uh . . . I mean, I hope this never happens, but if it was to happen—I mean, so many women have to go out to work, so handling these other matters would be—I'd have to go out to work, too, probably, but, I mean, these would be—not that difficult.

* * *

Lawyer: The next—you know—we'll just go down the list of contingencies. Now, if . . . uh . . . Katharine should happen to predecease you, you know, how would you want the property to go? We can assume, I suppose—

Francis: All to me [to Katharine] isn't it?

Katharine: Yeah. No [laughing] —I won't let you have it.

This was a direct, professional desk-side manner—the sort of thing I suppose these young lawyers will have highly developed as their wills practice begins to grow. This lawyer's approach, and the fact that Francis proved an exceptionally alert, well-informed client, resulted in a smoother handling of the subject of death than was characteristic of these interviews. This observation relates to the Crown, O'Donovan, and Thompson study; they found that most subjects prefer to see in others an unhealthy insensitivity to death, rather than an unhealthy sensitivity. "I don't believe I will die" is, in other words, preferred to "I fear death." But these subjects rated highest of all a *healthy* sensitivity, illustrated, perhaps, in this anecdote from a physician's life (reported by Lydgate):

> I go a long way with the man to whom I once had to say that his wife was dead. "Dead, eh?" he said; and then with a wistful glance into the middle distance, he said, "Dead, eh? Blimey, it's a funny old life."

A second fact indicating evasion of death discussion was the high incidence of raucous humor on the subject of death. Most of these people appeared to be normally delicate and refined, but their comments on death seem, out of context, almost callous. Here is a series of examples:

Lawyer: [After discussing Lewis's military service, and speaking to the other lawyers]: Always check that, fellows, because they'll buy you a tombstone, the V.A. will.

Lewis Eliot: That's right. Put you in the ground.

Lawyer: They're only paying about two hundred dollars for burial expenses and the undertakers are charging a thousand.

Margaret Eliot: Yeah, that's a scandal.

* * *

Lawyer: [during discussion of double-indemnity provisions of insurance policies] The best way for you to die would be in an accident.

Vernon Royce: That's right. [Laughter.]

Muriel Royce: How can we arrange it?

* * *

Lawyer: Do you have a reserve commitment?

Kurt Puchwein: No.

Lawyer: Which isn't a bad way to be this week. [Early spring, 1968.]

Lawyer: We hope we get a chance to finish your will. [Laughter.]

* * *

Lawyer A: [explaining V.A. death benefits] They pay toward funeral expenses and provide a nondescript tombstone and a flag—

Katharine Getliffe: Oh, they do?

Lawyer A: —and you [to Francis] can be buried in Arlington Cemetery free.

Katharine: [nervous laugh]

Lawyer B: You mean, when he dies—does he get a tombstone automatically?

Lawyer A: He has to ask for it.

Katharine: [nervous laugh]

[Everyone laughs.]

Lawyer A: The last I heard, they paid about two hundred and fifty dollars toward funeral expenses. Lawyers usually don't have to worry about that, though, because the funeral director collects it. . . .

Lawyer B: Can you do the same with the tombstone. . . . ?

Lawyer A: No, you have to take the one they give you. They're all the same. . . . Just like the shoes.

[Laughter.]

Lawyer A: . . . last name, first name, middle initial, rank and serial number. . . .

[Laughter.]

Lawyer C: Well, let's get on to something else.

* * *

[During a discussion of Francis's life insurance, one lawyer said he had some term insurance once and got nothing out of it.]

Lawyer B: That's because you didn't die. [Great emphasis on last word.]

120

Lawyer A: It wouldn't be worth anything to me then anyway.
[Nervous laughter.]

* * *

[One lawyer read the provisions of a term rider on a whole life policy.]

Lawyer B: You'd better die within the next five years. [Nervous laughter.]

Lawyer A: You get more money that way.

Katharine: I hope he lives to a ripe old age.

* * *

[Lawyers then began to discuss accidental death provisions of policies and exclusions for death in riots and insurrections.]

Francis Getliffe: How about if you're an innocent bystander. Still doesn't pay? [Katharine laughed.]

Lawyer: Well, it wouldn't pay for anything but accidental death. If somebody clobbers you with a brick, that's not an accident.

[Laughter.] . . . .

Roger Quaife: [discussing his life insurance] I tried to get more just before I went to Vietnam—

Caro Quaife: —and they wouldn't let him have it [laughing]. They said no.

* * *

[One of the lawyers asked Roger the amount of additional life insurance premiums he was required to pay in order to eliminate from policies the exclusion for death in private aircraft.]

Roger: Well, it's not much, because after you get above a certain flight-hour low, it isn't too much. There's a real big drop after you pass two thousand hours. It's nothing like the first hours, when you have to pay something like nine dollars a thousand.

Lawyer: A cheerful thought if you plan to learn how to fly. [There was a sort of nervous pause then, after which Roger again said, "Well, it's not too much."]

* * *

Lawyer: . . . A whole life policy is one on which you pay all your life—until age 100; then they'll pay you the face amount on the theory that if you're not dead you ought to be.

[Nervous laughter.]

Fox analyzed this phenomenon in a hospital ward devoted to experimental surgery and medication for serious and terminal patients. Of the physicians involved, who called themselves "the metabolic group," he reported:

[I]n its admixture of bravado and "blasphemy," the humor of the Metabolic Group resembled a type of humor known as "grim

121

humor" or "gallows humor." (*"Galgen-humor"*). This sort of joking typically occurs in situations where a group of individuals (more generally men than women) are faced with a considerable amount of stress—above all, firsthand contact with death.

He reports several instances involving jokes among the patients, which are perhaps closer to the prototype he describes. For example:

A group of . . . [patients] inflated some of the rubber tubing ordinarily used for tourniquets, and constructed a "kidney" out of it. They presented it to a patient who was in the advanced stages of a serious renal disease.

* * *

Remember that time when Mac was getting all that cortisone, and he kind of went off his rocker? He came, prancing down the ward one morning, flowers in one hand, a urinal in the other, saying, "I'm dead, and I'm going to Heaven with these in my hands!" It was a panic!

I reported, in Chapter 2, similar reactions in trial judges being exposed to gruesome real evidence.

A third factor indicating evasion of death discussion was the relatively greater comfort with which the clients returned to discussions of assets and family after death had been suggested. For example, Kurt Puchwein changed the subject abruptly from a discussion of guardianship for his (presumably) orphaned children to a discussion of assets. "We do have about a thousand dollars in savings," he said. "That should probably be mentioned. I didn't think it was enough to mention, but now that I think about it, a thousand dollars is plenty." He said this with more relish than he showed in discussing his own death. The change in subject also gave him, I thought, some emotional relief. And not only did members of each group tend individually to change the subject from death, but other members reacted positively to the tendency.

This retreat from the subject of death may resemble psychologically the trust exhibited in supporting persons (parents or siblings or even banks) as sources of care for their children. In other words, one way these clients have of coping with the unwelcome subject of personal death is to rely on the belief that both the people they love and their environments will live on after they die.

So much for evasion of the subject of death. What of the possibility that these clients also tend to deny that they will die? The difference is that denial occurs after the reality of death is confronted. Glaser and

Strauss found that terminal hospital patients tend to evade the mode of their deaths or the time of their deaths more readily than the fact of death itself, but this is probably, in the circumstances, a denial of the fact. It is a phenomenon familiar to life-insurance salesmen; Briggs reports:

> [I] n the life insurance sales situation, there are a large number of ways for the prospect to rationalize—to convince himself that he really does have enough insurance for right now. Naturally, he needs more, and he'll take it out later, but for now, he is OK.

One answer to the question is that "denial" is too strong a word. I can conclude from the interviews that the clients—with willing support from their lawyers—relied on a sort of indefinite mortality. They tended at least to expect that their personal lives would be suspended, and death could be postponed, beyond any focal point in time. The Quaifes' discussion of their furniture and appliances may be an illustration of this:

> [Caro listed the disposition of each item of her tangible personal property—stove, refrigerator, furniture, jewelry, etc.]
> Lawyer: Well, I tell you . . . my general attitude is that everything, every asset ought to be put in trust. That means the trustee has got to take care of some of this stuff. The cash realized from selling the stuff is—
> Caro: [interrupting] For the children.
> Lawyer: —cash that can be used for the support of the children. That is except, of course, things of peculiar personal value, like jewelry or paintings or something, but—just ordinary household stuff. . . .
> Caro: Well, the household things have some value now, but if nothing happened to either of us for some years, they wouldn't be worth anything. . . . So, if anything happened to us in the immediate future, I can see places for these things, but if nothing happened to us for ten of fifteen years. . . .
> * * *
> In a few years, it would cost more to get them anywhere than what they're worth.

It does not seem to have occurred to Caro that in ten or fifteen years she will own different, and probably better, furniture and appliances. She is extending the present and assuming that when she dies—an event she puts in the indefinite future—things will be as they are now. Another example of that mood is the almost uniform assumption, by these young parents of two, that their families would not increase in size. Only Francis Getliffe considered the possibility that he would father more children. Kurt and Hanna Puchweins' old wills provided only for one child, and did not mention or include by general reference the daughter who was born after the wills were executed.

The clients found it difficult to project their lives into the future, to a time when they would be older, more dependent perhaps, and less attractive. A good example of that, occurring in each interview, was the question of trust distribution if a child-beneficiary died leaving a spouse or children of his own. It was hard to conceive of their small children as adults, who were not dependent on the clients anymore—and that may have been, partly, because the conception implied age in the clients, a *memento mori* perhaps. Death and old age may have been associated in their minds, with the result—by no means inevitable—that old age for themselves was not an attractive prospect.

Burton reports the result of studying death attitudes among groups of (respectively) psychiatrists and clergymen. He asked them "What is the proper time to die?" The largest response from psychiatrists was that it is proper to die when one becomes a burden to others, but a large response from psychiatrists, and the largest response from clergymen, was that there is no proper time to die. He also asked what arrangements should be made for death. Nearly half of the psychiatrists listed arrangement for care of dependents, but the ministers' largest response was attention to the disposition of their property. Blauner surveys anthropological evidence that a culture devalues the humanity of those who are likely to die, citing examples from periods of high infant mortality in France; he concludes that our society devalues the old because devaluing them minimizes "the disruption and moral shock death ordinarily brings about." One might expect to find this association prominently in older clients; Jung observed, in that respect (in Feifel's anthology *The Meaning of Death*):

> Whenever possible our consciousness refuses to accommodate itself to this undeniable truth. Ordinarily we cling to our past and remain stuck in the illusion of youthfulness. Being old is highly unpopular.
>
> * * *
>
> Thoughts of death pile up to an astonishing degree as the years increase. Willy-nilly, the aging person prepares himself for death. That is why I think that nature herself is already preparing for the end.
>
> * * *

Objectively, it is a matter of indifference what the individual consciousness may think about it. But subjectively it makes an enormous difference whether consciousness keeps step with the psyche, or whether it clings to opinions of which the heart knows nothing. It is just as neurotic in old age not to focus upon the goal of death as it is in youth to repress fantasies which have to do with the future.

There is some evidence that when the context of death discussion is particularly affecting, denial is somehow surpassed and death faced with sadness, but without evasion. Care of children is, again, the most intense example of that. Here are examples from the interviews of Caro Quaife and Katharine Getliffe. Caro's expression of approval was quite emphatic at the end of this excerpt on a choice of trustee and guardian for her two small children:

> Lawyer A: I think it's pretty hard to have your father as trustee, because, you know, this might go on for thirty or forty years.
> [Pause.]
> Lawyer B: Of course, it ought to be over by then.
> Lawyer A: Yeah, but even if it goes on for ten or twelve years—How old is your oldest child now?
> Caro: Four.
> Roger: Four and a half.
> Lawyer A: Well, you would want to keep it until at least twenty-one.
> Lawyer C: That's not as critical with a trustee because the court will always appoint a substitute trustee. It's perhaps a little more critical with a guardian because there you've got physical care of the children. Anybody can take care of money, but you don't want just anybody to take care of your kids.
> Caro: Yeah!

Katharine Getliffe was closer to a confrontation with her own death at this child-centered point in the interview than at any other point:

> ... we've gone through—discussed this—and it's so—kind of a sad discussion to think who would take care of your children if you were ... weren't there to take care of them. And no one can—of course— take care of them as well as you can.

The psychotherapeutic aspiration is that a client has less anxiety when he faces, discusses and, if possible, resolves suppressed ideas. Death is, in these clients and in everybody else, both suppressed and anxiety

125

producing. Death tends to be conceived of in our culture as an accident, some kind of catastrophe, a modern version of the primitive attitude toward death as supernatural punishment. When clients and lawyers deal with death, as they did in Caro's and Katharine's will interviews, will interviews become a sort of therapy; this law-office therapy for death anxiety will probably tend, as will more advertent therapy, toward overcoming the denial of death, since denial is, in childhood and afterward, the way most of us come to terms with the horror of death. The law-office experience may then resemble the effect, noted by Southard, of friendly concern for the soldier's death anxiety. Even the terminally ill, as observed by Glaser and Strauss, experience peace and a realistic reconciliation with death when they are shown honest sympathy.

Death and Property

Relationship

Do these wills clients demonstrate that they are in a personal relationship with the property they own? There seems to be some evidence that they do, although I suspect that older, wealthier clients would present better evidence of the point. Furthermore, I suspect that the main evidence of relationship will appear in the next section, when the property relationship is discussed in reference to the client's death. There is, nevertheless, some evidence of the relationship without advertent and simultaneous consideration of death. This is illustrated by Roger Quaife's discussion of his coin collection and Caro Quaife's discussion of her paintings and art objects:

> [The discussion of assets came to an evaluation of jewelry, of which they have a relatively large amount. Roger had shown great interest in the value of this, and had had it appraised. *However,* Caro claimed no knowledge of its worth, even though most of it was what the couple would consider hers. While cataloguing various items of tangible personal property]:
> Roger: ... I've got about a hundred and forty dollars in coins. I've been throwing coins in boxes since I was a little kid.
> Lawyer: This is just, you say, the face value, Roger?
> Roger: Yeah, this is just pennies, nickels, dimes, and quarters.
> Caro: How about those mint sets? Are they worth very much?
> Lawyer: Are these proof sets?
> Roger: No, these are not proof sets. This is just—I have been throwing coins in boxes since I was three or four. . . . They're not real old; they're all American coins; but they're older.

126

Lawyer A: . . . Put the personal effects in the trust, then, and let the trustee—

Lawyer B: Well, it's up to the Quaifes.

Caro: . . . As long as the jewelry and the paintings and art objects go to my daughter. [Note that these items had significant value and that the daughter here was four years old.] Or my son. The rest of it—I don't care.

Roger: Yeah. All my coins and that, you know—I guess I would want that to—

* * *

I know they're worth more than a penny's worth of pennies and a nickel's worth of nickels. I know that they're worth more than a hundred and forty dollars in just raw coins. You know, I'd want that to go to the kids, but I wouldn't want that to get into the hands of my son until he had realized what he had.

The attitude toward personal property here is not economic, at least not to the person who has a relationship with it. Roger is willing to count Caro's jewelry, but Caro is not. And Roger is not willing to regard his coins simply as coins. Both parents wanted these bits of wealth—not as wealth, but *as things*—to be given to their children. They wanted these bits of personality to be *gifts,* to be expressions of love in a way that seemed to transcend, to be entirely other than, simple inheritance and any idea of support.

A similar attitude toward personal effects was found in the Eliot interview:

Lawyer: Lew and Margaret, how about personal property that you own yourself—any valuable rings, watch, something of particular—

Lewis: I wouldn't say—

Lawyer: You know, anything that you'd want given to a particular person?

[The Eliots then had a hushed conversation, and she answered the lawyer in a markedly subdued tone] . . . my wedding rings. . . .

* * *

Lewis: We don't have any inheritance . . . to give out to somebody else.

Margaret: Nothing of any value, just a lot of—junk.

["Junk" here is a contented sort of condemnation, though—like Christopher Robin's "silly old bear" or St. Francis's "Brother Ass."] And in the Getliffe interview:

[As part of a general inquiry into the value of assets, one of the lawyers asked about items of personal property.]

Francis: Really, the main things of value we've got would be (to Katharine) your rings—

Katharine: My rings [nervous laugh].

Francis: I guess that was about a thousand—right? [Katharine probably nodded.] About a thousand.

Katharine: And our furniture.

Francis: A couple of watches. [Laugh.] How are we doing?

Immortality

The possibility that wills clients usually think of their deaths as events in the indefinite future becomes clearer when the property relationship is included in their attitudes. The property relationship becomes clearer, too, when ownership is taken to be something that survives death. Goody, discussing post-mortem property disposition in an African society, remarks:

> The material goods with which he is associated are in fact part of the man himself as a social object; man, clothes, and tools are aspects of the unit of social relations, a social personality. It follows logically within this idiom that the flesh of man's cattle is his own flesh, just as a man's quiver is also in a certain sense part of himself.

Clients come more readily to the vague idea of surviving death when they approach it through the relationship they have with their property. The best example of that arises in discussions of trust arrangements for minor children. (With other clients one might find it in such things as spendthrift provisions, generation-skipping trust arrangements, and charitable dispositions which include pervasive and detailed provisions for disposition.)[3]

Most of the couples related their property to their (presumably) orphaned, pre-school children solely in terms of the "American Dream" of college education. They did not consider the support of a pre-school-age child first. In fact, they did not consider it at all until the lawyers reminded them of it. They considered first what the child would be doing when he was eighteen to twenty-two! Witness the Royce interview:

> Lawyer: Well, say you died right now. What's the first thing you would want done?
>
> Muriel: If I die right now [a note of incredulity]?
>
> Lawyer: Say both of you died.

128

Vernon: Set it up for the education of the children.
Lawyer: Would you want something before that?
Muriel: Well, make sure they had somebody to take care of them.
Lawyer: Okay, then, the first thing you would want is support of your children while they were minors.

Later in the interview, the group talked about the use of funds to support children while they are small, at the expense, if necessary, of college education. Vernon still had not received the message:

Vernon: I just want to clear up—there will be enough money, and so on. I want (to see that) they get a college education.
Muriel: Well, yeah. I don't see any reason—but what he said was if there wasn't enough money.

One of the lawyers explained that if they died soon the funds available to the children might prove to be insufficient.

Lawyer: ... We're talking about supporting them for fifteen years—both of them—before they're even near college age.
Muriel: Yes, that's the point.

And, finally, Vernon saw the light:

That makes a good point here, in terms of saying—If you were going to put into the terms of the trust that no more of the property that is given should be distributed for their support than is necessary, then there must be—the last four thousand dollars apiece must be given to each one for their college education. . . . [This] may bind the trustee in a way that is not very good for things that you can't foresee now. [This] allows the person who has the property to use it more or less as you would, you know, as things come up, he has a chance to do things more or less as if he were their parents, rather than, "I have to look to the trust instrument—spend this money here"—even though there's no money left.

The lawyers hastened to agree with him and to explain how prudent the trustee would be.

A similar dialogue occurred during the Eliot interview:

Margaret: ... and I don't know any more than that about what you do, with ... uh ... how the assets are disposed of. We want the kids to have a chance for college, to have that pretty much taken care of, and then any other things that would come up for them.

* * *

We've run into a couple of cases where kids, at a certain age, got a lot of money, went out and bought a big car, had no real idea, and then come to the point where that money ran out and they were done—and it was gone, and—you know—

The lawyers who dealt with Lewis and Margaret Eliot were somewhat more delicate than the lawyers who dealt with Vernon Royce, but the professional result was the same—a discretionary trust for minor children.

The Getliffe interview demonstrated, perhaps, a higher level of realism in the client, but even Francis Getliffe was a little worried about the division of his property when his children were adults:

> Francis: Maybe we should leave it up to the trustee to decide how much—
> Lawyer A: You want it entirely discretionary as to how much principal could be given out—
> Francis: Sounds like—
> Lawyer B: Up to his share.
> Katharine: What I'm wondering is—After they have both, or as many as you have, have reached that certain age where it is all divided, then the portion that the older child has received is deducted, right?
> Francis: Right.
> Lawyer A: Yes, we will specify that. . . .
> Francis: . . . Say, later on the principal goes way down and there's not much left. How would you work that, then? They would divide—

There, at the end of the interview, Francis had come to regard his limited resources in terms of support, rather than of dynastic distribution, and even rather than the "American Dream" of a college education for his two little boys.

The lawyers were also involved in the denial of death. They seemed to be actively interested in persuading clients that the law gave them a way to survive their mortality. This is a specific instance in the dynamics of law-office practice, of Shneidman's "psychosemantic" logic—the kind in which a person divides his own rational processes into two persons, one of whom will survive his own death. Wahl says, "It is as though they could remain behind to see and relish the discomfiture and remorse their act (death) would induce." The process probably has an infantile origin. Anthony reports a little girl who said, "How sad it is for that little girl that she is dead. I would be very sorry, too, if it was me that was dead." Hocking puts it this way:

> It is a simple matter to contemplate one's death. But when one does so, one does it *as a survivor!* Within oneself there is reproduced an element of social objectivity: it is the inclusive or reflective self which contemplates the death of the dated, excursive self, and is half able to accept it. The self does not contemplate nor know how to contemplate its own extinction.

Recall, in that connection, the emphasis with which the lawyers assured Katharine Getliffe that the state would not put her children in an orphanage. There are other examples of this reassurance in the interviews. Here is a sales-pitch for a contingent trust for minor support during the Getliffe interview:[4]

> Lawyer: ... In your will [to Francis]—this is talking about your will. You want it to go, you know—"if my wife is dead, when I die," you want it all to go to the children—
> Francis: Oh, I see. You mean, if we both—well, she, yeah—
> Katharine: The children, ...
> Francis: Yeah, but that's where the problem comes in, isn't it: They're too little.
> Lawyer: Well, right, That is where the problem comes in. [Another lawyer then completely changed the subject. He took the discussion to assets. Everyone went to this subject cheerfully, but the tangent amounted to no more than a moment of comic relief. The first lawyer then went back to the subject of death and care of children.]
> Lawyer: Well, I think ... uh ... if we want to talk about this a little more: In case Katharine would not be alive at your death, the children would be minor, now that is going to be the basic—really the basic problem we'd like to solve in a will. And the thing that a will allows you to do is to set up—to really set up what you want. You know, this is a thing nobody likes to think about, but it allows you to do what you want.

A similar episode occurred during the Royce interview:

> Lawyer: [explaining trust] ... It's a way of extending the use of your property, according to your wishes, beyond your death.
> Muriel: Mostly, don't trust and trust funds ... used by individuals who are quite wealthy ... instead of all of it to your children, part of it?
> Lawyer: I think that's kind of a common misconception, that trusts are for the rich.

131

                                    * * *

    Lawyer: One time in which [the trust] is almost always—or at
least very commonly—it's a good idea to set up a trust when you
have minor children, and will have minor children, for a substantial period of time. It's probably the simplest way of taking
your property, and sort of confining its use to your children. It's
using it more or less as if you were still alive, for their care and
support, in a way that you couldn't do—say, well, simply by
giving it in a will.

Finally, here is an example from the Quaife interview The group is
discussing care of orphaned children:

    Lawyer: Roger's parents are rather young, and—
    Caro: Yeah, and my parents are rather old—
    Lawyer: And they're not getting any younger.
    Caro: Right, but none of Roger's brothers and sisters are
married and I don't think my sister is even in a position to take
care of them. Possibly she would be in a few years, but—[pause].
If something happened to my parents, then she would.
    Lawyer: What would happen if all your parents were dead?
    Caro: Oh, [note of surprise], that's a possibility? The—I
suppose, my sister—[pause].
[Long pause.]
    Roger: What else could you do?
    Caro: ... Then you'd have to work down the line [of sibling
relatives].
[She listed the relatives in order.]

The lawyers then discussed the possibilities for trustees to manage
property for minor children—in terms of relatives and bank trust
departments:

    Lawyer: ... You see, Roger, [if you chose a corporate
trustee] you wouldn't have to change it, and you wouldn't have
to worry about the individual dying, or, you know, something of
this sort. They—
    Roger: Well, sure, why don't we do that, then.

This thought became even more cordial as the interview developed the
fact that an uncle of Caro's was a trust officer in one of the banks that
might be chosen for trustee.

Therapy

There was some evidence from these interviews that clients find the
experience of realistic, informed "estate planning" therapeutic. Al-

though the evidence is not overwhelming, when taken with secondary psychological literature it may sustain the conclusion that the professional relationship between wills client and lawyer, when pursued candidly and with realistic and thorough consideration of what is involved, helps to allay anxiety about death.

Both the Puchweins and the Quaifes came to their interviews with wills they had executed in the past. The Quaifes appear to have expected their lawyers to revise thoroughly what they had done, but the Puchweins did not. They had agreed to submit themselves to a student team only because they thought they might get some relatively minor advice on including their daughter in their wills scheme. They left the relationship, however, having completely discarded their old wills. They ended by executing more complex new ones.

The old Puchwein and Quaife wills were of the very simple, very short, all-to-my-wife-and-then-to-the-kids variety. Property was in each case given outright to children, either through the wills or by direct secondary beneficiary designations on life insurance policies. In the Puchweins' old wills, the secondary disposition was only to their son. On the face of the wills, their (presumably) orphaned daughter was given nothing; only by access to a pretermitted-heir statute could she have obtained her inheritance. Furthermore, in the Puchweins' arrangement beneficiary designations were secondarily in favor of grandparents, with the informal—hardly even stated—faith that the grandparents would use this wealth to support the (presumably) orphaned children. Most of these arrangements were, of course, unwise, and these lawyers advised their clients on this premise. The value of their advice is indicated by the fact that the clients made new arrangements. I think this value also present, although perhaps less obvious, in the fact that the clients obtained a certain reconciliation with their own deaths in having acted, and in having understood what they did. I detected a tendency to this in the Puchwein interview:

> Lawyer: Is that how your other will was set up—leaving your personal property to [Hanna's parents]?
> Kurt: I assume it was. I made that will out in about fifteen minutes one day. . . . I just went in and saw this lawyer that was the father of a friend of mine that I was in school with. And I just told him, "I don't have any problems or anything. I just—I'm married now and I'm raising a family and I just want a lawyer. So if I get hit by somebody in my car or something—and he says 'I'm going to sue you,' I don't have to go look in the yellow pages, you know."

So he said, "Yeah, I think that's a good idea." He said, "I think everybody should have some lawyer he can see."

So I said, "All right, will you be my lawyer?"

And he said, "Yes, I'm your lawyer."

And I said, "Okay, good-bye."

So, as I was leaving, he said, "Incidentally, do you have a will made out."

And I said, "No. A will? I'm only twenty-five," or something.

He said, "I thought you said you didn't need a lawyer."

And I said, "I don't."

And he said, "Well, sit back down." So, then, I just kind of—sort of—took care of [his newly-born son] at that time. And, again, I had just got out of undergraduate school then and I didn't have any assets or anything to consider. So I don't know if he really included [future children and arrangements for their care] or not.

The lawyers discussed a flexible trust arrangement. The Puchweins obviously had not thought of the possibility that the grandparents might die and that assets for children would then be part of the grandparents' estate. In this connection, Kurt said he had a substantial part of his funds earmarked for the children's college education. They talked and thought a good deal about these suggestions—with much verbal fumbling.

> Kurt: The same people would be in charge of the trust. There wouldn't be any reason to have them separated. Your reasoning— . . . What happens to my property if I should die or be killed or if Hanna and I should disappear?—die [nervous laugh]—in the next three years or four years or something like that, and they get this five thousand and the twenty thousand? . . . They don't just hold on to that twenty thousand until they become of age; they can use it, can't they?

The lawyers explained the consequences of outright grandparent ownership to them, and compared guardianship and trusts.

> Kurt: I just don't understand enough about these things. Just how flexible they can be—that the money would be put to good use—say, for education. I'm sure that Hanna's parents can afford to take care of—well, any problems that would come up for the children, financially, or any other way, for that matter. But I would still like to see the money that I have accumulated in my short time here to promote their education, rather than have them all of a sudden get it when they're twenty-one or become of age. . . . I don't think they need it. It wouldn't reap the harvest

that I would want it to. I wouldn't want that. I would rather that they would be able to use it. [It was clear here that he thought of trusts only as a way to keep funds static. The lawyers explained flexible trust disposition.]

* * *

Lawyer: . . . that's not the type of trust we're talking about.
Kurt: I know. I didn't realize that until—

* * *

Kurt: Another important thing that we've touched upon, but still doesn't ring clear with me, is that if . . . if Hanna and I die, and then Hanna's parents follow a short time thereafter, say two years, when the kids are only twelve and eleven—something like that—and my sister gets them, there's a possibility that, if I would just turn everything over to Hanna's parents, that money would be a long time in making that step from their death to my sister. It would be tied up for some time.

The lawyers explained to him, finally, how he might arrange his insurance policies to tie into the arrangement he had decided to make in his will.

Kurt: I'm glad [the first student he talked to about a will] mentioned this, about getting this will. Actually, we are not going to just renew this, but kind of put this one by the wayside and have them revamped. Is that the idea?

Kurt's realistic acceptance of death is clearer when one hears him during the interview than it is in the printed word. In the early part of his interview he was guarded and mildly skeptical. As he began to talk of the circumstances of his earlier will he sounded more interested in what we were doing, and by the time he announced his understanding of our plans for him he seemed to me genuinely concerned and open and *involved* in what we were going to do *together.*

Vernon Royce also proved reluctant to understand and appreciate what was involved in the professional services he asked for. He, like Kurt Puchwein—and like Lewis Eliot—came to the experience expecting some sort of black magic, a black magic he would not understand, and a consolation, if he experienced consolation, that was based on superstition more than on information. But the experience he had was not magic at all. It was more like a realistic consideration of his family, his property and his death. It is clear from the Royce interview—although, unfortunately, more in tone than in quotable language—that Vernon Royce benefited from a realistic consideration of these aspects of his life.

Francis Getliffe is a somewhat different case. He proved very realistic about such things as flexible trustee control of his funds. He asked searching questions and quickly absorbed information given in reply to them. Intellectually, he proved a different kind of client, but I doubt that his emotional condition during the experience made him as different as his interest in and comprehension of the law involved might suggest.

Conclusion: Two Problems With
Secondary Psychological Literature

These interviews were planned and carried out without reference to the psychology of testation. My purpose in recording them was to have material for a critique of the young "lawyers'" interviewing techniques. Months later it occurred to me to examine the tapes for psychological material. What I found for the most part confirmed the findings of those clinical and experimental psychologists who have in the last decade shown a burst of enthusiasm for thanatology. I found also some confirmation of classical psychoanalytic theories on death attitudes and generation reversal. These confirmations of secondary material are included here to show resemblances rather than to support my factual observations. (The structure of this chapter, including my theoretical interpretations of the data, was complete before I set out to find resemblances in secondary literature.)

There are, though, two features in these interviews for which I find little or no resemblance in the secondary literature. I discuss them here because they may indicate a gap in controlled psychological observation and in the insights of psychotherapy. The first of these areas is the property relationship; the second is the possibility that informed testamentary planning is a kind of therapy for death anxiety.

Property Relationship

There seem to be three clues in psychological theory to man's relationship to what he owns. None of them appears to have interested experimental psychologists, perhaps because white rats don't own things (or do they?). (Rats die, in any case, and Richter's work suggests some analogies to human death.) Two of the three clues seem to have come originally from Freud; scholars appear to have done little with these since Freud and his immediate circle (Jones, Ferenczi, and, later, Reik) worked them out. The third clue is a philosophical insight which seems to me full of promise, and which also has not been picked up by psychologists, largely, I suppose, because it comes from Jean-Paul Sartre.

The Faecal Theory. Freudians hold that infantile development proceeds out of a stage of omniscience, where the child makes no distinction between what he is and what is around him, into a stage where he concentrates on his body. His first experience with property is with his faeces. These are *his*, but they are not part of his body—*and* someone else wants them. He can please or displease, hoard or dispense, and he can enjoy himself in both ways or in neither, all in reference to the potty chair. The theory is extended—lucidly by Ferenczi—to explain a progressive interest in mud, sand boxes, rocks, *coins*, other forms of *money*, and even in *wealth*. It was used in a popular magazine a few years ago by our country's most illustrious pediatrician, Dr. Benjamin Spock, as a reference for counseling parents on allowances and piggie banks.

The faecal theory explains how it is that a man expresses himself in giving or refusing to give. It explains how a man can identify with what he owns—how property can rest, psychologically, somewhere between the *Mitwelt* (which he is not) and the *Eigenwelt* (which he is). Freudians divided the whole world into retentives and compulsives and thereby went a long way toward an analerotic explanation for generosity, fussiness, inefficiency, and even sadism and masochism. It is enough for present purposes to see the faecal theory as a means—a rigorously Freudian means, to be sure—of beginning to see if it is true that a man *is* what he owns.

My main difficulty with the faecal theory is that I cannot trace it, as Ferenczi suggests he can, from specific articles such as heirlooms, and Caro Quaife's jewelry and Roger Quaife's coins, to wealth—to the economic power and security one has, and to the tyranny one can exercise with intangible property. Ferenczi attempts to draw a straight line from potty chair to capitalism, but the link between coins, "filthy lucre," and capitalistic wealth is speculative.

The Psychopathology of Everyday Life. The second of the Freudian insights is not nearly so well worked out. In fact, I put it together from bits and pieces of Freud's book, and Jones's chapter, on silly mistakes, absent-mindedness, slips of the tongue, etc. (in each case entitled "The Psychopathology of Everyday Life"). Both are significant in psychological literature as instances of Freud's great insight that everything one does has significance, and that careless mistakes are windows into the unconscious. Many of these instances involve property-personality. In some instances an object is treated as if it were a person: A husband cannot find the book his wife gave him until he is able to feel love for her. People forget to pay bills they resent having to pay, or neglect sending money to relatives they do not really want to help. Servants break china if they are unhappy at the way they're treated. A bride who has been forced into marriage loses her wedding ring on the honeymoon.

Sometimes property represents the person acting; it extends his presence. Even without "psychopathology," consider the universal human custom of giving an old and valued piece of personal property as an expression of love, or the universal primitive religious sacrifice of valued property. Mauss demonstrates that anthropology is full of similar examples. Freud and Jones instance the man who leaves his umbrella or his coat in a place he does not want to leave, or who forgets the key to a place he does not wish to visit; the person who fails to wind his watch because he would prefer time to stop for him; and numerous, curious examples of unintended theft.

These examples—which fascinated Freud and Jones, I suspect, because they were a means, rare for them, to deal with the psychology of "normal" people—demonstrate that one tends to deal with *things* as a substitute for dealing with unreachable personality. That is true of the inner self of the actor, which can reach beyond the actor and *become* what the actor owns; it is also true of the hidden selves of others, selves that are not available, but selves that can *be* for the actor, in things.

Each of these Freudian theories can be projected also into a consideration of testation. The things a man owns do not die when he dies; his wealth—which is the *value* of his things—is relatively immortal. If he *is* what he owns, then he will, in a way, survive his own death. That is what testation is all about. That is why communities which protect some form of free testation, or pretend to it, are likely to talk about it as a "natural right." And that is why communities which deny or restrict free testation invariably develop evasive devices for allowing post-mortem property disposition without admitting it. A person *wants* to arrange his property for immortality and he feels better when he understands his arrangement, approves of it and thereby prepares to transcend the grave.

Sartrean Theory.* Sartre's theory begins at the most radical point in his metaphysics—the first principle that a person is not what he is. But he wants to be what he is. Freedom is a frustration and a curse because one can be whatever he wants, which means he is nothing at all except free (being-for-itself). This is not true, though, of an inanimate thing (being-in-itself); things are what they are; they enjoy a sort of metaphysical security. Man, who is not what he is and who has no metaphysical security, has an ontological envy for things. That is why he wants to own them—*to become them;* he wants them *to become him.* Freud, in theorizing a compulsion to return to the inorganic state, gives some clinical basis for Sartre's conjecture.

It is not sufficient to generalize ownership, as Sartre believes most systems of property law do, to use:

> I am not satisfied with this definition. In this cafe I use this plate and this glass, yet they are not mine. I can not "use" that picture which hangs on my wall, and yet it *belongs to me.*

Nor will it do to say that one owns what he is free to destroy:

> [A]n owner can possess his factory without having the right to close it; in imperial Rome the master possessed his slave but did not have the right to put him to death.

Both of those definitions are negative, "limited to preventing another from destroying or using what belongs to me." Even a thief regards himself as the owner of what he has stolen.

An adequate theory of property has to take into account the relationship between the possessed and its possessor:

> [T]he quality of *being possessed* does not indicate a purely external denomination marking the object's external relation to me; on the contrary, this quality affects its very depths; it appears to me and it appears to others as making a part of the object's being. . . . This is . . . the significance of primitive funeral ceremonies where the dead are buried with the objects which belong to them. . . . The corpse, the cup from which the dead man drank, the knife he used *make a single dead person.*

---

*Sartre's observations about property appear in *Being and Nothingness* and in two chapters published separately as *Existential Psychoanalysis.*

The explanation for this universal human phenomenon is in the free character of the possessor:

> [I]f we apprehend in things a certain quality of "being posses-sed," it is because originally the internal relation of the for-itself to the in-itself, which is ownership, derives its origin from the insufficiency of the being in the for-itself. It is obvious that the object possessed is not *really* affected by the act of appropriation, any more than the object known is affected by knowledge. It remains untouched. . . . But this quality on the part of the possessed does not affect its meaning ideally in the least; in a word, its meaning is to reflect this possession to the for-itself.
>
>   * * *
>
> The desire *to have* is at bottom reducible to the desire to be related to a certain object in a certain *relation of being.*

This human aspiration is also observable in the creative artist, the experimenting scientist, the sportsman (who sets out "to have" a mountain or a ski slope); "the 'mine' appeared to us then as a relation of being intermediate between the absolute internality of the *me* and the absolute externality of the *not-me,*" a relationship more fully realized at specifically legal levels of possession:

> I am responsible for the existence of my possessions in the human order. Through ownership I raise them up to a certain type of functional being; and my simple *life* appears to me as creative exactly because by its continuity it perpetuates the quality of *being possessed* in each of the objects in my possession. I draw the collection of my surroundings into being along with myself. If they are taken from me, they die as my arm would die if it were severed from me.
>
>   * * *
>
> Thus to the extent that I appear to myself as *creating* objects by the sole relation of appropriation, these objects are *myself.* The totality of my possessions reflects the totality of my being. I *am* what I have.

Sartre's theory has some clear implications for a psychology of testation, but a mere lawyer, mired as he is in for-instances, finds it hard to make it concrete in the lives of his clients. Sartre advanced the idea in psychoanalytical terms; he did it as part of a broad set of suggestions for analysis and therapy, and, no doubt, some medical practitioners have attempted to realize on his insights. But Sartre is neither therapist nor empiricist and none of the sources I read have subjected this work to clinical insight or to experimentation or observation. It would help if psychology were able to find and develop the idea of a person (being-for-itself) possessing a thing (being-in-itself) and possessing it in the fervent, serious aspiration that the possession will give him a godlike security. (The idea of God is the idea of someone who is being-in-itself-for-itself. He is a *person* who is who he is. Man is a person who is not what he is but who wishes to be what he is.)

One comes away frustrated from a consideration of property psychology, annoyed at psychologists because they have neglected the subject. The situation seems parallel to two earlier points in the history of that stormy science—the point at which Freud challenged psychology with the idea of unconscious, savage, sexual man, and the more recent point at which psychologists like Feifel and Shneidman, and psychiatrists like Lifton and Eissler, challenged Freudianism with the suggestion that it was afraid to talk about death. The present challenge, I think, is to a science which tends too far away from the material in human existence and which is annoyed at the unavoidable substance in the thought that a man is what he owns. Feifel suggested that one goes into the healing arts because of an early fear of death, and that this may explain why physicians are reluctant to discuss death with their patients or with anyone else. But why are they, along with nonmedical clinicians and research psychologists, reluctant to discuss property?

Therapy

The more modern research in thanatology results in a wedding of concepts—a link between the ancient idea of fearful death (expressed most often in our culture by regarding death as a catastrophe, an accident), and a world of modern devices for pretending there is no such thing as death. From the idea of death as fearful, of death as unmentionable, comes anxiety. Death is a suppressed idea and therefore a primary source of psychological disorder. Our cultural expressions of death neurosis include retirement cities and hospitals, where the dying are hidden and the old and ill are expected to die inconspicuously, and expensive, corpse-worshipping funeral rituals.[5] The individual expression of this neurosis in its less acceptable forms may be delinquency, crime and disabling illness; and in its more acceptable forms all sorts of petty emotional hang-ups.[6] Freud outlined (in *On Creativity and the Unconscious*) one of the mildest and broadest forms of these last in discussing the things we find uncanny:

141

> There is scarcely any other matter . . . upon which our thoughts
> and feelings have changed so little since the very earliest times,
> and in which discarded forms have been so completely preserved
> under a thin disguise, as that of our relation to death. Two things
> account for our conservation: the strength of our original emo-
> tional reaction to it, and the insufficiency of our scientific
> knowledge about it.
>
> It is true that the proposition "all men are mortal" is paraded
> in textbooks of logic . . . but no human being really grasps it, and
> our unconscious has as little use now as ever for the idea of its
> own mortality.
>
> Considering our unchanged attitude toward death, we might
> rather inquire what has become of the repression, that necessary
> condition for enabling a primitive feeling to recur in the shape of
> an uncanny effect. But repression is there, too.

The answer for neurosis is therapy, which is a pretentious word for care
and concern. And everyday neurosis, the kind we all have, is most likely
to be answered outside expressly therapeutic relationships. It is most
likely to be aired and dealt with realistically in a sort of everyday
psychotherapy—the sort that good lawyers have been performing for
their clients for centuries.

What this chapter is meant to suggest is the possibility that
advertent, informed planning for property settlement is therapy for
death anxiety. But the development of this possibility assumes stronger
contributions to the effort from practicing lawyers, who can both open
their experience to researchers,[7] and generalize upon it for their
brothers at the Bar. The development of a practical psychology of
testation assumes also relevant contributions from those whose special
vocation is human behavior—psychologists, sociologists, and even law
professors who occasionally tire of textbooks and appellate court
opinions. Lawyers cannot perform even everyday psychotherapy for
death anxiety if they continue to treat will-drafting as a form of black
magic, carried out in Elizabethan English, with canned forms and ten
minute interviews. And, with all of our best efforts, we stand in need of
reliable scientific information on the human side of property ownership.

Reading Suggestions

Feifel's and Fulton's anthologies are the best place to begin reading
about modern death attitudes; there is in each collection a certain
limited amount of material on young people and even a little on young

parents. Goody, Mauss, the psychoanalytic material discussed toward the end of the chapter, and Sartre are primary sources for some of the theories of property ownership; Sartre's work is separately published as *Existential Psychoanalysis,* but it is also in *Being and Nothingness.* Forster's novel, *Howard's End,* is a good literary source for some of the ideas suggested in this chapter, and for some of the moods behind the ideas. More specific leads are suggested in the text; complete references are in the table at the end of the book.

Notes

1. A note on methodology: The interpretation and range of information in these interview tapes has been compared for internal and external validity against the research standards suggested in D. Campbell & Stanley, Experimental and Quasi-Experimental Designs for Research (1963). The explication of the content of the tapes has been modeled to some extent on the suggestions in Becker, "Problems of Inference and Proof in Participant Observation," 23 *American Sociological Rev.* 652 (1958). The outline for analysis will, finally, bear some relationship to the "pre-supposed empirical relationships and interpretations" model suggested in Westie, "Toward Closer Relations Between Theory and Research: A Procedure and an Example," 22 *American Sociological Rev.* 149 (1957). I am grateful for these and other scientific insights provided me during the 1968 Institute on Social Science Methods in Legal Education, at the University of Denver College of Law; to the sponsors of the Institute, the Russell Sage Foundation and the Walter E. Meyer Research Institute; and to the distinguished faculty members of the Institute, Professors Harry Kalven, Jr., Allen Barton, and Stanton Wheeler.

A number of factors could here jeopardize external and internal validity; I used several items on the check-list suggested by Campbell and Stanley (D. Campbell & J. Stanley, supra, at 5-6):

The selection of subjects was accidental; they were persons available to students who were seeking real clients. Some of them actively sought legal assistance while others were relatives or friends of the "lawyers" involved. The unifying factor in the clients was their genuine interest in having the legal services offered by the project, in that these clients, like any clients in this area of practice, sought the legal services which were performed for them. That affords sufficient objectivity for an internal analysis of them. External validity is more doubtful, but I believe they were sufficiently representative of well-educated, young, middle-class, married parents to justify generalization to most clients in their category—and that category is an enormous, untapped one for legal services. I do not propose to generalize to older clients, childless clients, unmarried clients, poorer clients or clients whose children are older. Some of the attitudes suggested here would be paralleled in other groups, I am sure—but some undoubtedly would not.

There was some loss of subjects from this group. One couple's interview was not tape recorded. Another couple was unable to meet face-to-face with the "lawyers" involved; the latter couple's data was presented second-hand, through a relative. A third couple was one of the law students in the project and his wife; their interviews were conducted separately and were affected by the fact that the husband had a high level of legal sophistication. I eliminated the second and third couples because I thought they were atypical; I eliminated the first because I had no comparable data for them.

None of the five couples ultimately selected was pre-tested by these lawyers; the interviews reported here were first interviews. However, two couples had dealt with lawyers and wills at earlier points in their married lives and one couple had a fairly high level of sophistication in life insurance. This mixture seems to me nearly typical (two in five with prior experience, one in five with life insurance sophistication) and I did not eliminate or try to explain differences in their interviews. All of the data that is significant with regard to these couples is fully reported.

The arrangements for interviewing the couples were all similar. Four couples were interviewed in homes, in three cases with their children present or close at hand. One was interviewed in my office, with telephone contact with the home and a baby-sitter there (which, I think, simulated the presence of children).

I have followed Becker's suggestions (Becker, supra, at 659-60) with respect to the proof of my conclusions. I have, for instance, stated the information as fully as possible, eliminating for the most part what seemed to me routine in the interviews. As Becker notes, this permits the reader to form his own conclusions, because the evidence for the reader is substantially the same as the evidence presented to me. Where most of the audience, as here, is at least as experienced as the author in the participant observation involved, Becker's suggestion seems especially useful. I have added my own analysis, which most readers can test against their own observations, as well as against mine.

Finally, Westie suggests, in areas where "there is a high degree of theoretical incoherence" (Westie, supra, at 149), the procedure of stating alternative empirical relationships and interpretations of them in advance, and then selecting the relationship and interpretation which seem to come out of the data. I have found his system of analysis helpful in structuring my report on these interviews. Here is his general explanation of the model:

> This procedure involves (a) explicitly listing a comprehensive range of *presupposed empirical relationships,* many of them diametrically opposed to one another, *which might possibly turn up in the research at hand* and (b) explicitly listing a *range of interpretations,* many of them diametrically opposed to one another, for each possible empirical finding. Then, through empirical investigation the relationships that actually obtain are selected from the morass of "presupposed empirical relation-

ships" initially listed. All of the other initially proposed empirical relationships are discarded. The array of alternative interpretations attached to them in the original presentation are also eliminated from consideration as interpretation of the findings.

The final step in this phase of the research cycle involves the selection of the correct theoretical interpretations from the array of contradictory though "plausible" interpretations attached to the empirical relationships that have survived the research test. This last task, though difficult, is perhaps less difficult as well as more accurate than where the usual procedure is followed. Ibid., at 150.

It is probably unnecessarily technical to set out a "Westie" outline for each of my discussions, but the reader may be interested in an example:

Empirical Relationship 1-A: The experience of being interviewed by lawyers for the preparation of "estate-planning" devices is a relatively bland experience which does not significantly touch the clients' death anxieties. (Assumption: They have death anxieties.)
Interpretation 1-A-i: Death anxiety is a consequence of physical illness or some variable other than planning with respect to property.
Interpretation 1-A-ii: Death anxiety, while it may arise with reference to the possibly orphaned status of one's children, does not arise when the reference to children is their support.
Interpretation 1-A-iii: Death is relevant in discussion of "estate-planning" devices, but the levels at which death is discussed are not anxiety producing. (The anxiety arises from considerations of illness, the deaths of other loved ones, or some other area of experience which is not touched intensely in wills interviews.)
Interpretation 1-A-iv: Death anxiety is not likely to arise in circumstances other than those suggesting experience with death.

Empirical Relationship 1-B: The experience of being interviewed by lawyers for the preparation of "estate-planning" devices is an experience raising death anxieties. (Assumption: Clients have death anxieties.)
Interpretation 1-B-i: It is impossible to deal with the full range of property ownership without raising feelings about the personality of the owner—both in the owner and in the interviewer. Since this property-personality is discussed with reference to the cessation of the non-property-personality, suggesting in turn a radical separation of personality, death anxiety is inevitable and will be exhibited in evasion, euphemism and other psychological tactics of avoidance.
Interpretation 1-B-ii: Direct, unequivocal reference to the death of the interviewee raises his death anxiety.
Interpretation 1-B-iii: Reference to death words, which is inevit-

able even in the euphemism of the law office, raises death anxiety.

Analytical Preference: Empirical Relationship 1-B, Interpretation 1-B-i, with some collateral respect for the plausibility of Interpretation 1-B-iii.

2. "Will Drafting," distributed by the California Bar Association through the University of California at Berkeley.

3. See Friedman, *The Dynastic Trust.*

4. The students had, in this connection, studied Corcoran, *The Contingent Insurance Trust – A Hidden Bonanza for Minor Children,* and Shaffer, *Nonestate Planning.* Both articles indoctrinated them on the wisdom of trusts and the evils of guardianship.

5. Institutionalizing death tends to deny it; Fulton and Anthony elaborate the point; see also Jackson's article, *Grief and Religion.* It is the theme of J. Dunne, *The City of the Gods.* Murphy quotes Freud, "Consideration for the dead, who no longer need it, we place higher than truth – and, most of us, certainly also higher than consideration for the living."

6. Shoor and Speed and Stern, Williams, and Prados give some convincing examples, as do Hilgard, Newman and Fisk, and Weisman and Hackett. Hocking, Alexander, Colley, and Adlerstein, reporting serious social withdrawal, and Teicher, are also worth consulting on the point.

7. The ethical obstacles to access to behavioral information from will conferences are not insurmountable. Even if lawyers will not ask their clients to allow tape recording of the interviews, lawyers themselves can supply either specific (but anonymous) client information or generalizations on client behavior.

Part 3:
The Psychology of
Testation in the
Judicial Process

6　Psychological Autopsies in Judicial Opinions

The court's inquiry . . . is into the mind of the decedent, into that "heap or collection of different perceptions." Transfers prompted by the thought of death, even if they are also prompted by other motives, are includable in the gross estate. The tax law does not require us here to determine 'motive' . . . but it seeks an equally elusive shadow from the recesses of the mind of the deceased; did the thought of death prompt him to act? [T]he conclusion may not be wholly intellectual. Decision may result also from intuition, emotional reaction, and visceral response to the composite picture that results from the images imposed on each other in court by advocates with opposite motives, one bent on proving that the deceased, whatever his age or health, was convinced of his own immortality and impervious to thoughts of death, and the other seeking to show that the donor was weak of body and sick of mind, preoccupied by the converging approach of the grim reaper and the tax collector.[1]

It is surprising how many cases have been litigated under Section 2035 of the Internal Revenue Code, which imposes an estate tax on inter-vivos gifts in contemplation of death.* It is also surprising that

Dr. Robert S. Redmount and Dr. Herman Feifel contributed comments to this chapter. I am grateful to them for their contributions and for their suggestions on other material in this chapter.

*"The value of the gross estate shall include the value of all property to the extent of any interest therein of which the decedent has at any time made a transfer . . . in contemplation of his death. If the decedent within a period of three years ending with the date of his death . . . transferred an interest in property . . . such transfer shall, unless shown to the contrary, be deemed to have been made in contemplation of death within the meaning of this section. . . ."

those hundreds of judicial opinions embody rigid perceptions of human life and of attitudes toward death, perceptions which range from incisive to callous. They disclose a judicial system of death psychology which is detailed, systematic and sometimes, probably, accurate. This is an inquiry into those opinions (and decisions) as psychological autopsies. The inquiry has several practical possibilities:

1. It may indicate something about the legislative wisdom in retaining a tax provision which turns on a post-mortem assessment of the attitude a dead man had toward his death.[2]
2. It may indicate something about the judicial wisdom in construing a statutory word ("contemplation") literally.[3] Compare this, say, with the judicial wisdom in construing a similar word ("intended"), in a similar section of the same Code, to refer only to the mechanical operation of a property-transfer device.[4]
3. It may indicate something about trial tactics within a legislative and judicial system which continues to impose death taxes on transfers which are made in contemplation of death. (It is an open secret that the process as it now exists is chaotic and probably presents the only common factual issue in the federal estate tax on which taxpayers can usually expect victory.)
4. It may indicate something about the way men are as they approach death. That assumes, of course, that judges are able to detect human facts and to report them accurately. At least one can hope that the Section 2035 opinions will tell him how judges think men are as they approach death.

I make the inquiry against a model suggested by the eminent "suicidologist," Dr. Edwin Shneidman, who has recently worked at the National Institute of Mental Health, and as a Fellow of the Center for Advanced Study in the Behavioral Sciences. Dr. Shneidman proposed several years ago a "psychological post-mortem."[5] He designed his system primarily for death certification in suicide cases, but he developed it for all death certification, and he demonstrated that it is a model upon which attitudes toward death can be reconstructed after the man being studied is dead. And that is exactly what judges do in Section 2035 cases.

Dr. Shneidman's objective was "a psychologically oriented classification of death phenomena, an ordering based in large part on the role of the individual in his own death." His analysis had an affirmative premise that a man's death is a personal event and a negative premise that our culture, specifically those public officials concerned with death certification, accept "natural" death as an ideal. Both premises apply to the Section 2035 literature, where, because of *United States v. Wells,* the inquiry is a personal inquiry; and where judges make their decisions in reference to an ideal decedent who has lived his life to the end, with courage, and who has predicated what he did in his last days on his life rather than on his death. (One might call that ideal the "natural" attitude toward death.) This ideal death (or attitude) is what Shneidman calls "the idyll that living and dying are separate." It should be some consolation to lawyers and judges that Shneidman aims this "idyll" primarily at physicians and coroners.

This view of death, in Shneidman's world and in the chambers of judges deciding "contemplation of death" cases, assumes that death is something that happens to a man, rather than something a man does:

> What has been confusing in this traditional approach is that the individual has been viewed as a kind of biological *object* (rather than psychological, social, biological organism), and as a consequence, the role of the individual in his own demise has been omitted.

This leads Shneidman, as it led Freud, to forsake an analysis of death and focus instead on an analysis of *dying.* He avoids even the word "death" and substitutes instead four other words for dying: (1) *cessation* ("the last line of the last scene of the last act of the last drama of that actor"); (2) *termination* (a biological end which one might plan to survive, as Tom Sawyer did); (3) *interruption* (cessation, temporarily, without termination, as in sleep or a coma); (4) and *continuation* (the opposite of interruption: continuation relates to death because people may want to be delivered from continuation but not from life itself). These concepts are useful in a consideration of property disposition at, or "in contemplation of" death. Testamentary transfer is evidently a matter of termination without cessation; the testator expects to live on in his property. He may therefore view his death as an interruption, and he may view as continuation the aspects of property ownership which impose responsibilities on him.

Shneidman suggests that the decedent might have approached his cessation in any one of four general frames of mind: intentioned, subintentioned, unintentioned, and contraintentioned. Each category is further subdivided:[6]

Intentioned:
: cessation-seekers
: cessation-initiators (who would rather quit than be fired)
: cessation-ignorers (who contemplate cessation without termination)
: cessation-darers (who, for instance, "fly" airplanes without knowing how)

Subintentioned:
: cessation-chancers
: cessation-hasteners (alcoholics; people who refuse to use medicine)
: cessation-capitulators
: cessation-experimenters (who seek an altered continuation)

Unintentioned:
: cessation-welcomers (the ideal old person who is thought to welcome the end)
: cessation-acceptors (heroic acceptance)
: cessation-postponers
: cessation-disdainers (the supercilious death attitudes of some young people)
: cessation-fearers (for example, hypochondriacs)

Contraintentioned:
: cessation-feigners (for example, people who attempt suicide seriously)
: cessation-threateners (for example, people who "attempt" suicide as a way to manipulate others)

The decedent in every factually-detailed, reported Section 2035 case could probably be located within this scheme. I see an illustrative parallel in two cases Shneidman puts on the confusion involved in the psychopathology of suicide: The first case involved a woman who shot herself, with drastic physical damage short of death. The second case involved a woman

> who had cut herself with a razor blade. She had, she said, absolutely no lethal intention, but had definitely wished to jolt her husband into attending to what she wanted to say to him about his drinking habits.

Classifying both cases, as medicine has been likely to do, as "attempted suicide," would have "run the risk of masking precisely the differences we might wish to explore." The two classifications suggested in Shneidman's "contraintentioned" category preserve the distinction. An analogue is possible to (1) the person who makes testamentary transfers for vindictive reasons (the *March* case, below, in part), and to (2) the person who talks about or threatens testamentary changes (whether or not he makes them) for manipulative reasons (the *Dumay* case, below, in part).

Fitting Section 2035 cases into Shneidman's scheme will sometimes be the result of looking at the evidence objectively.[7] It will sometimes be the result of the subjective needs and views of death in the judge or judges deciding the case. The prototypes which arise from decided Section 2035 cases should in either event give way to a psychologically sophisticated view of death attitudes in the donors under judicial examination, and that will be analogous to the sophistication Shneidman suggests for the medical and paramedical professions in suicide treatment.

The prototype judicial view of a gift in contemplation of death case implies that the dead man expressly, overtly, considered death as the fact which would bring a series of plans into operation. Giving in contemplation of death is seen as goal-striving behavior which death will facilitate. I suspect and even hypothesize that this view is unsound because it equates "gift in contemplation of death" with "testamentary disposition." That equation is unquestionably at work in most of the cases. It is a judicial rule of thumb. But it is probably psychologically inaccurate. There is a difference between giving one's property away because one is going to die and making written plans for what is to be done with one's property when one is dead. I suggest, very tentatively, that the first is analogous to cessation-feigning and the second analogous to cessation-postponing.

In a second paper, Shneidman applied his system to Herman Melville. There is one aspect of his venture which is particularly interesting in the psychology of testation. Shneidman believes that Melville's preoccupation with death, combined with his almost obsessional resentment of literary critics, led him to a choice between protest and withdrawal. Melville chose withdrawal "disdainful, ignoring . . . critics as though they did not exist, as though they were dead, reducing them to the unimportant position of impotence by robbing them of their power to influence and especially of their power to hurt." Shneidman believes that Melville's withdrawal was a sort of death:

> [T]his maneuver, by its very nature, tragically can be executed only at the price of one's own total or partial self-ostracism and thus at the expense of the death of part of one's social and hence psychological self.

Melville was, in this view, focusing on a "post-self," on a future in which his real self (the self which he expressed in his work) would be vindicated:

> The self or ego relates to the core of one's active functioning, his cognitive and emotional masterings and maneuvers in the present life; the post-self, on the other hand, refers to the ways in which one might live on, survive, or have some measure of impact or influence after the event of his own physical death—for example, through one's children, or through one's published works. . . .

This is cessation *without* termination; and it is far better as a matter of human anticipation than cessation *with* termination: "To cease as though one had never been . . . to abandon any hope . . . of impact or memory . . . beyond one's death, to be obliterated . . . to be naughted . . . that is a fate literally far worse than death."

I mention this in introduction because the post-self concept has application in considering contemplation of death. A man survives his death (cessation) in those he loves and in the things he owns. He lives on (when the context is gratuitous transfer) in an expression that involves both those he loves and his property. He lives on in the act of giving property. And this is the same sort of living-on that Shneidman discovered in Melville; it is a part of things one contemplates when he contemplates death.

The format used here attempts to consolidate hundreds of Section 2035 cases into some kind of unified presentation, by proposing three prototype judicial opinions: Each of them is a composite of several cases; each contains within itself discussion of scores of precedent cases; and each demonstrates what I believe to be typical judicial perceptions of human facts on attitudes toward death. A series of comments follows each of the prototype opinions; the comments are meant to suggest what may become the law-review case comment ("or recent decision note") of the future—a new literary form which will combine close, logical analysis of what courts have done with a behavioral consideration of the process involved in the decision, and of the consequences the decision may be expected to portend for the profession and the people upon whom the law operates.

I have been generously assisted and encouraged in this and other aspects of the study of the psychology of testation by Dr. Shneidman and by two other distinguished clinical psychologists, Dr. Robert S. Redmount, who is also a lawyer, and Dr. Herman Feifel, who should probably be considered the founder of modern death psychology. Drs. Redmount and Feifel contributed comments to this chapter; these appear as the primary focus of the commentary section after each of the two composite cases.

Commissioner v. Estate of
Varner (Tax Court)

William Varner died at the age of 80 years, four months. At issue are three transfers he made during his life.[8] The first, made two years, ten months before his death, was of a summer cottage in Michigan; this transfer was made to his son, William Varner, Jr., "for the use of the grantor's granddaughter, Linda Snopes Cole." Linda Snopes Cole was the decedent's daughter's daughter; the decedent's daughter and her husband died in an airplane accident ten years before the transfer of the summer cottage.

The second transfer was of shares of stock in the Frenchman's Bend Realty Company, a corporation which owned and managed farm property in areas near the decedent's home. This transfer, made 18 months before the decedent's death, was of all the decedent's interest in the corporation; it was made, outright, to William Varner, Jr., the decedent's son.

The third transfer, made six months before the decedent's death, was of several parcels of real estate: two farms, ten acres of undeveloped land, and the house on which the decedent's home stood. This transfer was to William Varner, Jr., in trust for Linda Snopes Cole. It was accompanied by an extensive and complex trust instrument which contained detailed directions for managing the trust corpus, attempted restraints on its alienation, elaborate restrictions on the alienation of equitable interests (spendthrift provisions), and directions for the distribution of corpus and income to Linda Snopes Cole and to her children, if she had any.

William Varner, Jr., as executor of his father's estate, timely filed a federal estate-tax return, reporting these three transfers as not taxable, and a gross estate exclusive of these transfers of $15,000. Since the gross estate reported was well below the exemption allowed, the estate reported no taxable estate and paid no estate taxes. The values at death of the property transferred during life are stipulated in this Court and are:

the summer cottage, $65,000;
stock in Frenchman's Bend Realty Company, $150,000;
real estate in trust, $210,000.

The evidence is that these transfers had approximately the same values on the dates they were transferred inter vivos and that after the transfers were completed the decedent's owned property did not exceed $20,000 in value.

The Commissioner of Internal Revenue objected to the estate's position on the three inter-vivos transfers and issued notices of deficiency. He claimed estate taxes of $96,200, which assessments the estate protested. The case is here on the following issue: Were the three inter-vivos transfers includable in the gross estate under Section 2035 of the Internal Revenue Code of 1954, which provides:

> The value of the gross estate shall include the value of all property to the extent of any interest therein of which the decedent has at any time made a transfer . . . by trust, or otherwise, in contemplation of his death.[9]

This Court must decide whether the dominant motive of the decedent in making each of these transfers was prompted by the thought of death. The leading authority on the tests which are to be applied is the decision of the Supreme Court of the United States in *United States v. Wells*, which said that the question is whether "the decedent's purpose in making the gift was to attain some object desirable to him during his life, as distinguished from the distribution of his estate as at death." The Court there stated that the Congressional purpose in Section 2035 was "to reach substitutes for testamentary dispositions and thus to prevent the evasion of the estate tax." We have determined that the transfers were *not* in contemplation of death.

The cottage. The decedent was 77 years old when he transferred the cottage. The testimony is that he made the transfer in order to provide a restful, pleasant atmosphere for his granddaughter, so that she could spend her summer vacations there. The reason he transferred to his son, Mrs. Cole's uncle, rather than to Mrs. Cole, was that Mrs. Cole was somewhat unstable mentally. She had twice been hospitalized for "nervous breakdowns"; her husband had divorced her about a year before this transfer; she lived in the decedent's home when she was not on vacation; the decedent cared for her during periods of emotional tension in her life. The evidence is that Mrs. Cole found the summer heat in Frenchman's Bend oppressive and that she enjoyed staying at the Michigan cottage and had stayed there off and on during summers since she was a child. The decedent spoke many times before the transfer of making the cottage available to Mrs. Cole, so that she would not need to ask his permission to stay there.

Five years before he died and shortly after the death of his wife, the decedent stopped going to the cottage himself. Aside from a two-month visit there by Mrs. Cole, the cottage was in caretaker status for a year and a half after the death of the decedent's wife. About three and one-half years before his death, however, Mr. Varner visited the cottage on what he later referred to as an "inspection tour." When he arrived at the cottage he found that the caretaker had neglected it. In fact, Mr. Varner found the caretaker intoxicated and unconscious in one of the bedrooms of thè cottage. (This caretaker was replaced by William Varner, Jr., after the transfer which is at issue here.) Witnesses testified that this discovery disturbed Mr. Varner and that he decided to "get rid of the cottage." There is in evidence a letter he wrote William Varner, Jr., enclosing a copy of the executed, recorded deed; that letter said, in part:

> Your mother always preferred Michigan, but I have never liked it. Besides that, the worry of it has become too much for me; you have just got to go ahead and run it. I have had enough, and, besides, I need to reduce my tax bite. It has served its purpose so far as I am concerned. I have my home in Frenchman's Bend.

(As a matter of fact, Mr. Varner still had, at that time, extensive ownership of real estate other than his home, as well as 25 percent of the common stock of a real estate holding company there.) The letter said nothing of Mrs. Cole's use of the cottage, but the oral testimony was that William Varner, Jr., understood that the cottage "was really for Linda," that the deed made that clear to him, and that he managed the cottage for her and intends to continue doing so.

The decedent's health, prior to seventeen months before his death, was excellent for a man of his age. The first evidence of his terminal illness arose after the transfer of the cottage *and* of the corporate securities, when he visited his physician with the complaint that he was not able to hold on to things. The physician diagnosed his ailment as amyosthenic lateral sclerosis of the spinal cord, a chronic degenerative disease of the central nervous system which leads to the wasting away of the body from want of nourishment. The disease is usually fatal in from two to six years after diagnosis. The physician did not inform Mr. Varner of this condition; he told Mr. Varner that he had a nervous condition, that he (the doctor) would prescribe medication for it, and that Mr. Varner should return for "checking up" at intervals of one month. At the time of this diagnosis, Mr. Varner was active, cheerful, and optimistic. The physician never told him about his fatal condition, but he did tell William Varner, Jr., about seven months before Mr. Varner's death, and the testimony is that William Varner, Jr., told his father about the condition shortly thereafter.

We think that Mr. Varner, who made this transfer before he had any information on his illness—even partial, undisturbing information—was not significantly affected by an altered attitude toward life, that is, by thoughts of death. The evidence is that he was cheerful, pleasant, active, interested in many facets of life, sociable, and fond of many forms of entertainment, including circuses, card games, and, when he was in Memphis, burlesque shows. Few men many years his junior could match his zest for living, both physically and mentally. We find as a fact that the transfer of the cottage was not in contemplation of death.

The corporate securities. This transfer was made 18 months before death and one month before the decedent visited his physician for what turned out to be a diagnosis of fatal illness. The transfer was of all the decedent's interest in a corporate venture he had founded in 1928, and of which he had been variously president, secretary , and treasurer; he resigned from office in the corporation three years before his death, and turned the day-to-day management of the business over to his associate, Colonel V. K. Ratliff. He remained as a director and saw that his son, William Varner, Jr., (who was then a nominal shareholder) was employed as secretary and business manager for the corporation. Eighteen months before his death, Mr. Varner resigned as a director and transferred all of his shares (about one-third of those outstanding) to William, Jr.

Mr. Varner's health at this time remained good, although he had begun to suffer some muscular instability. His physician testified that there was nothing in his physical condition, at the time of the transfer of corporate securities, "which would lead any physician to anticipate his death at any time in the near future." Cross-examined about the spinal condition which was diagnosed a month later, the physician said he was not sure that a diagnosis would have disclosed this condition at the time of the transfer, and that in any event the prognosis at that time would have been survival for at least two years.

Mr. Varner's transfer of the securities was, of course, a part of his general retirement from business. Counsel for the Government contends that he was ' letting go, preparing to cash in his chips." That charming metaphor is not as apt as it may appear. Mr. Varner remained active in the management of rural real estate for another year; he climbed atop houses to inspect roofs, walked in fields which he owned to estimate crop yields, and even attempted minor repairs on his buildings. He began at about that time to make extensive plans for travel, and even to carry out some of them. He told his son and Mrs. Cole that he would make a sea trip around the world within a few months of retirement. He took an airplane trip to the World's Fair in New York City shortly after the transfer of securities, and he went on extensive automobile trips around his home region—some of them by himself. These travels were strenuous, and included hiking in the hills of his native state. Mr. Varner's only complaint about his trips was that he was unable to deduct their cost on his income-tax return. He took his physician on two of these trips into the hills; the physician testified that he (the physician) tired more readily in hiking that Mr. Varner did. William Varner, Jr., hired a servant to assist his father around the house, but his father resisted the servant and resented his presence. He never complained about his health or talked of death.

This evidence is similar to that on the cottage transfer. In the first situation Mr. Varner's manifest motive was to provide a pleasant summer retreat for his disturbed, unhappy granddaughter; in the case of the securities, the transfer was to provide a secure business future for his son, to reduce income taxes, and to enjoy, while he lived, his son's growth and success in a challenging business. Here, as in the transfer of the cottage, the dominant motives were living motives. Neither transfer was made in contemplation of death.

The real estate. Six months before he died, Mr. Varner transferred all of his remaining real estate to William Varner, Jr., as trustee for Mrs. Cole. The estate argues that this transfer, like the transfer of the cottage, was motivated by a desire to see Mrs. Cole provided for. The Government points to an additional circumstance, a steady, continuing deterioration in Mr. Varner's health. Beginning about eight months before his death (two months before this transfer), Mr. Varner had been forced to curtail his activity. He cancelled his world-wide trip. One month before this trust transfer, he was hardly able to walk; he had to use a wheelchair when he visited his physician. He ceased to complain about his servant and, in fact, became friendly with him. At the time of the trust transfer, he could no longer use either hands or legs. The physician continued to tell Mr. Varner that he had a nervous condition from which, he implied, Mr. Varner would recover. One month before the third transfer, however, the physician finally told William Varner, Jr., about the gravity of his father's condition. William, Jr., testified that he relayed this information to his father within two or three days. This was apparently before the second transfer. He said his father took the information calmly, and that his father's disposition remained cheerful. Not even then was Mr. Varner given to morbid thoughts; he did not refer to his condition again, not even in the final moments of his life. When he executed the trust instrument at issue, he told William, Jr., that his reason for the transfer was to see to it that Mrs. Cole was provided for. The estate argues that this fact, taken with Mr. Varner's continuing optimism about life, is evidence of a life motive, and we agree with that assessment. The size of the transfer, although significant, did not leave Mr. Varner without funds and is therefore not determinative, particularly in view of the fact that William Varner, Jr., as trustee, did not disturb his father's possession and use of the family home.

Mr. Varner is not shown to have entertained thoughts of death, even when he was dying.[10] He was not reticent about his physical condition, but he was not dominated by it either—that is especially apparent when one considers the transfers for Mrs. Cole, who was herself in poor health.[11] The gifts for her benefit were to establish her financial independence and to protect her from the eventualities of a life which had been cruel to her.[12] A person who retains a healthy mental condition normally does not make gifts in contemplation of death.[13] Mr. Varner's were not thoughts of death, nor were they thoughts which combined death and the desire to avoid estate taxes.[14] "Standing alone, the desire to avoid death taxes cannot be deemed conclusive of a mental state such as is contemplated by the statutory phrase."[15] His was a more cheerful, more "life-ful" frame of mind.[16] He was interested in the happiness of his children and in helping them financially.[17] He was determined to carry out "promises and plans that were unconnected with the thought of impending death."[18]

Conclusions of Law. The principal question in a gift-in-contemplation of death case is factual, but a consideration of precedent supports and confirms our factual conclusions.[19] The decedent's health, which was progressively worse at each of these transfers, is of course an important consideration.[20] But this Court has repeatedly held that health is not determinative of purpose in making life-time transfers. In *Coffin*[21] and

Beurman[22] we held that the existence at transfer of serious, even fatal, conditions was not controlling in the face of evidence of living motives. This attitude is mirrored in opinions and jury charges from the federal district courts, in which it is emphasized that cheerful demeanor and a disdain for morbid preoccupation indicate that a decedent has living motives even as he, quite literally, wastes into death.[23] The controlling test, as the court said in *Peck,* is whether the decedent "was motivated, moved, propelled, by the same considerations that cause one to make testamentary dispositions of property, and whether the gift made was a substitute for such testamentary dispositions, without awaiting death."[24] We find here that Mr. Varner's transfers were for the care of his granddaughter and the business success of his son and therefore not substitutes for testamentary dispositions.

An additional factor as to the first two transfers is that Mr. Varner did not know he was dying. Early decisions in the Eighth Judicial Circuit turn in part on the fact that the decedents had no knowledge of their fatal conditions.[25] In *Neal,* as here, doctors did not tell the decedent about his condition but did tell his family. The trial judge in *Delaware Trust Co. v. Handy* reached a similar decision where it was shown that the decedent suffered from arteriosclerosis but did not know about it.[26] Other cases in the federal courts are in accord, as are *Mills, MacDonald,* and *Bloise* in this Court.[27] The decedent in *Mills* was told he was ill but not how long he had to live. *MacDonald* turned on medical evidence that "the decedent may have been suffering from the disease for several years without any awareness of being ill."[28] There, as here, the fatal disease was serious but the life expectancy was at worst uncertain.[29] There, as here, the decedent did not talk about the condition even after he learned of it. *Bloise* held for the Commissioner, but is distinguishable because the condition there—terminal cancer—was diagnosed shortly before the transfers at issue (not, as here, after two of the three transfers) and because it was much more likely to bring speedy death.[30] Other decisions in this Court buttress our reliance on the rule that serious illness is only minimally relevant when it is not shown that the decedent knew he was ill.[31]

We detect in Mr. Varner's later life three features which emphasize that his thoughts were not thoughts of death. The first of these is the relinquishment of his business life in favor of a pleasant retirement, devoted to the care of his troubled granddaughter. The second is what we regard as an effort to draw closer to the two loved ones who remained to him. The third is his manifest desire to spend his last years in vigorous activity and travel. These factors combine, in our view, in a "life style" which seemed almost to turn away from thoughts of death; it was that life style which dictated the transfers here at issue.

This life style can co-exist with illness and even with concern about health, as we held in *Coffin,* in *Sachs* and in *Johnson.*[32] Transfers made in these circumstances tend to contemplate pleasant retirement from the burdens of life rather than from life itself. This is obvious, as we held in *Tetzlaff,* when one considers that careful and burdenless living *prolongs* life.[33] Mr. Varner's acquisitive years were over, but that is not necessarily a circumstance in which he would begin to contemplate death. On the contrary, he seemed to contemplate closer relations with his loved ones, a factor which tends to prove living motives for property transfer.[34] This factor is often present when the transfer is one to restore family harmony.[35] It can equally be present, however, where the family has been decimated by tragedy.[36] We think Mr. Varner was concerned more with what was thought of him while he lived than with happy memories after he was dead.[37] It is interesting to reflect how different the case might have been had he had no loved ones to draw near him in his last years.[38]

He was also determined to enjoy the life which was left to him. There are scores of cases in which physical activity, vigor, and, especially, travel and plans for travel, are held to be indicative of living motives. In *Delaware Trust Co. v. Handy* the federal district court was influenced by the fact that the decedent, at the time of transfer, contemplated a two-year trip around the world.[39] In *Heiner v. Donnan,* which was reversed on other grounds in the Supreme Court, the Circuit Court of Appeals took account of the fact that the decedent was an inveterate traveller, that he had, as Mr. Varner had, taken extensive automobile trips, and that he regularly went to Europe and travelled in the United States.[40] In *Commissioner v. Gidwitz's Estate,* the court noted that the decedent, despite a serious heart condition, "did not believe at that time that he was in danger of imminent death but . . . expected to live for a number of years."[41] Evidence of this, inter alia, was the decedent's habitual travel in the United States and abroad, his fishing and automobile trips, and the fact that he did his own driving. In that case the executor listed the decedent's last illness as lasting for 15 years; the transfer involved was one that did not in fact benefit beneficiaries until after the decedent's death. Despite these factors the court found that Gidwitz's cheerful attitude toward life, his energetic interest in travel and activity, was determinative evidence of living motives for the transfer involved. Finally, in the *Old Colony Trust* case, the federal district court in Massachusetts, deciding a case in which the decedent took his own life, held that an active business life and domestic and foreign travel within the year before death indicated living motives in a trust transfer for children.[42] The case resembled Mr. Varner's in several respects and differs notably only in the fact that Mr. Varner held onto his life until the last. A number of decisions for the taxpayer in the federal courts of appeal have relied on the fact that the decedent's general pattern of travel and activity indicated that he had no thought of death at the time of transfer.[43] Decisions from federal district courts and from this Court are essentially similar on this point.[44] In many of these cases the decedent had been actively traveling at the time of the transfer in question.[45] In others he was making plans for future travel.[46]

We are aware of the limitations of our process in cases such as this. We are not so much determining here what William Varner was like as we are determining what the evidence shows he was like. "We cannot be certain that our portrait . . . is a lifelike replica . . . but we are confident that it accurately reflects the portrait . . . drawn by the evidence in the record."[47] We find that none of the transfers at issue was made in contemplation of death.

Commentary by Dr. Redmount

In *Commissioner v. Estate of Varner* the Tax Court very skillfully wove evidence, interpretation and opinion, and precedents from other judicial reasoning, to produce a plausible and perhaps a reasonable decision and outcome. However, as the Court is careful to note in its concluding statement, "We are not so much determining here what William Varner was like as we are determining what the evidence shows he was like. We cannot be certain that our portrait . . . is a lifelike replica . . . but we are confident that it accurately reflects the portrait . . . drawn by the evidence in the record." It might be noted, too, that the interpretations and opinions relating to William Varner and his attitudes about death are those of men of certain age whose views of life and of death are also relevant if not directly articulated.

Not only are there general reservations or uncertainties about the judgment reached in the Varner case, but there are particular reservations about the way the court arrived at or "found" its result and about the result itself. Judicial decisions, as with much decision making, are the result of selection and rejection of emphasis and avoidance and of neglect and oversight as well as belief and acceptance. It is on both sides of the antinomy that one will find the true case, albeit that political expediency requires a decision in one direction. Let us consider the judicial neglects in the Varner case.

Firstly, the court failed to attach any significance to, and even failed to discuss, the fact of Varner's age, 77. One may reasonably inquire (since judicial precedent on the issue is not cited) whether a man of 77 contemplates, or consciously or unconsciously avoids the contemplation of, death and its consequences. Perhaps the men of the court, no more than Mr. Varner, *like not to think* about death but that does not mean that persons of middle or advanced age *do not think* about death.

The problem may be an evidentiary one. The vagaries of the adversary system being what they are, perhaps nobody thought or chose to inquire about evidence as to how Mr. Varner felt about his age and its implications and what he did about it. Even granted an effort to garner evidence on the matter, thought and contemplation on such a sensitive issue may as readily lead to suppression as to expression. Mr. Varner might very well contemplate death and choose not to think further or in any way talk about it. In fact, his whole mode of life, an active, physical life, may be evidence of a strong desire to try to consciously avoid troubling contemplation about death.

On a matter closely related to age, namely health, the Tax Court appears to have avoided its senses in judging statements about Mr. Varner's health, his terminal illness, and how the latter was perceived, experienced, and handled. Sense and reason should alert a contemplative court to the possibility, even the likelihood, that a mentally normal man, nearly 80, who is ill, severely incapacitated, and deteriorating fairly quickly, would have some thoughts of death. However, the evidentiary fabric for the Court's decision could not very well incorporate the thrust of such a view. Since comments about Varner's attitudes toward and awareness of his health reveal a merely heuristic collection of statements conveniently selected and placed, it is conceivable that there was, by this system, no verifiable evidence made available of contemplation of death, even though the fact of quickening life failure was inescapable.

The Tax Court relies upon and uses the rationale of the Supreme Court decision in *United States v. Wells* to frame its questions in the case. The requirement read from the Wells case is that " . . . the question is . . . " whether " . . . the decedent's purpose in making the gift was to attain some object desirable to him during his life, as distinguished from the distribution of his estate as at death." One cannot question the Tax Court's judgment in following precedent, according to the traditions of our judicial process, but one can question the kind of judicial reasoning manifest in the precedent or in the use of the precedent. The higher court, by offering the kind of distinction it indicates on which to base decision, and without further qualification as to how the matter is to be weighed, provides more pegs at which to throw rings in hope that one may hit. The political expediency of this procedure is clear but the effect of the precedent as used in this case is to say that any evidence of a certain kind that serves a decision is good enough, whether or not the evidence was very substantial or important in the larger scheme of things. One could be finished with the issue of contemplation entirely by making the literal argument, with whatever minimal proof might be needed, that the decedent's purpose in making a gift is *always* personal happiness and satisfaction in some form, clearly "objects desirable to him during his life." The Court in the *Varner* case virtually followed this cue with repeated references to some acts and thoughts in Varner's life, both clearly relatedto and unrelated to the transfer of his property, that served his pleasure.

Other precedents the Tax Court uses may also be challenged for their verity. The Court offers the charge to the jury in a case with a similar issue, *Peck v. United States,* where that court is interpreted to say that " . . . a person who retains a healthy mental condition normally does not make gifts in contemplation of death." One may as readily and perhaps more validly offer the opposite proposition that a person who retains a healthy mental condition, given sufficient personal circumstances, normally does make gifts in contemplation of death. Various cases are cited to the effect that "cheerful demeanor, and a disdain for morbid preoccupation, indicate that a decedent has living motives." It is not facetious to state that some living motives are to be found in nearly every, if not every, living person, if that is to be an evidentiary criterion. Much is made by the Tax Court of a series of precedents indicating that evidence of illness has no bearing if the party did not know of his likely and impending death. It would be incredulous that many dying persons, and especially elderly dying persons, would not feel, sense or otherwise be aware of, or would not consider, subsequent death. It may be fairer to the Tax Court and to the courts it follows to say that they choose not to find evidence of this, or they may have difficulty finding evidence addressed to the point. The courts may feel that public policy is better served and decisions come out "right" when this line of evidence and decision is not followed.

If the object in *Varner,* as in other litigation is to make a "case," one could also make a case against the decision with evidence, opinion, and interpretation to support conclusions opposite from those reached by *Varner.* Perhaps in a logical sense and within the limits of available or acceptable trial evidence, the case would not have been as strong, meaning, not so well documented for apparent facts. However, in terms of truth as it relates to human behavior concerning death, as well as in terms of public policy preference, the "better" decision may be opposed to the *Varner* result. The need may be for better ways to arrive at a better decision.

Commentary by Dr. Feifel

There is a presumption in the *Varner* opinion that the psychological influence of death is necessarily proportionate to the temporal nearness of actual death. This is not so. For example, you can be in good physical health and, yet, fear of death can significantly guide your behavior more than it guides one who is seriously ill. My research indicates, for example, that fear of death as a dimension is not something which is limited specifically to the aged, terminally ill or combat soldier, but can be directing at any age.

The observation that Mr. Varner was "cheerful, pleasant, and active" does not inevitably imply that he was not contemplating death. What we may be dealing with here is his reaction to or coping with the idea of death. Death is a multifaceted symbol which can be "terrible to Cicero, desirable to Cato, and indifferent to Socrates." For instance, a good proportion of the terminally ill patients I studied, in response to the question "How would you use your time under the threat of death?", answered "continue on as usual," "draw closer to loved ones," "travel," "do and accomplish," etc. Mr. Varner's physical activity, travel, and zest for life could also reflect his preparation for obtaining closure with regard to certain facets of his life in anticipation of oncoming death. The fact that he never complained about his health or talked of death to others cannot, from a psychological vantage point, be construed as necessarily demonstrating lack of interest or concern about death. Not only could he be consciously or deliberately withholding his "true feelings" from others but thoughts and anxieties about death could well be a steering variable for him on a below-the-level-of-awareness plane, hidden from his own cognizance. Psychological defenses which we term "denial" and "repression" might well be at work here. This is particularly relevant in an area such as attitudes toward death where our culture generally fosters an orientation of camouflage and expulsion. Differing levels of awareness and knowledge have to be considered.

Concerning Mr. Varner's "retirement": one must also weigh the possibility that retirement can mirror a means of disengaging from life and preparing for death. What is viewed as being indicative of "living motives" may be in the service of possessing as much of life as possible under the goad of feeling that Charon is near to ferrying one away, although that feeling may not be verbalized or readily available to one's consciousness.

Commentary by Professor Shaffer

The Tax Court's opinion in *Varner*, and Dr. Redmount's and Dr. Feifel's comments on it, suggest that the judiciary is finding in precedent and then applying six "group norms" about death and property. They are something like this:

1. *Contemplation is Surrender.* The court is at some pains to point out that the transfer of the cottage was a relatively insignificant transfer in terms of Mr. Varner's total assets, even though this point should, logically, embarrass the court when it talks about the cumulative effect of all three transfers. The court also labors the fact that Mr. Varner had enough to support a gracious retirement after transferring the corporate securities, and even enough to keep body and soul together (given his son's permissiveness in letting him live in the house) after all three transfers. Finally, the court finds that, since Mr. Varner could and did live in the house until he died, its transfer was not death-motivated. In other words, a death-motivated transfer is one that lacks present-day operation; this last point could as well be made in reverse in other words, since Mr. Varner wanted the house to be used for his grand-daughter and at the same time to live in it until he died (a clearly "testamentary" frame of mind), the transfer was within the statute. It is interesting to compare the judicial assumption, that dying people give up, with clinical information discovered by Zinker and Fink:

> [I]ndividuals on the brink of death or individuals who knew they were to die in the near future experienced the greatest insights, the greatest joys, and important re-evaluation of their past lives . . . greater religious strength, greater love . . . integration and closure of their past lives and sometimes "grew."

167

We have found . . . that many patients often are . . . concerned with being respected as human beings, with being loved, and with understanding the nature of their illness. We have come in contact with several critically ïll patients who showed signs of psychological growth. These individuals seemed to accept the fact of their coming death and, having freed themselves from the burden of fighting for physical survival, felt free to feel close to their fellow patients, to be creative, and to experience greater religious strength. . . .

[D]espite the fact that some dying individuals get "stuck" on certain basic needs and often deteriorate psychologically, other individuals begin to think in a more fluid way and are stimulated to examine their past lives, to examine their beliefs, and to examine afresh the nature of things around them. For the first time, they are able to cope with questions that continually have plagued them.

2. *Death is a medical matter.* Civilized western man is the only animal to whom this norm is applied; it is assumed that other animals, such as elephants and birds, Eskimos and Indians, know enough to prepare for death without being told to do it.[48] The medical-death norm had two applications in the *Varner* opinion, both well justified by the precedents. The first application assumed that Mr. Varner, even though he was almost 80 years old and declining physically, would not be biologically or psychologically aware that his condition portended death. The second and corollary application of the medical-death norm is the court's treatment of the fact that a physician (at the time the securities were transferred) did not know Mr. Varner was dying, and therefore Mr. Varner cannot have known. The insight supporting both applications is that dying is not a matter of human experience, or of instinct; it is a matter of medical information. Behavioral research is to the contrary; there is now good clinical evidence, and some more systematic evidence, that dying people often foresee their deaths at a virtually conscious level, and even more often sense death unconsciously and begin an almost instinctive preparation for it.[49]

3. *Travelers Forget Death.* This norm relates to the first two norms and is applied whether or not the traveler is dying or, if dying, knows that he is dying. The *Varner* court is candid about its assumption, both in terms of negative evidence (Mr. Varner's surrender of the cottage was actuated by compassion for his granddaughter, who arguably gained nothing by it), and in terms of affirmative evidence (Mr. Varner continued to climb atop houses, go hunting, and take trips, even when he was dying). The genesis and growth of this travel-and-activity norm

is probably related to the death-is-surrender norm (or to a general attitude that death is something that happens to a man, rather than something he does). There is a substantial amount of literary indication that it is not true (which is relevant because judges often adhere to literary insight even though they usually spurn psychological insight). Tolstoy's story, *Three Deaths,* in which a dying consumptive woman believes she will survive if she can make her way out of Russia, is an example. (And, incidentally, her family and doctor think she doesn't know she is dying.) O'Connor's recent memoir on the last days of the Irish poet and editor, George Russell, relate the fact that Russell suddenly left his home in Dublin, gave away his possessions, and moved to London. Yeats remarked that this was a matter of his "giving up the world to go on a world cruise." But O'Connor thought not:

> Of all the men I have known, Russell was most a creature of habit, and for him to give up everything—his house, his books, his pictures, his friends—was already a sort of death.

And there is solid behavioral evidence to support the poetic insight.[50] Even practicing lawyers know that travel and death are psychologically related; those I have interviewed said that the prospect of a trip is the usual reason clients come in to have wills prepared.

4. *Dying People are Sad.* This norm has a tacit assumption—that people who are dying may make gifts in contemplation of death—but the court did not state it because it would have tended to undermine the court's conclusions on the house transfer. In explaining the cottage transfer the court was almost intemperately anxious to mention Mr. Varner's contemporaneous optimism, even though the evidence also indicated sadness at the relatively recent death of his wife and disgust at the fickleness of caretakers. In explaining the house transfer, the most difficult part of the opinion, the court relied almost exclusively on Mr. Varner's optimism in the face of a death which was obvious by this time even to Mr. Varner himself. Mr. Varner's disapproval of the servant his son provided for him was taken by the court to indicate that the servant symbolized death; life-centered man's reaction to symbols of death is resentment. The court did not express that assumption, possibly because Mr. Varner later grew closer to the servant, and even then, according to the court, did not contemplate death.

5. *Support Is Only For Life.* Following what is perhaps the most commonplace of all platitudes in these cases, the court gave it as the law that a person who is concerned about the support of loved ones is

not concerned about his death.[51] The norm has a couple of subnorms. One is that no one worries about how his loved ones will be taken care of after he is dead (the life-insurance industry to the contrary notwithstanding). The other is that satisfactions derived from providing support are seen in terms of one's lifetime. This is a judicial denial of the insight represented by Shneidman's "post-self" concept.

6. *Dying People Withdraw.* This norm seems superficially to resemble Shneidman's analysis of Melville's "social death," but the resemblance is only superficial. The factual basis for it in this case is the conclusion that Mr. Varner's retirement—retirement, ultimately, even from the ownership of the roof over his head—was carried out so that he could devote more time and attention to those he loved and so that he could, by giving them property, entice them into unfamiliar intimacy with him. The court takes this aspiration for togetherness to be the opposite of withdrawal. Melville, by contrast, withdrew *toward* his work (and would, Shneidman says, have withdrawn toward his family too, if he could have). Melville and Mr. Varner did similar things, but Shneidman's conclusion from this fact is that Melville was dying; the court's conclusion is that Mr. Varner was not dying, at least not in the tax sense.

Estate of Ruth March v. United States
(United States District Court)

This is a claim for refund of estate taxes paid, brought by the executor of the will of Ruth March, deceased.[52] The taxes were assessed on the theory that a single set of inter-vivos transfers, made by the decedent on April 1, 1960, were made in contemplation of death and were therefore estate taxable under Section 2035 of the Internal Revenue Code of 1954. The case is before this Court on submission to the Court after trial without jury. Briefs have been filed by the executor and by the Government.

The late Mrs. March was the widow of Leonard March. He died in June, 1959; she died in August, 1962. While they were both alive, very little of the family's considerable wealth (in excess of $500,000) was owned legally by Mrs. March. Leonard March's will provided that all of his property (i.e., all of the family's property) was to be placed in trust; the income from the trust property was to be paid to Mrs. March during her life, and she was to have a testamentary power to appoint one-half of the principal at her death. The other half of the principal—or all of principal if Mrs. March did not exercise her power—was to be paid to

Leonard March's brother, Philip March. Mrs. March elected against this will, under applicable provisions of state law and was awarded one-half the estate of her husband; the other half accelerated and was distributed to Philip March.

After this transaction Mrs. March owned approximately $250,000. This was distributed to her in March, 1960; within less than a month she conveyed almost all of it ($232,000 according to the stipulation) to her two children, Charles March and Katharine March Getliffe. At her death she owned only about $8,000 and was living in a house which she had deeded to her son as part of the transfers here at issue. The question is whether the March, 1960 transfers (of approximately 95 percent of her wealth) were made with living motives or with testamentary motives. The estate has the burden of proof on this issue. The question is not whether the transfers were made in contemplation of death, but whether they were not made in contemplation of death.[53]

Both Charles March and Katharine March Getliffe lived in their father's house until they were into their thirties. Both married somewhat later than is common in our society; both were married to persons of whom their father disapproved. In Mrs. Getliffe's case, the marriage was disapproved because her husband was not of the Jewish faith. In Charles March's case the marriage was disapproved because Charles' wife, Ann Simon, although Jewish, had been at some point in her youth a member of the Communist Party. Charles also incurred the disapproval of his father several years before his marriage when he abandoned the profession for which he was trained, the law, and decided to enter medical school. Charles is now a practicing physician. Although the late Mr. March paid for the education of these children (even including Charles March's medical education) and provided for them generously, he vowed to disinherit them after these marriages were performed. That, obviously, he did.

The personality with whom this Court must primarily be concerned is that of the decedent, Ruth March. But it is difficult to examine this lady's purposes without examining also the character of her late husband. He was a patriarchical father who lived in almost constant tension with his son; it is possible to conclude from testimony of Charles and of Philip March that Leonard March's disagreement with his son's choice of profession, and even his disapproval of his son's marriage, were not the real emotional reasons for his disinheriting Charles, but that their differences ran deeper. On the other hand, the disinheritance of Mrs. Getliffe was more "normal" and even to be expected in a Jewish family. In any event, it appears that Mrs. March felt that the disinheritance of Mrs. Getliffe was justified, but that the disinheritance of Charles was not. She determined, almost as soon as Leonard March was dead, to right the wrong she felt had been done Charles. She was heard to say that she intended to carry out her late husband's "moral obligations," and that she prayed God that she would live long enough to do it.

Mrs. March had a cheerful disposition and did not complain of illness, although she was not particularly well and was, at the time of these transfers, 78 years of age. She was never morbid and did not discuss the prospect of death or future life with members of her family (or, so far as appears, with anyone). She had been, in her early married life, a jovial person, talkative, fond of expensive clothing and jewelry. However, her first child, a son, died in early infancy (before either of the children in this case were born); the testimony of her brother-in-law, Philip March, in this Court, is that she was severely affected by this unexpected tragedy and that she thereafter showed less interest in social life and, when her other children were born, concentrated her life on them.

She was a thrifty, frugal woman who did not, for instance, own a car. She does not appear to have worried about her health. Although she appeared not to mourn her husband excessively at the time of his death, she physically collapsed about three months after the funeral. She was hospitalized then and found to suffer from "general depression, arteriosclerosis, and fatigue." The physician who attended her then testified that the principal causes of her illness were "old age and grief." She was released and treated as an outpatient after one week in the hospital and did not become seriously ill again until about two weeks before her death. She was then hospitalized a second time, declined rapidly, and died. The cause of death is listed on the death certificate as "hypostatic pneumonia, cerebral hemorrhage and arteriosclerosis."

She was generally calm and pleasant during the years following her husband's death. Her condition, prior to the last illness, was not so bad that the Court can infer that it caused the idea of death to possess her mind, nor was it good enough to constitute that sound health from which I could infer purposes entirely associated with life.

In January, 1960, when the distribution from her husband's estate was imminent, Mrs. March invited her children to her home and announced that she intended to "do right by Charles." Both Charles and Mrs. Getliffe objected to her plans because they did not include equal treatment for Mrs. Getliffe. Mrs. March resisted them, stating that Mrs. Getliffe knew why she had been disinherited and that nothing could be done about it. They were in complete disagreement on the matter, with one relatively minor exception: both children agreed with Mrs. March's plans to deed the family home at Bryanston Square to Charles so that he and his wife would "have the security of a Jewish home in the event of the ever present possibility of one kind of an emergency or another."

The three members of this family then entered into a two-month period of bickering, an unusual circumstance for Charles, who had not resisted his mother in the past. He apparently pursued the issue with the zeal of one who has found a cause in which he can be unselfish, and in which he can challenge the older generation.

In March, 1960, without notice to either of her children, Mrs. March called her lawyer to her home and announced that she wanted transfers made of all of her share of her husband's estate, to the children equally. Only at her lawyer's insistence did she even retain the $8,000 in cash with which she died two years later. Her lawyer reported that she said both children had insisted to her that they were entitled to their father's money and that, although she did not agree with them, she was weary of argument and wanted the lawyer to arrange the transfers. As the lawyer left her that day she said, "I am glad to stop all this talk. It will be a relief to get it off my mind. They can have it." The instruments of transfer were prepared within two or three days and conveyed to the children, with a terse cover letter, prepared by the lawyer but signed by Mrs. March, stating that the transfers were "out of love and affection and in order to assure your independence and support." Mrs. March's lawyer filed a gift-tax return for her for the calendar year 1960 which listed the motive for the gifts as "betterment of beneficiaries—peace in family."

Both children replied to Mrs. March's letters with gratitude and attention, which was, at first, spurned by Mrs. March, who told them she had made the gifts so that she would not consider herself obligated to her children and that she wanted no more calls for money from them and that she hoped they were satisfied. However, Mrs. March's natural affection for her children soon overcame this apparent resentment, and the family grew closer over the following year or so. The children spent holidays with their mother during those months; she rejoiced at the birth of a son to Mrs. Getliffe; Charles provided for his mother's support and made no claim to the house at Bryanston Square which she had deeded to him; both children were at her hospital bedside when she died.

The Government contends that these transfers were testamentary in character and that the critical motivation in making them lay with the children, especially with Charles March, and not with the decedent herself. The intentions of the two children, in the Government's view, overbore the will of Mrs. March; and *their* intentions were clearly testamentary. The executor contends that both transfers fall within the pattern of cases involving transfers to establish the independence and provide for the support of donees.[54] The Court cannot help but notice that the two theories are not necessarily inconsistent. But of course the results to which each body of precedent supposedly points are inconsistent. It may therefore be helpful to examine the factors that appear to have been prominent in Mrs. March's mind, to decide which of them is dominant, and then to decide what result is indicated by this dominant factor. (The Government's allusion to the intention of the children is relevant only insofar as the Court can infer that their intention became Mrs. March's.)

Pressure from Children. An easy answer to this difficult determination would be to say that Mrs. March transferred virtually everything she owned in order to stop the family argument. Transfers to avoid the importunities of relatives have been held not in contemplation of death.[55] However, I believe the executor is incorrect in his reliance on the *Higgins, United States Trust,* and *Jacobsen* cases.[56] The transfers in those cases were, to be sure, responsive to family pressure; but none of them was like the transfer here. In *Higgins,* the decedent transferred to protect her property from her husband. The evidence was that she did this in order to have it for herself and in order to diminish pressure on her which was literally destroying her health. She transferred in order, physically and materially, to stay alive.

In *United States Trust,* the decedent transferred *to* her husband, in order to avoid the importunities of two of her 12 children; she did so in order to prevent the dissipation of the estate at the hands of the importuners. In *Jacobsen* the decedent transferred in order to establish the independence of his wife, after considerable pressure from her. The decedent there wrote his wife a letter after the transfer explaining that he made it "so that from now on throughout our lives this one cause of misunderstanding may be altogether absent. . . . It is what I am anxious to do for you and for our life together." The court did not feel that the disposition was testamentary. That situation is somewhat similar to Mrs. March's, but it seems to me to differ in one crucial particular; a husband who transfers property to his wife still, in a very real sense, retains it. As a matter of fact, one of the decedent's motives in *Jacobsen* was to remove the necessity for his wife's asking him for money for personal and household needs; he was providing by the transfer what he would probably have had to provide in any event. That is not true of transfers to adult children. While I cannot say that the family-pressure consideration here proves that Mrs. March's gift was in contemplation of death, neither can I say that it proves the contrary.

Family Unity. The executor points to the fact that Mrs. March's transfers operated to pull her small family together after the death of the head of the household—a living motive. The Government contends that the transfers were testamentary in effect, because they operated, as a will would have, to establish the financial independence of the children. The Government also points to the fact that Mrs. March's transfers were within nine months of her husband's death, and within six months of her collapse from grief and depression. Transfers soon after the death of a loved one, which are temporally related to disabling grief, are arguably death-related, although this is not a factor that has been significantly discussed in the cases.[57] *Fatter v. Usry* is a compelling instance of the phenomenon.[58] Both husband's and wife's estates were at issue there; they had died close together, and the husband, who was the second to die, had apparently wasted away after his wife, who cared for him like a child, was gone. In that case, though, and in *Budd,* the death of a loved one was an expressed, obvious, health-related obsession in the decedent.[59] In *Budd,* where the decedent mourned her dead daughter, there was even evidence that she did not want to live. This was an important part of what the court found to be "a general attitude of mind inviting contemplation of death." In a way, her transfer of property was suicidal. *Coffin,* finally, makes a point which seems important here: The decedent there had been depressed virtually all of his life because of the death of his father.[60] His change in personality was doubtless related to the effect of parental death, but his was not shown to be a death-contemplating personality. The court held for the taxpayer. I find here, as the court found there, that the deaths of Mrs. March's first child, and the more proximate death of her husband, did not cause her to contemplate her own death.

The fact that she made these transfers in order to benefit her children economically seems clearly established. This sort of transfer is similar to the transfer in *Stinchfield*.[61] There a wife conveyed to children in discharge of her husband's moral obligation and to secure isolation of assets from the risk of her husband's business, and to that in *Kaufman v. Reinecke,* where the transfer was to remove assets from the operation of a corporate buy-sell agreement.[62] It resembles *Kroger's Estate* and other cases in which a father transfers property to insulate it from the demands of a second wife.[63] In *Kaufman* the court spoke of a gift in contemplation of contract; and in *Kroger* of a gift in contemplation of marriage. What did Mrs. March's gift contemplate? It won't do to answer that it was intended to establish the financial independence of her children, because that is factually ambiguous and an observation which begs the question. (It is important to notice that this was not simply one of lifelong series of transfers to children, which would present a different case.[64])

There are cases in which the gift was held not in contemplation of death because the decedent desired to see the donee made financially independent.[65] In *Wishard* the court thought that a transfer to make a wife and sister independent of the financial vicissitudes the decedent might encounter was with lifetime motives. But the risk factor is not present here. Mrs. March's only risk was the risk of death. In *DesPortes* the court held purchase of single-premium life insurance not in contemplation of death, but that case relies heavily on the decedent's good health.[66] As I noted above, the state of Mrs. March's health is of no probative value one way or the other. In *Hinds* the issue of health was closer but the court—erroneously in my view—held it determinative.[67]

This case seems to me to more closely resemble *Igleheart* and *Neal*.[68] The *Igleheart* court distinguished between a transfer for the economic health of the donee during the transferor's life and a transfer to secure economic health after the decedent's death; the latter is in contemplation of death.

The *Igleheart* court also relied on the fact that the arrangement was to provide for the donee in the event the donor was "absent," which under the circumstances was held to mean "dead." The same conclusion is possible here, with reference to the transfer of the house "in the event of the ever present possibility of one kind of an emergency or another." I place no particular weight on the letter Mrs. March sent her children, which was drafted by her lawyer;

circumstances are more important than a lawyer's words, and the circumstances here, as in *Neal,* are testamentary.[69]

The executor insists, however, that this was a transfer to "pull the family together" after the death of a strong and vengeful father. Family harmony as a purpose of gift-giving is usually conceded to be not in contemplation of death.[70] However, the contrary has been held where there is strong evidence of death-centered motivation, as, for instance, where poor health is shown.[71] An excellent treatment of the point is to be found in *Russell,* in which the decedent, a lady, had transferred property to her son in order to induce him (and his wife and children) to remain in her apartment building.[72] That situation is somewhat like Mrs. March's, and were it not for evidence of testamentary motive, coupled with the statutory presumption against the taxpayer, might be determinative.

Reward-Revenge. The executor argues, finally, that these transfers were made to reward Mrs. March's children and to redress the wrong done Charles by the late Mr. March and possibly to obtain some measure of retaliation against a domineering husband and father. There are several cases in which the transfers involved were vindictive, but they seem wide of the mark here.[73] It may be that Mrs. March was vindictive, but that is conjecture, and there is no evidence of anything but positive motives in both her desire to restore Charles' patrimony to him and her ultimate decision to treat Katharine equally. The same can be said of the argument that she was fulfilling a moral obligation of her husband or rewarding the children for something.[74]

In the view I take of the case—which is that, on balance, Mrs. March's transfers appear to be the sort of transfers she could have made by will—this consideration is ambiguous. A parent may reward and punish his children and redress past wrongs as fully in a will as in inter-vivos transfers. When a factor in a gift-in-contemplation-of-death case is ambiguous, the case must be decided on other factors. In my opinion, the testamentary factors, discussed above, point to the application of the statute in this case.

The burden of deciding what was in the mind of a person long dead, at a point in time months before her death, is almost too much for Congress to have required of the judiciary:

> It is unfortunate that the Congress, in the estate tax law, used the phrase "in contemplation of death," without defining its intended meaning; and it is equally unfortunate that courts should undertake the legislative function of defining the legislative intent.

The fact that every person of sound mind knows that he will eventually die makes it indefinably difficult to determine when persons act in contemplation of death and when they do not. The best that can be said of such a decision is that the judge, having the duty of deciding, exercised his best judgment. The decision on such a problem is inherently difficult.

In the last analysis it is sufficient to hold, and this Court does hold, that the executor has not met the burden of proving that Mrs. March's transfers to her children were not in contemplation of death.

Commentary by Dr. Redmount

In *March* some of the matters with which issue is taken are in many respects very much like the neglected matters of the *Varner* case. The effects of age and illness on the "contemplation of death" are reoccurring considerations. In *March,* as in *Varner,* one might think that the issue is over and the decision is gainsaid when the court, following precedents thus frames the matter: "The question is not whether the transfers were in contemplation of death, but whether they were not made in contemplation of death." It is not hard to realize and not hard to prove, using the thinking of the *Varner* case, that every or nearly every person in some manifest way contemplates life as well as or more than death. Perhaps, the judicial result one comes by with such thinking is no more than the execution of legislative intent but, if so, then why bother to insert Section 2035 of the Code? The court in the *March* case does better. It seeks the "dominant factors," thus seeking to balance the possibilities, rather than any available peg on which to hang its decision.

In the effort to balance life and death motives the court seeks to establish something about Ruth March's contemplation of death from her relationships with her children. Almost inevitably, the court must enter the realm of psychological speculation about family relationships. The court seems to be aware of the intricacy and subtlety of family relations. It does not oversimplify. It recognizes that to understand Ruth March's attitude in transferring property to her children it is also relevant and important to understand her relationship with her deceased husband and his attitudes. It also recognizes a distinction between real or more meaningful and apparent attitudes. It speculates that the father's "disagreement with his son's choice of profession, and even his disapproval of his son's marriage, were not the real emotional reasons for his disinheriting Charles, but that their differences run deeper."

The court gives further evidence of psychological sophistication in the recognition that ostensible acts may be ambiguous as to their meaning and purpose, and inconclusive on their face. Seeking conclusions, or perceiving the impossibility of it, the court recognized that the status of Mrs. March's health could be valued in terms of both a life interest and a death interest. It decided that Mrs. March could have transferred wealth because of pressure from her children, that she could have done so to create or preserve family unity, but it still recognized that her decision in either instance might as readily have reflected testamentary motives at the same time. Finally, the court reached to a procedural point to arrive at a solution, and passed the buck. It decided, under statutory authority, that the executor had not satisfied the bùrden of proof that Mrs. March did not make a transfer in contemplation of death.

The court, in the concluding statements of an astute decision, identified the culprits who saddled it with a problem of psychological analysis and decision making that it was not prepared to handle. "The burden of deciding what was in the mind of a person long dead, at a point in time months before her death, is almost too much for Congress to have required of the judiciary." It quotes *DesPortes v. United States,* where the court states, "The fact that every person of sound mind knows that he will eventually die makes it indefinably difficult to determine when persons act in contemplation of death and when they do not."[75] Perhaps *DesPortes* makes the point with exaggeration, but the matter of finding precedence in life or death motives is a difficult evidentiary task. It assumes, with the possible exception of findings relating to suicide, more systematic or certain knowledge about psychological experience relating death, and to death versus life, than now exists.

Section 2035 of the Internal Revenue Code puts in issue the matter of the transfer of property in contemplation of death. The issue is one of great behavioral and psychological complexity and even ambiguity.

The Matter of Contemplation. To contemplate, a mental act, is "to have in view" or to give "attentive consideration." One must determine that contemplation has taken place, more from logic than from observation. And one must rely on evidence from behavior sufficient to support a conclusion.

If we regard the matter as procedural, the decision making may not be difficult. The process of inference allows great latitude in speculation, especially where all the acts and events to which the logical process applies are not clear and certain. And, if one regards behavior ex tempore and not as part of a system, any and all behavior can be used freely in speculation and interpretation. One can build a neatly contrived cardboard pyramid of seemingly purposive behavior from passing remarks, momentary stresses, exaggerated dispositions, circumstantial occurrences, and the like. And the mortar of interpretation that accounts for the pyramid derives not from close validation of individual experience within a careful scientific framework but from logical implications of selected events, general or reasonable meanings attached to personal phenomena, juxtapositioning of events to reduce or to emphasize absurdities, and the like. In short, if one searches for "contemplation" as a matter of juridical procedure one likely can make a case for contemplation and, if one chooses to recognize it, one can make a case against contemplation. The issue turns on which way the judge wants to come out or on purely impressionistic phenomena that seem to strike him most vividly and tend to tilt his thinking.

Contemplation from a substantive point of view may be another matter. And, it may be more properly and reasonably the province of the psychologist who truly seeks to examine behavior than of the jurist whose essential effort and responsibility is to somehow pass judgment. Contemplation, from this view, is part of a system of behavior. Contemplation may be goaded by external events, by internal stresses and needs, or by both. It may be evidenced in verbal and expressive behavior, in symbolic behavior, or it may not be observably evidenced at all. It may be an intense, meaningful, and continuous experience or it may be relatively brief, passing, or unimportant. If the system of behavior in which contemplation is regarded is to be complete, then the reasons and circumstances for non-contemplation may be just as important as the causes and phenomena relating to contemplation. A person who is too anxious may suppress rather than contemplate, because the issue that concerns him is too important and disturbing rather than unimportant and unnoted. One may contemplate a particular event or circumstance because one is, relatively, a contemplative person. Or, one may not contemplate important events or circumstances because one is not, temperamentally or for other reasons, disposed to such a kind of thinking.

The Concern About Death. Even given the study of "contemplation" by a jurist in a life-probing sense, there are yet other difficult shoals in the interpretation of mental acts-and-behavioral phenomena. The contemplation in this instance is the contemplation of a phenomenon called death. Death is a behavioral event, a matter of psychological interpretation, a social phenomenon, and a theological construct. It has legal implication, social significance, and consequences of various kinds. In personal terms death is "in the eye of the beholder." It is either thought of, or perhaps deliberately not thought of, by the octogenarian. It is a matter of recklessness and some indifference to some younger persons. It is a prospective event to be reasoned for the more thoughtful person but it is also one consciously to be avoided by the more anxious individual. Death attaches to soul, psyche, relation, and property but it likely does so in different ways for different people. And, as if this were not difference or difficulty enough, there is even an implied behavioral norm in our culture that shuns the open and conscious contemplation of death. Thus, in itself and in its attending features, it is an experience ripe for more intense and specific psychological and social investigation.

Mostly, it is fear and anxiety that attaches to death or to the thought of death. Fear and anxiety may be expressed or revealed in different ways. There may be preoccupation in particular thought and feeling, so that there may be considerable evidence of concern about death. There may be suppression of feeling so that there is little or no apparent anxiety or contemplation about death. There may be denial, and reactive behavior to deny any contemplation of death when there is really great concern about it. There may be a displacement onto other concerns, such as a concern about one's property or an interest in religion, which may be a preoccupation in place of or on top of stronger and possibly more terrifying concern about death. There may be a substitution from an interest or concern about death to an interest and exaggerated involvement in having fun or maintaining health.

The Importance of Property. Finally, in the juridical questioning of matters possibly relating to future interests, it is not only the mental act of contemplation and the phenomenon of death that are to be comprehended in some terms. It is also the social and legal datum and, in this context, the psychological meaning of property that should be identified. Property as an extension of individual personality, defining and affecting intimate as well as business relationships, is not clearly understood. The value and the meaning of property may be akin to the incidents to a drive in certain personalities. The "acquisitive or possessive drive" may function not unlike sexual or aggressive drives. To some personalities, it may be one of the less important modes to personality expression and interpersonal relationship. The point is, property is an important psychological phenomenon on which many human relationships in our society turn. It is used in the exercise of power, of love, of guilt and remorse, of hope and resignation, and in many other ways. The character as well as the use of property can be in large part an idiom of personality. There are psychological dispositions, social conventions, and legal conventions regarding the character, the value, and the use of property. Psychological dispositions in this matter are hardly illumined. It is an act of sheer intellectual creativity when jurists probe motives regarding the meanings and uses of property thought to be exercised possibly in the contemplation of death.

Policy Choices and Means of Decision. Whatever the status of our system of inquiry and our knowledge about transfer of matters of personal right and value in contemplation of death, sooner or later some policy choices must be faced. In the matter of estate taxation, so important to social control, it may be a form of abandonment and irresponsibility to say there is insufficient knowledge or inadequate procedure on which to act equitably or intelligently. Legislative enactments and judicial process are best thought of as approximations, that is, most reasonable or best available means for dealing with some complex social problems. The issue is not "should there be" enactments on estate taxation but "what kind," not "should it be decided" but "who is to decide" and "how."

In the matter of statutory enactment, the issue regarding Section 2035 of the Internal Revenue Code may present itself on the question of whether objective or subjective criteria should be utilized in deciding about transfers before death, considering the current state of our knowledge about motivations leading up to death. It is at least easier, if not possibly more reasonable or more accurate, to accept only (1) evidence of age (any person over 60?), (2) professional certification of health (determined evidence relating to terminal illness), (3) transfer of property executed shortly before death (within a year of death, unless this presumptive evidence of death transfer is conclusively refuted "beyond a shadow of a doubt"), and perhaps some other, similar tests to determine whether a testamentary transfer has occurred.

The issue in Section 2035 regarding judicial determination, especially on the matter of "contemplation of death," may be thought to raise a question as to whether a panel or commission of behavior experts may be used best to advise the court on this consideration. The question, if it is not semantically modified, largely voided of substance through legal fiction and convention and the like, or abandoned to fairly unrestrained logical exercise, presents a profound psychological problem. The most expert judgment and advice is likely to lack full understanding and agreement but, again, it represents a truly best effort on which a judge could more comfortably and veritably rest his *ratio decidendi.*

This "panel of experts" idea really addresses itself to two issues regarding trial procedure in the matter of Section 2035 of the Code. Such panels may be used as part of the end process in decision-making machinery, in this case as an adjunctive or advisory function in deciding the outcome of a case. They may be used also to augment or replace the adversary process in the matter of acquiring and presenting evidence. The relative efficacy of the adversary process in dealing honestly, reasonably, thoroughly and reliably with complex social and psychological behavior is the subject of a brief that in itself would overshadow the issues presented by Section 2035 of the Internal Revenue Code. It may be easier to grant, for the moment, that experts as well as laymen, and evidentiary procedures used in psychology and in other forms of science as well as those used in law, should be systematically used, presented, and evaluated on all matters of social and psychological behavior before the courts.

Commentary by Dr. Feifel

A finding of mine which I think has relevance for the *March* case and makes things somewhat more thorny is the information that attitudes toward death can oscillate in the same individual from strong avoidance to calm acceptance. The point in time one centers on can be crucial. My data underline the coexistence of contradictory attitudes toward death, i.e., realistic acceptance of death and its simultaneous rejection in a subtle equilibristic balance in numerous persons.

[There follow portions of the text of a brief report, "Perception of Death as Related to Nearness to Death," by Dr. Feifel and Mr. Robert B. Jones of the Veterans Administration Outpatient Clinic in Los Angeles. It is reproduced here with permission of the authors and of the American Psychological Association. The research reported was conducted on 371 persons in four major groups: seriously and terminally ill (92), chronically ill and physically disabled (94), mentally ill (90), and healthy (95). Their ages ranged from 12 to 89, with a mean age of 40. All groups were average in intelligence, educated at the high school graduate level, and of average socioeconomic status. About half were male and a few more than half were Protestant. The data were secured by psychologists and psychiatrists using tests, rating scales, and open-ended questionnaires. Qualitative answers were scored by investigators who showed a percentage of agreement ranging from 81 to 96 percent. These findings, especially as to denial defenses, are as important for *Varner* as for *March.*]

Man is a creature in time and space whose consciousness permits him to nullify their strictures. Anticipation steers many of his deliberations, and expectation serves as a principal mediator of goal-directed and purposeful behavior. One cogent aspect of this capacity, it seems, would be the influence on the individual of temporal nearness or distance from probable personal death. One's perception of the world and attitudes toward death might not be quite the same next week as it is at present if one were then to learn of a metastasizing cancer.

With regard to consciously verbalized fear of death, a majority (71 percent) of all the groups, denied fearing death primarily because "it's inevitable." Those who admitted to fear of death did so essentially because of fear of the unknown. Frequency of thoughts about dying and death was dominated by "rarely" (44 percent) and "occasionally" (42 percent). Almost half (49 percent) stated that no changes had occurred in their attitudes toward death since their illness (patients) or in the past five years (healthy), with another 30 percent actually indicating less fear now than heretofore. Additionally, a majority in each group assessed their overall attitude toward death as "positive," with the physically ill patients ranking highest in this respect.

A somewhat contradictory and contrasting picture emerged when other conscious material and below-the-level-of-awareness measures were examined. Interviewers' assessments of the patients' attitudes toward death underlined an ambivalent rather than positive outlook. Forty-four percent of the population reacted with rejection to the idea of personal death, with acceptance indicated by only 30 percent. Analyses of color-word interference and word-association tests showed greater interference, increased reaction times, and more recall errors on death than on neutral words. Scrutiny of dying and death imagery data disclosed negative imagery as regnant. Further, denial was the major (63 percent) coping technique used to deal with the idea of personal death.

Certain significant differences were manifest among the groups. "Own illness" was reliably more important for the patients than the healthy in bringing death to mind and in making a lasting impression on them. Anxiety and depression characterized the seriously ill and terminally ill patients more than the healthy. The seriously ill and terminally ill also blocked significantly more often than the healthy when asked to conceptualize death verbally and graphically. Additionally, they used denial as a coping defense relevant to death thoughts reliably more often than the healthy. The healthy, on their side, resorted to intellectualization as their prevailing coping technique.* This does not imply, naturally, that denial was not available to a substantial number of the healthy or intellectualization to the patients, not to mention such other shields as reaction formation, isolation, and displacement.

Concerning general view of self and the world, no sharp overall differences among the groups were evident. "Feel fulfilled" was rated "yes" by 42 percent, "no" by 41 percent. As expected, however, more of the healthy reported "yes" than did mentally ill patients. Self-description was generally positive, with the mentally ill bringing up the rear. Major personal assets were designated as "friendly and sociable" (57 percent) and "helpful and sympathetic to others" (52 percent). Major liabilities were "personal defects" (57 percent) and "lack of emotional control" (39 percent). The most important thing in life now was "health" for the physically ill, "family" for the healthy, and "being a better person" for the mentally ill. The world itself was delineated as "OK" (39 percent) and "good" (38 percent), along with a pronounced minority vote of "messed up" by the mentally ill. The path of life ranked highest by all groups emphasized "integration of diversity," that is, accepting things from all paths of life as needed and appropriate. This was followed closely by the path stressing "group participation in achieving common goals." The paths least favored were

---

*Dr. Feifel supplied for this chapter some underlying data from the study on the use of intellectualization and denial as techniques for coping with death:

The percentage of occurrence of denial and intellectualization in the four groups (I–seriously and terminally ill; II–chronically ill; III–mentally ill; IV–normal) as judged by clinically trained interviewers were as follows:

Percent	I	II	III	IV
Denial	84.8	56.4	51.1	57.9
Intellect.	47.8	51.1	40.0	56.8
Total N	92	97	90	95

In the case of denial, the *difference* between groups when adjustments are made for differences in age, sex, socioeconomic status, marital status, intelligence, number of children, education, and religious denomination, are such that they would occur by chance less than once in a thousand.

In the case of intellectualization, when the same adjustments are made, the differences would occur by chance less than once out of 20 times.

"being a quiet vessel through whom others work" and "the rich, inner, contemplative life." Passivity and the meditative life as dominant guides were eschewed.

Concerning personal fate after death, 55 percent of the present population adopted a religious orientation, the physically ill being more partial in this direction than the other two groups. The physically ill also manifested a significantly more conventional religious outlook than did the others. Nevertheless, scores for all four groups on this variable centered broadly in the average range. No significant differences were noted on the intrinsic-extrinsic religious dimension. Self-rating in the area was primarily "somewhat religious." Major reasons for being religious were "tradition" (31 percent) and "belief in God" (22 percent); for being nonreligious, "false teachings" (24 percent). The impact of religion on behavior was reported as "improves me" (48 percent) and "makes little difference" (39 percent).

Time was considered "valuable" by most, but also "meaningless" by a good proportion of the seriously ill and terminally ill patients. The future was the time period of most concern to the patients, particularly the seriously ill and terminally ill; the present to the healthy. "Personal gratification" (58 percent) and "social orientation" (56 percent) governed the essential use of time under the threat of death.

Strong contrasts are apparent in attitudes toward death. Both acceptance and rejection coexist, with acknowledgement and manageable fear generally commanding verbal conscious considerations, denial, and dread, the "gut" level. Avoidance and evasion strategies tend to become intensified, particularly at the non-conscious level, when a person realizes that death is possible in the near future. Undoubtedly, this counterpoise serves adaptational needs. This is increasingly understandable in an era of dissolving beliefs and traditions when one no longer possesses unquestioned conceptual creeds which transcend and integrate death or furnish one with sustaining continuity and meaning. Nevertheless, it also mirrors unhealthy expulsion and inadequate binding of fears and anxieties concerning death. Expanded communication and openness concerning death rather than suppression is called for in providing emotional support, especially for the seriously ill and terminally ill. The expressions of gratitude and relief verbalized by many of the interviewees suggest its pertinence for all. Closer affinity with the notion of death is required in developmental perspectives. One also needs to comprehend more penetratingly varying and fluctuating meanings of death within as well as between individuals.

Additionally, one faces the task of unraveling more intelligibly bonds existing among verbally expressed ideas, fantasy musings, and unconscious concepts concerning death.*

Commentary by Professor Shaffer

The *March* opinion is as ambivalent as the *Varner* opinion is assertive. Since ambivalence is less useful in the judicial science than it is in the psychological, the court is therefore driven to resolving its problem as all difficult factual problems are resolved by judges: by the application of a presumption. ("Presumption" in this sort of case means a policy determination to be applied in deciding the unproven; it is not here a matter of factual inference.)

At least one of the *Varner* opinion's group norms, *Contemplation Is Surrender,* is implicit here; the court is at some pains to suggest that all of the things that happened to Mrs. March are consistent with its (statutory) presumption that she had surrendered to the grim reaper. Two other of the *Varner* norms are clearly rejected: the fifth (*Support Is Only for Life*) and the sixth (*Dying People Withdraw*). Aside from these areas of resemblance or difference, though, the mood of the *March* opinion is uncertainty. The uncertainty can be stated in terms of five variable principles:

1. *Moral Obligations May Be Satisfied After Death.* The *Varner* court, on solid authority, distinguished between transfers in contemplation of death and transfers to satisfy moral obligations. *March,* on almost equally solid authority, takes the view that satisfaction of moral obligations is not necessarily a living motive. (Even classifying this as a satisfaction of moral obligation is debatable, of course. It is possible that Mrs. March reacted out of hurt at Charles' reaction to her attempt to satisfy moral obligation. She withdrew, in a

---

*These data tend to indicate two facts which are contrary to the almost universal assumptions apparent in Section 2035 opinions: (1) the most common coping technique for all groups, of all ages, and in all conditions of health, is denial ("I am not going to die"), rather than intellectualization ("We all die sometime"); (2) the older the subject is, or the poorer his health, the more likely it is that he will select denial, rather than intellectualization.

Dr. Feifel adds two caveats to these data:

(1) These are just group statistical findings, i.e., the seriously ill can make use of intellectualization just as well as the healthy. They do so, however, significantly less often, (2) Both denial and intellectualization, as coping techniques, can coexist within the same individual (one does not necessarily exclude the other) be the individual sick or healthy.

way, and thereby possibly put herself within Shneidman's "social death" generalization.) "Rules," such as they are in these cases, are like that. There is almost literally no rule which is not, like some sort of law of physics, matched by an equal and opposite contrary rule. This is a familiar phenomenon in the law of the dead, or at least in that part of it that turns on the intent of a dead man. It is almost impossible to confront the judiciary with what seems to be a doctrinal inconsistency, because it is always possible for the judge to say or infer that precedent counts for very little when intention is the central inquiry.[76] This rejoinder is used by the judiciary even though it is perfectly obvious that courts do not with any sincerity or seriousness attempt to find out what the dead man's intention was. The judge in *March* is refreshingly candid about that.

Another aspect of moral obligation as producing a life-centered motive (or ambivalent motive) is the distinction which the facts here present. Mrs. March seems to have made the transfers to Charles because she thought he had been wronged, and to have made the transfers to Katharine to settle a family squabble. The court regards both motivations as doubtful, and resolves the issue in the case by reference to a presumption rather than by reference to either motive. If the presumption were not used, the court might then have to inquire into the relationship between Mrs. March and each of her children, and this especially in reference to her relationship with her late husband and to the apparently radical change in her life which followed the death of her first child. That sort of inquiry might be characteristic of a serious attempt to find out her intention.[77] It would undoubtedly have to involve the kind of interdisciplinary inquiry Dr. Redmount suggests. The alternative of using a presumption is an easy out, and one for which the court cannot be criticized, of course, since Congress provided it. Another alternative might be to abandon the venture the *Wells* case began nearly forty years ago and have taxation turn on the manifest operation of transfers rather than on the hidden contents of the hearts of dead men.

2. *Grief Reactions Color Behavior, But It Is Impossible for Judges to Know How They Do It.* However honest this reaction might have been, and despite what seems to be Dr. Redmount's acceptance of it, I suspect that the conclusion is wrong. And the failure is not really the court's; it belongs on the shoulders of the lawyers who try these cases. An impression I have from reading hundreds of Section 2035 cases is that the taxpayer estates win them too easily and the Internal Revenue

Service doesn't really try to win them. One can read all of the cases under Section 2035 without detecting the slightest indication that Sigmund Freud and his precursors ever lived or the further fact that substantial numbers of clinical and research psychologists and psychiatrists have devoted volumes of work to death research in the past decade. It is possible to inquire into the effect of relatively tangible psychological trauma and to inquire into it with the clarity and certainty required for judicial decision. Dr. Feifel's exacting work is particularly encouraging on that score. The inquiry could be undertaken as a result of procedural reform, possibly the interdisciplinary board Dr. Redmount recommends. It could be undertaken within existing procedures by using judicially noticeable data in Section 2035 trials. There is now, I think, a sufficient body of clinical, experimental, and survey research to justify judicially cognizable scientific opinion in Section 2035 trials. This can be demonstrated in terms of reported clinical cases and in terms of reported research generalizations.[78]

3. *Manipulative Property Transfers May or May Not Contemplate Death.* This point is nicely illustrated by the court's comparison of its case with the facts of the *Russell* case. It was fairly clear in *Russell,* on the facts as reported, that the decedent there (also a widowed lady) had made transfers so that her children and grandchildren would be close to her as she grew older. That was a possible conclusion in *March,* but it was certainly not inevitable. Mrs. March may have wanted her son and daughter emotionally close to her so that her old age could be spent in satisfaction and peace, but her motives may have been more indefinite than that. They may, specifically, have involved a redress of wrongs she felt her late husband had done, and this in turn may have involved a manipulation of their emotional attitude toward her and toward their late father. The operation of a transfer to manipulate affections would have been important after her death, as well as until her death. This was very much the Government's view, which was sustained by attempting to attribute to Mrs. March the motives of her children. But the Government's case apparently presented only legal precedent in support of this psychological conclusion. The Government finally relied on the statutory presumption, which worked out well for it in this case but which has failed it more often than not in other cases. Could the Government have offered data from which the judge might have concluded that (1) Mrs. March's were manipulative transfers, and (2) in contemplation of her own death?

4. *"Just in Case" Transfers Are In Contemplation of Death, But May Not Be A Dominant Factor.* This principle has a doctrinal side. The doctrine that transfers "in case anything happens" are in contemplation of death is one of those "principles" Dr. Redmount recognizes as essential to the business of judging. Facts do not have to support a principle like this with precision. It is sufficient that they seem to come pretty close to supporting it. It is probably a good doctrine, not so much because it is invariably correct as because it is in reasonable approximation to correctness—as reasonably approximate as any general principle can be when it is to be applied in every case. But the court, even though it identifies a useful general principle, fails to apply it because it finds that factor not dominant on the facts of this case. Again, ultimate decision is based on the statutory presumption rather than on the facts. Is it possible to separate out donative factors, and to isolate the dominant one, on the basis of scientific information? If scientific assistance is not acceptable, the alternative is to pile a doctrine (that a given factor is or is not dominant) on another doctrine (that the factor designated dominant is a contemplation-of-death factor). In a case where the factor is found to be dominant, the result will then be like what Professor Leon Green said "proximate cause" is in tort cases; the judiciary will have delimited a zone of liability, out of policy considerations, with only indirect allusion (if any at all) to scientific information.[79] In a case where no factor is designated dominant, the primary doctrine will, as in this case, have failed of its purpose and the case will be decided on the statutory presumption. If it were possible to sort out and weight factors scientifically, cases could be decided either on a single doctrine (that the factor so isolated is a contemplation-of-death factor) or on the basis of no doctrine at all (when the factor so isolated is itself capable of scientific evaluation in terms of contemplation of death). Some of Dr. Feifel's careful research may very well point the law to this weighting of factors.

For example, scientific information might be available here to demonstrate that the "just in case" motivation behind Mrs. March's transfer of the house was a contemplation-of-death motive. This information would be substituted for the use of precedent. Facts would be used rather than policy. And I mean here, of course, what students of Brandeis call "legislative facts": facts of the sort developed in Dr. Feifel's research. The court would then have to decide whether, on the peculiar facts of this case (judicial facts), this motive was dominant. If scientific evidence could demonstrate that it was or was not dominant, the case would be decided on the basis of facts (in both senses), rather than on the basis of presumption and doctrines.

5. *Vindictive Transfers May Be Life-Related But They May Also Be Focally Suicidal.* This of course overstates what the court said: What it said was that in the *Budd* case the transfer seems almost to have been suicidal. The *Budd* case was then identified as not helpful in resolving the issues in the case before the court. But the insight, which was not stated in the *Budd* opinion, seems to be a useful one. It is probably accurate to say that some inter-vivos property transfers are suicidal. The reasoning would be this: (1) the transferor identified himself in some significant way with his property; (2) he transferred his property in a suicidal frame of mind; (3) suicidal frames of mind are within the statutory phrase "contemplation of death." Points 1 and 2 are case-by-case factual inquiries. Point 3 is a conclusion based on inquiry but applied more or less generally: it is a "legislative fact." There is and has been for a generation a significant amount of psychological groundwork for the inquiry: the groundwork is more solid every year, as clinicians and experimenters reach large areas of consensus on suicidal behavior. An exploration of this factor in Section 2035 cases, and in the psychology of testation generally, may be worthwhile, and may result in the conclusion that psychological information on suicidal property transfer would be useful in the general process of replacing doctrines and presumptions with facts.

Estate of Dumay v. United States
(United States Court of Appeals)

John Richard Dumay, had a wife, a son, and a daughter. He also had a business and a fine old house in the city, a brother who was his business "angel", and a large policy of life insurance. This appeal is about the last days in his life with these people and these things.[80]

Mr. Dumay's life was divided between his home and his business. At home were his wife Janet and his disabled, unmarried daughter Millicent. Mr. Dumay spent his weekends in this home environment. He grew a garden there, an unusual avocation for a businessman who lived in the city. He made routine repairs around the house. He bought the house, which had been constructed in 1881, in his early married life, at a time when it was beyond his means. He appears to have maintained it at considerable sacrifice of other interests which might have been normal to a man growing in prosperity: business connections, life at the country club, and some of the status of middle-class respectability. It

191

was and is an impressive house, and Mr. Dumay undoubtedly had an unusually strong attachment to it (and, we think, to the people who lived in it).

Mr. Dumay also had a business: the manufacture of embalming fluid. He came into the business in his youth and took it over when its founder died in 1934. He built it by thrift and diligence from a tenuous venture to a respected, dependable concern. Of course, he found the economic aspects of doing that difficult. When he took over the business from its founder's estate he borrowed some $40,000 from his older brother, then and now a successful real estate broker in California. When he expanded it in 1938, he returned to his brother for financing. His brother observed that none of the principal of the 1934 loan had been paid, and Mr. Dumay countered with an offer to discharge the 1934 debt and cover new capital by incorporating the business and giving his brother one-third of the stock in it. His brother agreed to this arrangement and has retained 333 shares of the 1,000 shares of outstanding stock in the company (Dumay Embalming Fluid Company, Inc.) since 1938.

As part of this 1938 transaction, Mr. Dumay and his brother, Arthur Dumay, entered into a cross-purchase "buy and sell" agreement. This was a simple arrangement, apparently set up as an afterthought to the larger transaction and probably traceable to the diligence and thoroughness of counsel who supervised the transaction. In any event the agreement provided that either shareholder had a right of first purchase at book value, of the other shareholder's holdings at death, *and* in the event either shareholder sought to sell any of his holdings to an outsider.[81] This agreement would undoubtedly have required that the Estate of John Richard Dumay offer all of the stock in the corporation to Arthur Dumay at book value. The evidence is that book value of these shares is $150 and that their fair market value (although that is disputed) is at least $600 a share.

The business prospered after 1938. Mr. Dumay was able to pay himself an adequate salary as its president and to reinvest earnings and put the company on a solid footing. He did not move from his house, even when his circumstances might have justified that, and he continued to live the home-and-business, simple life he had always led. He did not invest his personal savings in either frivolity or the stock market, but he did buy a life insurance policy in 1954, in the face amount of $100,000, and was able to pay all premiums on the policy within three years. That life insurance policy, the house, and two-thirds of the stock in the family business are at issue in this appeal.

Mr. Dumay's relationship with his family was apparently normal. His son Brian attended college and law school and became an attorney in his home city. His daughter Millicent also progressed into her college years, but she had a tragic automobile accident which left her disabled and disfigured and, as it turned out, indefinitely dependent on her loving father. (Millicent lived in the parental home until her father's death, and still lives in it. She is not employed but is able to "do things" around the house and to help her mother. The family has never had servants.) It is reasonable to infer that the purchase of life insurance in 1954, the year after Millicent's accident, was related to Mr. Dumay's concern for her welfare.

In 1964 Mr. Dumay discussed his business situation with his son Brian. The gist of that conversation was that Mr. Dumay needed help with the expanding business, that he hoped to reduce the time he spent in in his work and devote more time to his garden and home, and that he could offer Brian a secure future in the business. He orally offered Brian managerial authority and a share in the business if Brian would give up his law practice and devote all of his time to the company. Brian accepted this proposition and, since early 1966, has been secretary and general manager of the company. His father remained active in the office, however, until his death and was, at his death, president of the corporation. Mr. Dumay died December 10, 1967.

Mr. Dumay did not immediately transfer stock to Brian, as he had promised, and Brian (with support from Mrs. Dumay and from Millicent) pressed his father to begin stock transfers in performance of the bargain. There is no evidence that this pressure was either protracted or intense, but there is no doubt, either, that it was a matter which weighed in some way on Mr. Dumay's mind, and on the minds of Brian, Millicent, and Mrs. Dumay.

In 1965, Mr. Dumay consulted an independent attorney for "estate planning" services. This attorney pointed out that Mr. Dumay's death would result in the sale of his corporate shares to his brother for about a fourth of their value; that the house would, under local law, be divided among wife, daughter, and son; and that the life insurance proceeds would be given entirely to the wife (pursuant to the policy's beneficiary designation). He also pointed out that the cross-purchase agreement with Arthur Dumay was binding only as to inter-vivos sales and to disposition at death; Mr. Dumay in other words, was free to *give* the shares away during his life.

Mr. Dumay's situation at that time was typical of many businessmen of his age (64). His son had promise and a good future in the family business, and Mr. Dumay was frequently reminded of general and specific obligations toward him. His wife and daughter, on the other hand, were in need of continued support and protection and were of no economic value in the business. If Mr. Dumay's situation as an "estate planning" client was unusual at all it was in the fact that he also had a valuable home and a substantial amount of life insurance. His attorney advised him that any planned transfer of corporate shares to Brian should be undertaken promptly, so that those shares would be removed from the cross-purchase agreement with Arthur Dumay; that the life-insurance policy afforded protection for Mr. Dumay's wife and daughter, but that it should be removed from the risks of the business (which it bore so long as Mr. Dumay owned it); and that Mr. Dumay could and should take steps to guarantee that the family home would be controlled by his wife and daughter.

Mr. Dumay did not act on this advice for more than two years. There is no clear evidence explaining the delay, but we assume the sort of procrastination familiar to any lawyer who draws wills. In any event, Mr. Dumay returned to his lawyer in 1967 to relate the fact that he had "signed over" the shares of stock—all 667 of them—to Brian and that he wanted to take care of the house and life insurance. Within a week the lawyer prepared, and Mr. Dumay executed, a conveyance of the house to Mrs. Dumay and a conveyance of the insurance policy to an irrevocable trustee who had directions to apply insurance proceeds to the support of Mrs. Dumay so long as she lived and then to the support of Millicent. Mr. Dumay did not, however, make a will. He died six weeks later, intestate.

Mr. Dumay's death was sudden. He was not unusually old and he had not been ill until stricken with last illness shortly before he died. He had been under the care of a physician, for arthritis, but this ailment was not unusually serious. He had not consulted a physician otherwise, except for routine physical examinations (which he had taken since early in his life once a year, and took in the last three years of his life four times a year). The cause of death was listed as "short term coronary thrombosis."

The question here is whether these three transfers—the stock (approximately $400,000); the house (approximately $85,000); and the insurance policy (worth about $65,000 at transfer) were gifts in contemplation of death, under Sec. 2035 of the Internal Revenue Code of 1954. The Commissioner prevailed in the Tax Court as to the house transfer and as to the insurance transfer; the Tax Court found for the taxpayer on the stock transfer. The Commissioner appealed from the last finding; the taxpayer estate appealed from the rest of the Tax Court's judgment.

The Stock. We affirm the Tax Court and hold that the transfer of stock was not in contemplation of death. The test, we think, is that suggested by the court in *Lockwood v. United States:* "[T]he question is whether the decedent made this gift for a purpose which would reasonably be effected during the lifetime of the decedent, or is the gift a substitute for testamentary disposition."[82] In that case, as here, the purpose was one which could not possibly be effected after the decedent's death. In *Lockwood,* the motive was saving income taxes; here it was placing property beyond the operation of an agreement *which could only have operated after death.* This is the usual holding where income taxes, as distinguished from death taxes, appear to be the decedent's principal concern.[83] This is altogether different from the result where saving of death taxes is indicated as a dominant motive.[84]

The Government emphasizes, though, that Mr. Dumay delayed the conveyance of these securities to his son—until, the Government argues, the imminence of death added a decisive consideration to those motives he already had. The Government points to three factors—the desire to avoid the buy-sell agreement (a living motive), the desire to transfer the business to the son (a death motive), and the desire to retire from the business (an ambivalent motive which is arguably made a death motive by a process of morbid contamination). We think the Government places too much emphasis on its own conjecture. Transfers of business, during life, to the next generation, are not necessarily testamentary. In *Flynn,* the court considered the fact that the objectives of retirement and new business management could have been accomplished by some method other than stock transfer, but held that the decedent was not bound to choose those nontransfer methods in order to avoid Section 2035; nor was it enough that the decedent obviously must have had in mind the continuation of the business after his death.[85] The jury charge in *Mollenkamp* was even more emphatic: "[I]f the trans-feror . . . desired to avoid the cares and burdens of continuing to manage the property . . . such a purpose would be consistent with the enjoyment of life. . . ."[86] Whether the *Mollenkamp* court's language was stronger than an objective consideration of the precedents would justify is unimportant in this case because we have here additional evidence of living motive—especially evidence that Mr. Dumay, who was in good health and not unusually old, planned to devote his time and energies to home and garden rather than to business. What he seems to have contemplated, in other words, was a transition *in* his life not a transition *out* of his life.[87]

Another factor—Mr. Dumay's delay in effecting the transfer—explains the Government's argument on the stock. Mr. Dumay was reluctant to turn over his business, even when it was explained to him that failure to do so would frustrate his plans with respect to his son in the business. That reluctance was understandable; we are talking after all about the surrender of his life's work. That was a momentous event for him, one he came to slowly, but not, we think, necessarily one that can be explained only by an apprehension toward death. Here, as in *Goldberg,* his attitude toward his son, toward his retirement, and toward the buy-sell agreement, all point toward living motives for the delay, rather than death motives.[88] We do not believe that this case falls within the well-established line of authorities which equate "gift in contemplation of death" with "testamentary transfer."[89] It falls instead within precedents which overcome that conclusion—and even, sometimes, strain a bit to do it—with evidence that there was more in the transfer than merely testamentary motivation.[90]

The Life Insurance. We reverse the Tax Court and find that the transfer of life insurance to the trust was not in contemplation of death. The dominant motive in this situation, a motive which realistically dates from the *purchase* of the insurance and which was merely carried one step further in the *transfer* of it, was provision for the support of Mr. Dumay's disabled daughter Millicent.[91] It is true that life insurance transfers seem by their nature to be death-centered, since the insurance will not usually ripen into any sort of economic benefit for anyone until the insured is dead. But an insured may purchase or maintain insurance because he wants to have economic values for the support of his family which are not subject to business risk.[92] It is possible, as we think in the case here, for him to transfer ownership of existing insurance in order to increase and protect that economic immunity.[93] This is a case where concern for support overcomes concern for death (which is to say that the statute compels us to *assume* the existence of concern for death and then determine whether evidence of other concern overcomes the assumed concern). The life-insurance trust is a familiar situation in the cases: In *Want,* the decedent was concerned about the physical care of an infant daughter.[94] In *Colorado Bank* an adult dependent daughter was important, and Mr. Justice McReynolds said for the Court: "Broadly speaking, thoughtful men habitually act with regard to ultimate death, but something more than this is required in order to show that a conveyance comes within the ambit of the statute."[95] There is, in other words, a difference between disposing of property as in a will and disposing of property as one would provide for the medical expenses of a dependent child, and this is true even though the provision may have an effect after the parent is dead.[96]

The House. Two factors compel us to affirm the Tax Court and to hold that Mr. Dumay's transfer of the house to his wife and daughter was a gift in contemplation of death. The first factor is that we can find no non-testamentary purpose in the transfer; he could have accomplished the same result by making a will. Second, we think the evidence shows an attachment, or an involvement, with this asset which is more intense, more personal, than his involvement with his business shares or with his life insurance. This involvement leads us to conclude that his transfer was death-centered.

It seems to be the case that property owners have a stronger personal identity with residential (or agricultural) real property than they have with relatively impersonal economic interests in businesses and insurance investment. (Perhaps our common-law property heritage disposes us to believe that whether it is true or not, but in this case we believe there are indications that it is true.) Mr. Dumay was in every way an old-fashioned householder, the sort of man who takes pride in discharging a mortgage quickly, growing a handsome garden, in remaining in his home even after industrial expansion and changing neighborhood patterns have driven his more transient neighbors into the suburbs. Why, then, did he give his home away? There seem to us to be three explanations: (1) He wanted the home to be immediately and easily available to his wife and daughter (a "how to avoid probate" motive which is inherently testamentary). (2) He wanted the home to be available to them and not to his son, who did not live in it; he may also have intended an equalization for the stock transfer to his son. (3) He had begun to think of the home as less the place where *he* would live than the place where his wife and daughter would live. All three possible explanations seem to us to point to the application of the statute. There is some authority to the effect that transfers "to make sure the property stays in the family" (our first hypothesis) are not death-motive transfers.[97] But that authority seems to us wrong; the only way property leaves a family in circumstances such as this is when the owner dies and it is given to persons outside the family; concern over that very eventuality seems to us precisely a matter of concern about "what will happen . . . to . . . property at . . . death."[98] There is some resemblance between the situation in which we find Mr. Dumay when he transferred his house and the man who disposes, inter vivos, of virtually everything he owns. In the latter case, the courts have almost uniformly held that the transfer was in contemplation of death.[99] Without applying that kind of quantification to Mr. Dumay, we think the same result follows here. Real estate transfers seem especially indicative of this death-centered transfer—as in *MacDonald*, where the court charged the jury to consider, in a case involving transfer of real estate, "the amount of property transferred in proportion to the amount of property retained."[100] In *Heiner v. Donnan*, where the court reached an opposite conclusion but was impressed by the fact that the transfer related to residential real estate.[101]

The insight attempted here is that there are circumstances in which a decedent seems to have obliterated a part of his personality, a sort of property personality. They seem to us likely to occur, and, in any event, to have occurred here, when the subject of transfer is a home in which the decedent was without a doubt personally involved. This should explain our motive in using precedents which involve transfers of all the decedent's property. Both circumstances suggest an obliteration of property logically related to death more than they suggest a calculated dispensation of expenditure of property.

We therefore find that (1) the transfer of securities was not in contemplation of death; (2) the transfer of life-insurance ownership to the trust was not in contemplation of death; and (3) the transfer of residential real estate was in contemplation of death.

Commentary by Dr. Redmount

The Court in *Dumay* appears to show a rare intelligence about human behavior, even though it may not have conveyed this intelligence in terms of some systematic framework of behavior explanation. It recognizes, as in fairness have other courts, that there is a dominance of motives in relation to acts. A decision about stock transfer is not a matter of either life motive or death motives. Both may be relevant and the question is which kind of motive is substantially stronger. The Court also recognizes that vital decisions about oneself in relation to one's family and in relation to one's wealth or property (an extension of personality) do not come easily. In fact, decisions may be piecemeal and delayed. By the way in which the decisions are formed and expressed they may reflect indecision and uncertainty extended in time rather than clear, consistent contemplation followed by decisive action. This appears to be the case in decedent Dumay's handling of his business transfer and perhaps his home transfer as well. The Court recognized the true significance of delayed and seemingly belated decisions that all too glibly might have been construed as fear, panic or concern because of the increasing imminence of death. The Court, in fact, is ahead of the psychology of its time in recognizing and differentiating the importance of property of various kinds as an important attribute of personality around which or through which some needs, feelings, thoughts, and actions grow. It offers the pregnant thought that a person's attachment to his residential property is heavily invested with acquisitive, possessive, or protective feelings much like some of his attachment to his family. It thinks, correctly or not, that this is not as true or vital in the case of a person's interest in his business, commercial investments and the like.

The essential thrust of the court's style of thinking can be put in the form of a sound proposition. The character and purpose, the timing and direction, and the meaning of a person's actions are validly comprehended only in terms of a cohering system of behavior. One must understand or at least appreciate the person's system of needs, his modes of expressing or revealing himself, his ideas about life, his feelings and practices relating to family, to career, to property and wealth, to health, etc., and contemplate all of these in relation to one another before one can make meaningful and reliable statements about any one facet or important behavior in the person's life. This approach and analysis the court approximates in the *Dumay* case, though it does not articulate a systematic framework of behavior. It acts more intelligently than many and perhaps most other courts where the judicial vogue is to take a behavioral event, roughly isolated, and then make fragmented and spurious speculations about persons and other matters relating to and deriving from the event.

Commentary by Professor Shaffer

The judicial sophistication which Dr. Redmount finds in the *Dumay* opinion is a composite of insights from a relatively small number of cases. It is accurate; it compiles real judicial behavior. But it is an aspiration, too, because it represents a stronger concentration of psychological insight than I have found in any one opinion. It also suggests a limit; it is as far into the psychological as the judiciary is likely to go. In reference to Dr. Redmount's observation that the judges in *Dumay* "may not have conveyed this intelligence in terms of some systematic framework of behavior examination," I think it unlikely that American judges will ever be open about their adherence to systematic psychological examination. But I think they can engage in psychological examination more frequently and more deeply than they have in most Section 2035 cases.

Which is to say that the *Dumay* opinion exemplifies what judges can do, do well, and get away with when they are commissioned to divine human feeling. I see this as illustrated in this opinion in three respects: (1) The court identified a relationship between John Richard Dumay and his property. (2) It recognized that this relationship varied depending on what the property was and how owning and giving it affected human relationships in Dumay's family. (3) It began to move toward some understanding of the role property plays in attitudes toward death; in this case it seems to have realized judicially what Drs. Weisman and Hackett have realized clinically in their "appropriate death" concept. My discussion of these points may serve as a conclusion and summary of this venture into the judicial use of the psychological autopsy. psychological autopsy.

1. *Property relationship.* The court sees Dumay as in a personal relationship with the three kinds of property transferred: the business shares, the life insurance, and his house in the city. It seems to me that there are several levels at which this insight might have been worked out in Dumay's life and dying. The unifying factor would have been that all of his property was centrally involved in what psychologists would talk about as Dumay's ego life, in his conscious living. Some of his property might have been involved in his life as a part of himself, a personal extension. An example of that might have been Dumay's favorite hammer and saw, or the tools he used in his garden, or the desk fixtures which he had on his desk throughout a difficult business career. I have tried to demonstrate in Chapter 5 that property held in this intensely personal way is not seen as economically significant but is regarded almost as a physical extension of the self. This personal character seems to have extended in this case to Dumay's house, not only on the symbolic level, as *representing* something in his life, but also on the level of identity. In a very real way the house was Dumay and Dumay was the house. And those of us who think we understand the testamentary behavior of wills clients might add that the house *is* Dumay now, long after his death.

There are less intense levels of identity with property. The business shares, for example, seem not to have a quality of personal extension. I believe this sort of asset is best described in a client's life as representing his *work,* and I have found indications that clients in Dumay's situation tend to regard their family businesses less as assets (economic value) or personal things (identity) than as projects, as what they do. If that is true—and the court's opinion assumes that it is—Dumay's disposition of the business shares can be related to his interest in having the work continued, and in this sense his work is a part of his life. His work life ended at retirement; retirement can be a traumatic event, but, absent a psychopathology which is probably prevalent in our society, it is not necessarily a death-related trauma.

The life insurance seems to have been seen by the court as occupying a third kind of property relationship in Mr. Dumay's life. If the house was a matter of personality, and the business a matter of personal project, the insurance was a matter of personal power. It is possible for a man to be in a doing relationship with one part of his property and in a power relationship with another. A hypothetically "pure" capitalist, for instance, would probably not occupy either a personal relationship or a project relationship with his shares of stock in public corporations and his government bonds. But he might be in a personal relationship with them in the sense that capital is a source of power with which he can provide for and influence the lives of others. If that was true as to Dumay's life insurance—and the court appears to have treated it that way—then the question is whether his transfer of it related to the lives of others during Dumay's life or to their lives after his death. The court—fairly it seems to me—decided on the former characterization.

In each of these senses property has become real and personal in the life of the dead man. In some sense each of these aggregations of things has been loved, and in being loved has become real, like the toys in the children's story ("The Velveteen Rabbit" by Margery Williams Bianco):

> "What is REAL?" asked the Rabbit one day, when they were lying side by side near the nursery fender. . . .
> "Real isn't how you are made," said the Skin Horse. "It's a thing that happens to you. When a child loves you for a long, long time, not just to play with, but REALLY loves you, then you become Real."
> "[O]nce you are Real you can't become unreal again. It lasts for always."

2. *Differences in Property Relationships.* The Court assumed a

personal relationship between Dumay and his property, and built upon the assumption a theory for treating each of the three assets differently. There is no other way to explain its three-part decision. (And I repeat at this point that its three-part decision fairly represents one kind of judicial behavior in Section 2035 cases.) The two ways one might explain the psychological process of differentiation are in terms of giving as goal-striving behavior, and in terms of death as something Dumay did rather than something that happened to him. The latter point is covered in the following section.

Property disposition is goal-striving behavior. It could be that death is a necessary condition in the goal toward which the donor is directing his effort. This is true when one makes a will; it is often true, as Briggs demonstrates, when one purchases life insurance. (However, purchasing life insurance may have lifetime objectives, and its transfer, as in this case, may aim at protection or isolation from lifetime activity.) A sub-species of death-centered property disposition which might have been involved in the *March* case involves suicidal behavior; Shneidman's characterization of the death of Captain Ahab is an example of that, as is his pragmatic advice that sudden irrational property disposition may be a clue to suicide.[102]

The court seems to have considered these factors in deciding that Dumay's goal in transferring the business was related to his retirement, and to his promise to his son, and to his desire to maintain the family business. These factors are also involved in the court's deciding that the isolation of life insurance and the equalization of patrimony were related to lifetime goals more than they were related to objectives to be accomplished after Dumay's death. One can disagree with the results in cases such as this without disapproving of the psychological considerations involved.

The court did not do what courts commonly do when faced with significant human motivations. It did not ignore its own behavioral insight and decide the case on unstated, even unconscious assumptions which are patently unsound. The scores of decisions like *Varner*, which regard frantic physical activity and frenetic travel as evidence of life-centered motivation, belong under that indictment.

The Dumay court did not, on the other hand, surrender its decision to the "experts." That would have added a new chapter to the long, unwholesome list of judicial problems which are falsely centered on a misuse of psychiatric and psychological information. The gift-in-contemplation-of-death problem is a legal problem; if psychology is relevant to its solution, it is a psychology which is embedded in the legal problem and which must be understood and applied by the officers who are commissioned to solve legal problems. Psychology is indispensable in bringing data to the process, but psychology as it is presently derived in the adversary system, through adversary expert witnesses, often dilutes its scientific integrity, and does not serve the law well.[103] This is not to disagree with Dr. Redmount's creative suggestion that courts seek the cooperation of behavioral scientists in solving factual problems in cases which involve human behavior. It is to disagree with the common reaction that the solution to problems which fairly involve psychological science is to assign the decision to competing expert witnesses. One sound alternative would be to develop general legislative and judicial policies around the available "legislative facts" on the way people develop and act upon their attitudes toward death. Dr. Redmount's suggestion aims instead at evidentiary fact finding; but neither suggestion—and I am pleased to note that we seem to agree on the point—involves the expert witness.

3. *Appropriate Death.* "[T]he purpose of living," according to Weisman and Hackett, "is to create a world in which we would be willing to die." And an appropriate death is a death in that kind of world; it is a death which the dying man sees and accepts as his own. This insight is at work in the *Dumay* opinion, particularly when the court discusses the transfer of the house; the house is seen as involved in Dumay's appropriate death.

Weisman and Hackett developed their concept out of three years of clinical psychiatric practice on the surgical wards of Massachusetts General Hospital; it is the product of thorough examination of five cases; the five cases are the product of some 600 consultations. Each of the five patients analyzed had predilection of death—a realistic acceptance of death. The predilection is not necessarily psychopathological; the patient is "firmly convinced of approaching death but regards it as wholly appropriate and shows little depression and no anxiety." These were not cases of psychic death, where anxiety (at, for instance, impending surgery) *causes* death; the predilection patient had, on the contrary, "come to terms with life and with people." His attitude was the opposite of suicidal, even though some of the patients suffered intensely and without hope of survival. These unfortunate people were what Shneidman classifies as unintentioned toward death (cessation-welcomers or cessation-acceptors) rather than intentioned (cessation-seekers or cessation-initiators). They were people who knew and accepted and imminence of death, and sometimes even the time and manner of death; one of them resisted his psychiatrist's attempts to console him; "he considered it strange that anyone should attempt to talk him out of death when everything in his experience pointed to its appropriateness at this point in his life." It was almost characteristic of these patients that family and physicians were the ones who needed to be consoled. It was often the patient himself who acted as consoler.

Death in these cases was not necessarily related to the ailment which caused hospitalization. One patient was being treated for ovarian carcinoma (cancer), but died of a myocardial infarction (heart attack); another was being treated for bone fractures and died of pulmonary embolism (blood clot in the lung).

These patients accepted dying as part of living and participated in their own deaths. "Life *as it is lived* has more parameters than there are laboratory methods available to use them; death encompasses the human personality as much as life does." The evidence is that the distinction between dying and living gradually fades in this sort of "natural" (human?) death, and that anxieties about death, fantasies of rescue from it, depression, and suicidal impulses also fade.

Weisman and Hackett accept the Freudian dogma that it is impossible to conceive of oneself as dead. This makes it difficult for them to explain how the appropriate-death phenomenon works. The explanation they choose is derived from their conclusion that subjective death (death seen as happening to me, and not simply as a process but as a subjective reality) always involves some fantasy of survival.* "If there is some meaning or emotion in the phrase, 'When I am dead,' there is also a trace of psychological survival in which 'I' continue to exercise an influence in some form or other. . . . The notion of 'I am dead' is a paradox." (An interesting instance of this among their patients was a career woman who felt humiliated by her illness and who welcomed death because it would restore her dignity.) With this explanation, Weisman and Hackett see the appropriate death as involving these features:

> . . . (1) there is quiet acceptance that death is a solution to abiding problems, or that few problems remain at the time of death;

---

*They see death as personified in any one of three ways: (1) impersonal ("it," a corpse, is dead), (2) interpersonal ("he," a person, is dead), and (3) intrapersonal ("I," a subject am dead). This last category has a dual aspect, which they treat as (a) attitudes toward the process of dying and (b) attitudes toward subjective death.

(2) superego demands [the demands of conscience] are reduced; (3) optimal interpersonal relations are maintained; and (4) the ego [consciousness] is encouraged to operate at as high a level as may be compatible with the physical illness.

"Appropriate death" is therefore, in their view, a uniquely personal way to approach the grim reaper. Everyone's death is (or can be) his own. This scientific conclusion supports the federal judiciary's attempt to resolve gift-in-contemplation-of-death cases one at a time, in what we have been calling a psychological autopsy. It may not, of course, support the legislative wisdom of imposing that pathologist's office on judges.

The judges in this third composite case appear to me to have thought that John Richard Dumay died an appropriate death, a death in which the house transfer was central to his predilection. The court, without any systematic disclosure of its psychological processes, appears to have concluded that Dumay calmly accepted his death; that he saw it as problem-resolving rather than problem-creating; that he was not found to be tense or anxious or ambivalent about it; that he maintained "optimal interpersonal relations" with those he loved as the end of his life approached; and that he continued to live his conscious life at a high level.

Appropriate death rests on some personal conception of immortality, though, on what Weisman and Hackett see as a survival fantasy, and on what Shneidman's treats as the post-self concept. That part of Dumay's death seems to have involved his house and plans in reference to his house which were psychologically similar to will-making, to testamentary activity.

The court seems to have been sound, as a matter of judicial policy, in holding that testamentary activity is in contemplation of death. The mistake other courts have made is in adopting the converse view, that contemplation-of-death activity is always testamentary. The statutory concept seems to me to have been broader than that, but Dumay is seen here as being well within both concepts. The court sees him as attached to his children and anxious to provide for them appropriately (for his daughter's care and for his son's business future). He was personally involved with his house; it was somehow a part of, an extension of, his personality.[104] In giving it to his wife and daughter, he reached out to them, and expressed love and concern for them, and envisioned a human relationship with them (care at least and maybe love) which would survive his own death. It was a very beautiful example of what will-making is all about, and it was accepted by the court as beautiful. The house transfer was an appropriate part of Dumay's appropriate death, just as his growing vegetables or painting the front door was an appropriate part of his life.[105]

Notes

1. Fatter v. Usry, 20 A.F.T.R.2d, para. 147,154 (E.D. La. 1967) (Rubin, J.).

2. See generally Lowndes and Kramer; Lowndes and Stephens; Riecker; Kimbrell; Hochman and Lindsay.

3. United States v. Wells, 283 U.S. 102 (1931).

4. Shukert v. Allen, 273 U.S. 545 (1927); see Lowndes and Kramer, note 2 supra at 81-82; Wishard v. United States, 143 F.2d 704 (7th Cir. 1944); Estate of Hofford, 4 T.C. 542, 790 (1945).

5. Shneidman, *Orientations Toward Death: A Vital Aspect of the Study of Lives;* Shneidman, *Orientation Toward Cessation: A Reexamination of Current Modes of Death.*

6. Shneidman uses the word "psyde" as a prefix to these classifications, but he explains that he uses the Greek word as a synonym for "cessation"; when writing for lawyers, he uses the word "death."

7. See Mills, *Medicolegal Ramifications of Current Practices and Suggested Changes in Certifying Modes of Death,* which suggests a parallel between familiar elaborate systems of arriving at intention in negligence and criminal litigation (contributory negligence, assumption of risk, subtleties in workmen's compensation, etc.) and the prediction of levels of "self determinism" in attitudes toward death. This is similar to what judges do in Section 2035 cases, although judicial classifications have not yet been subjected to anything resembling Shneidman's elaborate rational taxonomy.

8. This ·is a composite of the following cases: Fatter v. Usry, 20 A.F.T.R.2d para. 147,154 (E.D. La. 1967); Kniskern v. United States, 232 F. Supp. 7 (S.D. Fla. 1964); American Trust Co. v. United States, 175 F. Supp. 185 (N.D. Cal. 1959); Estate of Want, 29 T.C. 1223 (1958); Estate of Hinds, 11 T.C. 314 (1948) *aff'd* 180 F. 2d 930 (5th Cir. 1950); Estate of Atwater, T.C.M. 44,375. The notes which follow the text are, through the end of the *Varner* opinion, the court's.

9. The same section in S2035(b), creates a statutory, rebuttable presumption that transfers within three years of death are in contemplation of death, and an irrebutable presumption that transfers

more than three years before death are not in contemplation of death. In addition to these specific presumptions, determinations of the Internal Revenue Service are presumptively correct. See Neal v. Commissioner 53 F.2d 806 (C.C.A. 8, 1931).

10. See Moylan v. United States, 18 A.F.T.R.2d 6240 (N.D.N.Y. 1966) (jury charge).

11. Tetzlaff, T.C.M. 43,034, *aff'd* 141 F.2d 8 (8th Cir. 1944); see Estate of Neilson, T.C.M. 67,219.

12. Neilson, Ibid., involved a trust for a retarded child, which is similar to the trust for Mrs. Cole in this case.

13. See Peck v. United States, 16 A.F.T.R.2d 6125 (M.D. Ga. 1965) (jury charge).

14. See Stiles v. United States, 2 A.F.T.R.2d 6391 (S.D. Fla. 1958) (jury charge).

15. Rhoads v. United States, 12 A.F.T.R.2d 6195 (E.D. Pa. 1963) (jury charge); see Farmers Loan and Trust Co. v. Bowers, 68 F.2d 916 (C.C.A. 2, 1934), *cert. den.* 296 U.S. 649 (1935); Denniston v. Commissioner, 106 F.2d 925 (C.C.A. 3 1939); Estate of Higgins, T.C.M. 50,132.

16. The decedent of Altendorf v. United States, 14 A.F.T.R.2d 6134 (D. N. Dak. 1964) (jury verdict for taxpayer), was a cheerful 85; in Estate of Johnson, 10 T.C. 680 (1948), he was more than 90; and in Metzger v. United States, 181 F.Supp. 830 (N.D. Oh. 1960), he was an optimistic alcoholic. See Carlson v. United States, 7 A.F.T.R.2d 1825 (D. Minn. 1960) (jury verdict for taxpayer).

17. Estate of Bond, T.C.M. 66,021; Estate of Flynn, T.C.M. 44,387.

18. Metzger v. United States, 181 F. Supp. 830, 834 (N.D. Oh. 1960).

19. Kentucky Trust Co. v. Glenn, 217 F.2d 462 (6th Cir. 1954).

20. Estate of Johnson, 10 T.C. 680 (1948).

21. T.C.M. 54,338.

22. T.C.M. 65,114.

23. For example, Gordon v. United States, 163 F. Supp. 542 (W.D. Mo. 1958); Peck v. United States, 16 A.F.T.R.2d 6125 (M.D. Ga. 1965) (jury charge); Stiles v. United States, 2 A.F.T.R.2d 6391 (S.D. Fla. 1958) (jury charge).

24. Ibid. at 6129.

25. Neal v. Commissioner, 53 F.2d 806 (C.C.A. 8, 1931); Willcuts v. Stoltze, 73 F.2d 868 (C.C.A. 8, 1934).

26. 53 F.2d 1042 (D. Dela. 1931).

27. Commissioner v. Gidwitz's Estate, 196 F.2d 813 (7th Cir. 1952), citing and quoting Allen v. Trust Co., 326 U.S. 630 (1946); United States Trust Co. v. United States, 23 F. Supp. 476 (Ct. Cl. 1938); *cert. den.* 307 U.S. 633 (1938); First National Bank of Birmingham v. United States, 25 F. Supp. 816 (N.D. Ala. 1934) (knowledge in family, but not in decedent); Estate of Wolfe v. United States, 10 A.F.T.R.2d 6292 (E.D. Tex. 1962) (jury charge); Seattle-First National Bank v. United States, 11 A.F.T.R.2d 1824 (W.D. Wash. 1963): "The decedent did not at any time have any serious thought of death or the imminence thereof. . . ." T.C.M. 46,216; T.C.M. 51,326; T.C.M. 66,044.

28. See Estate of Larsh, T.C.M. 49,221; Estate of VanDever, T.C.M. 52,352.

29. See Estate of Martin, T.C.M. 43,498; Estate of Burr, T.C.M. 45,364.

30. See Estate of Awrey, 5 T.C. 222 (1945).

31. Estate of Delaney, 1 T.C. 781 (1943); see Estate of Vardell, 35 T.C. 50 (1960); Estate of Macaulay, 3 T.C. 350 (1944); Estate of Fry, 9 T.C. 503 (1947); Estate of Fleishmann, T.C.M. 54,111.

32. T.C.M. 54,338; see Estate of Hite, 49 T.C. 580 (1968); T.C.M. 55,239: "A man who is not in good health may, nevertheless, make a transfer which is . . . for purposes connected with life"; 10 T.C. 680 (1948).

33. T.C.M. 43,034, at p. 43-107: "[H]is interest in and care for his health indicates that he was devoting his attention and thought to the extension of his life as long as possible."

34. See Peck v. United States, 16 A.F.T.R.2d 6125 (M.D. Ga., 1965) (jury charge).

35. For example, Estate of Jacobson, T.C.M. 50,301.

36. See Estate of Neilson, T.C.M. 67,219.

37. Estate of MacDonald, T.C.M. 51,326: "We cannot overlook the fact that the decedent appears as interested in what his family thought,

during his lifetime, but indifferent to their views after his death."

38. See Estate of Maxwell, T.C.M. 44,366, and compare it with Metzger v. United States, 181 F. Supp. 830 (N.D. Oh. 1960).

39. 53 F.2d 1042 (D. Dela. 1931). See also Dunn V. United States, 1968 Prentice-Hall para. 147,235 (S.D. Ill. 1968) (jury charge); Estate of Mills, T.C.M. 46,216; Rea v. Heiner, 6 F.2d 389, 391 (W.D. Pa. 1925); "The week before she died, she drove to Pittsburgh three times, was preparing to go to Canada for the summer, making arrangements for building a boathouse and seawall there, and for changing the barn and building a dairy on the farm at home"; Beeler v. Motter, 33 F.2d 788 (D. Kan. 1928).

40. 61 F.2d 113 (C.C.A. 3, 1932); 285 U.S. 312 (1932).

41. 196 F.2d 813, 815 (7th Cir. 1952).

42. 15 F. Supp. 417 (D. Mass. 1936).

43. Bradley v. Smith, 114 F.2d 161 (C.C.A. 7, 1940); Tait v. Safe Deposit and Trust Co., 74 F.2d 851 (C.C.A. 4, 1935); Brown v. Commissioner, 74 F.2d 281 (C.C.A. 10, 1934). This factor was held not determinative, though, in United States v. Tonkin, 150 F.2d 531 (C.C.A. 3, 1945); Buckminster's Estate v. Commissioner, 147 F.2d 331 (C.C.A. 2, 1944); Northern Trust Co. v. Commissioner, 116 F.2d 96 (C.C.A. 7, 1940); Updike v. Commissioner, 88 F.2d 807 (C.C.A. 8, 1937); cert. den. 301 U.S. 708 (1936); and Stubblefield v. United States, 6 F. Supp. 440 (Ct. Cl. 1934). See United States v. Wells, 283 U.S. 102 (1931).

44. In re Kroger's Estate, 145 F.2d 901 (6th Cir. 1944); Flannery v. Willcuts, 25 F.2d 951 (C.C.A. 8, 1928); Poor v. White, 8 F. Supp. 995 (D. Mass. 1934); Welsh v. Hassett, 15 F. Supp. 692 (D. Mass. 1936), rev'd on other grounds 90 F.2d 833 (C.C.A. 1, 1937), aff'd 303 U.S. 303 (1938); Estate of Ridgely v. United States, 20 A.F.T.R.2d 5946 (Ct. Cl. 1967). Estate of Fleischmann, T.C.M. 54,111; Estate of Hinde, T.C.M. 52,016; Estate of O'Neal, T.C.M. 47,167; Estate of Cook, 9 T.C. 563 (1947); Estate of Burr, T.C.M. 45,364; Estate of Koussevitsky, 5 T.C. 656 (1945).

45. Estate of Vardell, 35 T.C. 50 (1960); Estate of Ackel, T.C.M. 58,027; Estate of Weir, 17 T.C. 409 (1951); Estate of Macaulay, 3 T.C. 354 (1944).

46. Estate of Green, T.C.M. 45,086; Estate of Bickerstaff, T.C.M. 42,358.

47. Estate of Johnson, 10 T.C. 680 (1948).

48. Lorenz discusses and compares the Freudian "death wish" theory with his ethological findings and relates both to Margolin's study of Ute Indians. Goody discusses property transfers *propter mortem* in primitive societies in Africa.

49. See Hutschnecker; Glaser and Strauss; Eissler; Joseph; Weisman and Hackett. Some federal judges demonstrate similar insight. See Gregg v. United States, 13 F. Supp. 147 (Ct. Cl. 1936); Kengel v. United States, 57 F.2d 929 (Ct. Cl. 1932). The facts in Estate of Kent, T.C.M. 47,233, are the kind of facts these psychological researchers talk about.
    Ridden v. Thrall, 125 N.Y. 572, 26 N.E. 627 (1891), is an interesting, largely implied judicial recognition of the fact that men somehow foresee in their tissues not only the time of death but maybe even the occasion of death. The decedent there had given property *causa mortis* as he was about to undergo a relatively minor operation. He died from a heart ailment, shortly after surgery. The question was whether he contemplated the cause of death and the court held that he did, even though his physician did not. See also CALIFORNIA CIVIL CODE §§ 1150-53 (codifying property rules on gifts "in view of death").

50. Feifel, *Attitudes of Mentally Ill Patients Toward Death;* Jung, *The Soul and Death;* Stern, Williams, and Prados, *Grief Reactions in Later Life.* Rogers reports a course of psychotherapy which took a sudden, sharp turn for the worse when the patient ("client") was about to leave for a vacation trip. The reported interview and diary material surrounding this event is filled with allusions to death. See the psychological sources in note 69 supra, and Fox.

51. The collection of suicide notes in Shneidman and Farberow, *Clues to Suicide,* is a heart-rending evidence to the contrary.

52. This is a composite of the following cases: Hoover v. United States, 180 F. Supp. 601 (Ct. Cl. 1960); Abbett, 17 T.C. 1293 (1952); Carr, T.C.M. 52,118; Estate of Belknap, T.C.M. 51,243; Estate of Davis, T.C.M. 52,238; and Estate of Goldberg, T.C.M. 51,303. The characters and, to some extent, their personalities, are taken in part from C.P. Snow's novel, *The Conscience of the Rich* (1960). The footnotes which follow, through the end of the opinion, are the court's.

53. The statute seems to compel this negative formulation. See the forms of verdict used in Jefferies v. United States, 19 A.F.T.R.2d para. 147,125 (D. Tex. 1966), and the court's explanation of the issue in Smith v. United States, 4 A.F.T.R.2d 6108 (D. Utah 1959). See also Estate of Brockway, 18 T.C. 479 (1952); MacDonald v. United States, 12 A.F.T.R.2d 6191 (E.D. Tenn. 1956).

54. Allen v. Trust Co., 326 U.S. 630 (1946); Llewellyn v. United States, 40 F.2d 555 (D. Tenn. 1929); Vaughan v. Riordan, 280 Fed. 742 (W.D. N.Y. 1921); Estate of Hopper, 22 T.C. 138 (1954); Estate of Coffin, T.C.M. 50,303; Estate of McCulloch, T.C.M. 49,023; Estate of Engel, T.C.M. 47,104; Estate of Burr, T.C.M. 45,364; Estate of Smith, T.C.M. 43,053.

55. Estate of Weaver, T.C.M. 52,320 (decedent's husband had died two years before the transfer at issue); Estate of Hofford, 4 T.C. 542 (1945).

56. Estate of Higgins, T.C.M. 50,132; United States Trust Co. v. United States, 23 F. Supp. 476 (Ct. Cl. 1938), *cert. den.* 307 U.S. 633 (1938). Estate of Jacobsen, T.C.M. 50,301.

57. See Neal v. Commissioner, 53 F.2d 806 (C.C.A. 8, 1931), where the decedent's rapidly declining health was undoubtedly related to the recent death of his wife. United States Trust Company v. United States, 23 F. Supp. 476 (Ct. Cl. 1938), *cert. den.* 307 U.S. 633 (1938), is a similar situation, but the court held for the Government. Estate of Spiegle, T.C.M. 52,299, is also similar on the facts but the court does not discuss this factor.

58. 20 A.F.T.R.2d para. 147,154 (E.D. La. 1967).

59. Estate of Budd, T.C.M. 45,192.

60. Estate of Coffin, T.C.M. 54,338.

61. Estate of Stinchfield, T.C.M. 45,168, *rev'd on other grounds* 161 F.2d 555 (9th Cir. 1947).

62. 68 F.2d 642 (C.C.A. 7, 1934); see also Brown v. Commissioner, 74 F.2d 281 (C.C.A. 10, 1934).

63. In re Kroger's Estate, 145 F.2d 901 (6th Cir. 1944). Lippincott v. Commissioner, 72 F.2d 788 (C.C.A. 3, 1934); Terhune v. Welch, 39 F. Supp. 430 (D. Mass. 1941), *rev'd on other grounds* 126 F.2d 695 (1st Cir. 1942) ("a present arrangement of his affairs in view of his coming marriage"); Estate of Want, 29 T.C. 1223 (1958) (in which transfers were to protect the decedent's daughter from a lady-friend); Estate of Barad, T.C.M. 54,082. See Studebaker v. United States, 211 F. Supp. 263 (N.D. Ind. 1962); Estate of Rosebault, 12 T.C. 1, (1949); Estate of Henry, T.C.M. 57,079.

64. Belyea's Estate v. Commissioner, 206 F.2d 262 (3d Cir., 1953).

65. Wishard v. United States, 143 F.2d 704 (7th Cir. 1944); DesPortes

v. United States, 171 F. Supp. 598 (E.D. S. Car. 1959); Estate of Hinds, 11 T.C. 314 (1948).

66. DesPortes v. United States, 171 F. Supp. 598 (E.D. S. Car. 1959).

67. Estate of Hinds, 11 T.C. 314 (1948).

68. Igleheart v. Commissioner, 77 F.2d 704 (C.C.A. 5, 1935); Neal v. Commissioner, 53 F.2d 806 (C.C.A. 8, 1931).

69. Ibid., at 808 the court quoted a letter *written by the decedent* which accompanied the gift: "I hope you will keep this present intact as much as possible, and will enjoy the income therefrom the rest of your life. I trust you will see fit to, in turn, divide this gift between your children when you get ready to provide for their welfare when you are gone." See the factors outlined in the jury charge in Robinson v. United States, 8 A.F.T.R.2d 6082 (N.D. N.Y. 1961).

70. Wishard v. United States, 143 F.2d 704 (C.C.A. 7, 1944). Estate of Metz, T.C.M. 51,302.

71. Igleheart v. Commissioner, 77 F.2d 704 (C.C.A. 5, 1935); Estate of Hite, 49 T.C. No. 64 (1968).

72. Russell v. United States, 260 F. Supp. 493, 503 (N.D. Ill. 1966): "The dominant motive prompting the transfer was that of insuring that her grandchildren, whose presence was a source of happiness to her, would remain as tenants of the building in which she resided." See Estate of Baxter v. United States, 22 A.F.T.R.2d 6047 (D. Ark. 1968).

73. United States Trust Co. v. United States, 23 F. Supp. 476 (Ct. Cl. 1938), *cert. den.* 307 U.S. 633 (1938); McGregor v. Commissioner, 82 F.2d 948 (C.C.A. 1, 1936); Estate of Barad, T.C.M. 54,082; Estate of Haley, T.C.M. 51,244.

74. Willcuts v. Stoltze, 73 F.2d 868 (C.C.A. 8, 1934) (promise to late wife); Studebaker v. United States, 211 F. Supp. 263 (N.D. Ind. 1962); Estate of Rosebault, 12 T.C. 1 (1949). See Dunn v. United States, 22 A.F.T.R.2d para. 6039 (S.D. Ill. 1968). Belyea's Estate v. Commissioner, 206 F.2d 262 (3d Cir. 1953) (involving, however, a series of lifetime gifts); Estate of Cowan, T.C.M. 1965-113; Estate of Baxter v. United States, 22 A.F.T.R.2d 6047 (D. Ark. 1968).

75. DesPortes v. United States, 171 F. Supp. 598, 602 (E.D. S. Car. 1959).

76. See Schuyler, *The Art of Interpretation in Future Interests Cases,* 17 Vanderbilt L. Rev. 1407 (1964); Halbach, *Stare Decisis and*

Rules of Construction in Wills. 52 Calif. L. Rev. 921 (1964).

77. "Intention" can be given a medieval definition in this context: "Intentional characteristics represent above all else the individual's primary modes of addressing himself to the future." Allport, *Becoming* 89 (1955).

78. One might start with Feifel, Fulton, Shneidman and Farberow, and Farberow and Allport. And one should not neglect Eissler, Joseph, and other clinical information. Federal tax lawyers seem to eschew these subtleties in favor of trying the decedent as a tax evader. See Robinson v. United States, 8 A.F.T.R.2d 6082 (N.D. N.Y. 1961).

79. Green, *The Rationale of Proximate Cause* (1927); Green, *Judge and Jury* (1930).

80. This case is based upon the following: Hull's Estate v. Commissioner, 325 F.2d 367 (3d Cir. 1963); Garrett's Estate v. Commissioner, 180 F.2d 955 (2d Cir. 1950); Kaufmann v. Reinecke, 68 F.2d 642 (C.C.A. 7, 1934); Yeazel v. Coyle, 21 A.F.T.R.2d 1681 (N.D. Ill. 1968); Estate of Casey, 25 T.C. 707 (1956); and Estate of Howard, 9 T.C. 1192 (1947). The names are taken from Iris Murdoch's novel, *The Red and the Green* (1965). The remainder of the footnotes, through the end of the opinion, are the court's.

81. The parties have stipulated as controlling value for estate-tax purposes the value specified in the agreement.

82. 181 F. Supp. 748, 750 (S.D. N.Y. 1959).

83. In Safe Deposit and Trust Co. v. Tait, 3 F. Supp. 51 (D. Md. 1933), *aff'd* 70 F.2d 59 (C.C.A. 3, 1933), an income-tax saving, on advice of counsel, of about 20 percent, was held to override even evidence of age and ill health. Estate of Howell, T.C.M. 43,047, Estate of Ackel, T.C.M. 58,027, and Harrison T.C.M. 58,157, are similar. Here health and attitude were good—see Estate of Rosebault, 12 T.C. 1 (1949)—which adds, as in Estate of Sheldon, 27 T.C. 194 (1956), a potent additional factor. See Becker v. St. Louis Trust Co., 296 U.S. 48 (1935); Commissioner v. Hofheimer's Estate, 149 F.2d 733 (2d Cir. 1945); Rowe v. Fahs, Prentice-Hall Tax Reporter (1968), para. 120,353.4 (D. Fla. 1954); Poor v. White, 8 F. Supp. 995 (D. Mass. 1934); Vaughan v. Riordan, 280 Fed. 742 (W.D. N.Y. 1921); Estate of Minzesheimer, T.C.M. 54,222; Estate of Hinde, T.C.M. 52,016; Estate of Haley, T.C.M. 51,244; Estate of Farnum 14 T.C. 884 (1950); Estate of Cook, 9 T.C. 563 (1947); Estate of Bendet, T.C.M. 46,098; Estate of Stinchfield, T.C.M. 45,168; Estate of Howell, T.C.M. 43,047.

84. Vanderlip v. Commissioner, 155 F.2d 152, 154 (2d Cir. 1946) (L.

Hand, J.):

> [A] donor, interested in saving [estate] taxes, is not concerned with the donee's enjoyment while he himself lives; he is interested in relieving his legatees from taxes after he dies, and, not only may his legatees not be the donees, but when they are, their relief will not concern their enjoyment of the property while he lives. Such a motive is necessarily testamentary. . . .

85. Estate of Flynn, T.C.M. 44,387.

86. Estate of Mollenkamp v. United States, 11 A.F.T.R.2d 1819, 1821 (D. Kan. 1963). This is not like Estate of Goar, T.C.M. 50,242, where the court felt the dominant motive was post-death support for children and discounted the probative value of evidence that the decedent was concerned about the management of his business.

87. This may resemble anthropological information about certain primitive farmers who gradually turn over parts of their farms to their sons as they retire; see Estate of Pearson, T.C.M. 52,092, an American analogue; the court held that the transfers there were not in contemplation of death: "The decedent enjoyed life, resented being thought of as old and never spoke of death." See Estate of Baxter v. United States, 22 A.F.T.R.2d 6047 (D. Ark. 1968).

88. Estate of Goldberg, T.C.M. 51,303.

89. Becker v. St. Louis Trust Co., 296 U.S. 48 (1935); Pate v. Commissioner, 149 F.2d 669 (8th Cir. 1945); Koch v. Commissioner, 146 F.2d 256 (9th Cir. 1944); Smails v. O'Malley, 127 F.2d 410 (8th Cir. 1942).

90. Welch v. Hassett, 90 F.2d 833 (C.C.A. 1, 1937), aff'd 303 U.S. 303 (1938); Lippincott v. Commissioner, 72 F.2d 788 (C.C.A. 3, 1934); Schwab v. Doyle, 269 Fed. 321 (C.C.A. 6,1920); Estate of Hopper, 22 T.C. 138 (1954); Estate of Macaulay, 3 T.C. 350 (1944).

91. The distinction between purchase and transfer was determinative in Aaron's Estate v. Commissioner, 224 F.2d 314 (3d Cir. 1955).

92. Estate of Israel, T.C.M. 44,401.

93. Estate of Mudge, 27 T.C. 188 (1956).

94. Estate of Want, 29 T.C. 1223 (1958).

95. Colorado Bank v. Commissioner, 305 U.S. 23, 27 (1938).

96. Clear testamentary equivalence should result in judgment for the Government. Pate v. Commissioner, 149 F.2d 669 (8th Cir. 1945); Oliver v. Bell, 103 F.2d 760 (C.C.A. 3, 1939); Purvin v. Commissioner, 96 F.2d 929 (C.C.A. 7, 1938); Anneke v. Willcuts, 1 F. Supp. 662 (D. Minn. 1932); Estate of Gidwitz, 14 T.C. 1263 (1950: *but see* Estate of Farnum, 14 T.C. 884 (1950). However, time, or concern for support, or the size of the gift, may indicate a contrary result. Denniston v. Commissioner, 106 F.2d 925 (C.C.A. 3, 1939); Routzahn v. Brown, 95 F.2d 766 (C.C.A. 6, 1938); Estate of Smith, T.C.M. 43,053. See Smails v. O'Malley, 127 F.2d 410 (8th Cir. 1940).

97. Estate of Selnes v. United States, 1 A.F.T.R.2d 2141 (D. Minn. 1957).

98. Ibid.

99. In Stubblefield v. United States, 6 F. Supp. 440 (Ct. Cl. 1934), a similar situation we think, the decedent was almost unbalanced in the literal obliteration of his property ownership. This sort of obliteration was determinative in Buckminster's Estate v. Commissioner, 147 F.2d 331 (2d Cir. 1944); Northern Trust Co. v. Commissioner, 116 F.2d 96 (7th Cir. 1940); Purvin v. Commissioner, 96 F.2d 929 (C.C.A. 7, 1938); Updike v. Commissioner, 88 F.2d 807 (C.C.A. 8, 1937), relying on Igleheart v. Commissioner, 77 F.2d 704 (C.C.A. 5, 1935), and on Rengstorff v. McLaughlin, 21 F.2d 177 (N.D. Cal. 1927); and in Tait v. Safe Deposit and Trust Co., 74 F.2d 851 (C.C.A. 4, 1935). Welch v. Hassett, 15 F. Supp. 692 (D. Mass. 1936), *rev'd on other grounds* 90 F.2d 833 (C.C.A. 1, 1937), *aff'd* 303 U.S. 303 (1938), and Lippincott v. Commissioner, 72 F.2d 788 (C.C.A. 3, 1934), are to the contrary but seem to turn on special circumstances. See Koch v. Commissioner, 146 F.2d 259 (9th Cir. 1944); Llewellyn v. United States, 40 F.2d 555 (D. Tenn. 1929); Vaughan v. Riordan, 280 Fed. 742 (W.D. N.Y. 1921); and Gaither v. Mills, 268 Fed. 692 (D. Md. 1920).

100. MacDonald v. United States, 12 A.F.T.R.2d 6191 (E.D. Tenn. 1956).

101. 61 F.2d 113 (C.C.A. 3, 1932), a chapter in the leading case reported at 285 U.S. 312 (1932).

102. This comes from Dr. Shneidman's lecture at the University of Notre Dame, April 27, 1969.

103. Halleck, *The Psychiatrist and the Legal Process*, Psychology Today, February, 1969, p. 25.

104. Here is the sort of judicial insight I have in mind, from Kengel v. United States, 57 F.2d 929, 935 (Ct. Cl. 1932):

It is abundantly proved that Joseph Kengel was a frugal and astute businessman; he knew full well the value of property and the consequences which might follow his parting irrevocably with title to it in his own name, and as we view it must have appreciated what it meant to him to deed it to another; a transaction of such consequences to such an active, careful, and prudent man justifies the inference, to say the least, that the time had arrived when he confidently believed he would have no further use for it.

See also Welch v. Hassett, 15 F. Supp. 692 (D. Mass. 1936), *rev'd on other grounds* 90 F.2d 833 (C.C.A. 2, 1937), *aff'd* 303 U.S. 303 (1938); Estate of Henry, T.C.M. 57,079. It is important to distinguish this view of death as appropriate from what Shneidman calls social death. The two are opposites; one is realistic and one not. Withdrawal, social death, is neurotic. Jung, *Psychological Reflections:*

The neurotic who tries to escape from the necessities of life gains nothing and only takes upon his shoulders the fearful burden of age and death tasted in advance, which must be especially cruel because of the total emptiness and pointlessness of his life. When the libido is denied a progressive life which also desires all dangers and decay, then it follows the other road and buries itself in its own depths. . . .

The predilection patient sees death coming when it really is coming. He, in a way, welcomes it. Jung, *Modern Man in Search of a Soul:*

I am convinced that it is hygienic—if I may use the word—to discover in death a goal towards which one can strive; and that shrinking away from it is something unhealthy and abnormal which robs the second half of life of its purpose.

105. Four purposes were suggested at the beginning of this chapter, any one or more of which I thought might be served by applying the psychological autopsy to cases under Section 2035. The first of these purposes related to the wisdom of retaining a provision taxing "gifts in contemplation of death." A conclusion on that score is relatively simple: Section 2035 is troublesome and wasteful. It has probably not produced enough revenue to pay the court costs for the hundreds of losing cases the Internal Revenue Service has brought under it. And it has never had the *in terrorem* effect it was designed to have. It rests on what is undoubtedly an archaic view of the federal government's constitutional power to tax and should probably be replaced with a resurrected provision imposing a tax on all transfers within three years of death.

The second purpose of the inquiry was to test the judicial wisdom of a subjective test for the word "contemplate" (as compared with an objective test for the word "intended"). That judicial response to

Section 2035 has been administratively unsound; a test based upon the mechanical operation of Section 2035 would probably have produced less litigation than the subjective test has produced. Even a test which narrowed the question to whether or not the decedent intended to evade death taxes would probably operate more smoothly than Section 2035, as interpreted in *Wells*, has worked during the last thirty-eight years. The litigation has been a boon to the legal profession and a fertile source of conjecture for legal scholars, but it has probably not redounded to the public good—partly because it is uneconomical and partly because many judges have proven themselves to be callous psychological pathologists.

The third and fourth purposes of the chapter—inquiries into planning and trial tactics for Section 2035 cases, and behavioral inquiry into attitudes toward death and judicial attitudes toward attitudes toward death—are more fully illuminated by a psychological analysis of the cases and by the comments of the psychologists who contributed to this chapter. Both of those purposes seem to me to be summarized in the *Dumay* opinion and in the judicial opinions on which it was based. This composite case suggests a realistic psychological point of view. Advocates have almost literally never used psychological learning in building cases under Section 2035; judges have not consulted psychological information. The result has been a wide array of attitudes and assumptions which are either untested or patently unsound; recent psychological research on attitudes toward death is correcting similar errors in the behavioral sciences; this scholarship is useful to advocates who are able to build their cases on accurate psychological theory, and to judges who are able to decide cases on the basis of scientific conclusions. Judges and lawyers who bother to look will find this data available to them directly. They will find that they need not sift their interest through expert witnesses.

The fourth purpose is the most interesting to a lawyer who looks upon contemplation of death as something relevant both to his law-office practice and to his life in the courts. Judges in Section 2035 cases, even if they are often inaccurate, are not always callous men. Many of their opinions are searching inquiries into the way men feel about death, inquiries into how we relate our property to our deaths and to the people we love. These judicial opinions, in other words, are research reports on how the decedent felt about his death; and they are exhibitions as well of the way the judge feels about his own death. They range from the insensitive (*Varner*) to the confused and defensive (*March*) to a judicial openness that is instructive and even inspiring (*Dumay*). The *Wells* Court caused lawyers and judges more effort and dismay than it could have predicted when it decreed that "there is no escape from the necessity of carefully scrutinizing the circumstances of each case." As a matter of tax policy, the struggle has not been worth the grain of objective inquiry it has provided. But as a means of exploring what Judge Rubin called the "heap of collection of different perceptions," the "elusive shadow from the recesses of the mind," which make up a personal psychology of death, the cases are important to lawyers as counselors and as thoughtful men.

7   Testamentary Relationships and the Transference Concept

This chapter attempts to describe a common human relationship as it has been developed in two traditions which are today largely separated from one another. The relationship is referred to as "confidential" in the law and as "transference" in psychoanalytical psychology. Legal insight on the phenomenon is found mainly in the appellate literature on gratuitous transfers obtained by undue influence; psychological insight occurs in the practice and speculation of therapists who have discovered the phenomenon in psychotherapy. Both traditions are useful in understanding the confidential or transference factor in human interaction. The interaction itself has impact beyond the appellate cases or the practice of psychotherapy. It is, for one relevant instance, of central importance in legal counseling.

A Psychiatric Case Study of Transference and the Law

One of the clinical case reports in Dr. K. R. Eissler's book, *The Psychiatrist and the Dying Patient*, suggests a model that might integrate both aspects of the prototype undue influence case—the legal tradition and the psychodynamics of what is known, in the legal tradition, as "confidential relationship."

Dr. Eissler treated a dying, middle-aged woman during the last three years of her life, from an early point in her last illness until she died. He

I am grateful for assistance in this chapter given by Mr. Patric Doherty and Mr. Richard Farina of the staff of the *Notre Dame Lawyer*.

then became defendant in a lawsuit involving her will; her family contended he had exercised undue influence on his patient.

Dr. Eissler treated this lady during three periods in the last three years of her life. She first consulted him, for about three months, while her husband was dying. A second treatment period of about eight months commenced after the husband's death and terminated when the patient moved away from Dr. Eissler's city. When she returned, about ten months later, treatment was resumed. This final phase ended with the patient's death fourteen months after the latest resumption of therapy.

Treatment during the periods immediately before and after the husband's death consisted largely of resolving the woman's "slavish dependency" upon her husband and converting her from a "social doll" to a self-reliant and competent businesswoman able to take over her dead husband's affairs. Dr. Eissler's prognosis was optimistic when she left his care to build a new life in another state.

The terminal phase of treatment began when the patient returned to her husband's old home and again consulted Dr. Eissler:

> When I met her, her physical appearance alarmed me. She was paler than usual, underweight, and short of breath. She coughed from time to time but was sure that her physical symptoms as well as the nightly attacks of anxiety which had started a few weeks earlier were psychogenic. She had been carefully examined in O ——— as well as upon her arrival in C———, but no physical pathology responsible for the cough had been detected. She spoke with great anger of her relative, reporting a few incidents which had made her stay in O———unbearable and reproached me for ever having her go to O———. She was determined to stay in C———, never to return to O———, and to stand on her own feet from then on. She felt independent and was certain that she could now manage her affairs successfully, because she had left O———against her family's advice, had prepared the move alone, and had traveled alone, something of which she had previously been afraid. She was disturbed only by the reappearance of anxiety at night and by the cough. She begged me to help her in getting rid of these symptoms so that this time nothing would stand in the way of her fulfilling the great wish which she had had since early youth, namely to live an independent life. A brief exploration revealed that shortly before the onset of her nervous cough and anxiety, a person who had played an important role in her life had died. This suggested a connection between the nervous cough, the return of anxiety, and a feeling of guilt which she habitually tended to develop after the death of a person close to her.[1]

Dr. Eissler referred the patient for further physical examination, despite indications that she was not physically ill, and learned that she had "an inoperable malignancy. . . . [D]eath would prematurely stop the patient who had, against heavy odds, rallied all her resources in order to realize finally some of the potentialities which seemed to have been dormant in her."

Dr. Eissler and the internist who examined the patient agreed that she should not be told she was dying; they conspired in what they thought benign deceit and told her that she had a minor disorder. They decided that "she should be kept ignorant of the gravity of her state, encouraged to maintain her optimism and her morale, and prevented from falling into a depression." Dr. Eissler believed that a more candid relationship "would have precipitated severe psychopathology." (Dr. Eissler thinks that this involves a denial of death and a strong motivation to be free of the pain of death. This means that the patient wants the doctor to keep the fact of impending death a secret, even though the patient may in his fibers know that death is coming.)

At about this time (and possibly as evidence against Dr. Eissler's belief that she didn't know she was dying) the patient began to talk to him about her will:

> Shortly after her return from O _____ the patient had told me that if she knew she were dying, she would change her will instantly and distribute part of the money which had been allocated in a previous will to her quasi-adopted daughter to other relatives, who were in need of financial assistance. But since she was assured that her sickness was benign, she did not see any reason to proceed in a hurry. Pointedly—and evidently in order to test me—she added that she was certain that I, since I had never let her down, would tell her to make a will now if her life were in danger. A decision to make myself instrumental in the preservation of the patient's illusion of approaching recovery thus might have had detrimental consequences for some of her relatives, inasmuch as they would obtain less of her estate if she died prior to executing a new will. However, I decided that the patient's mental and emotional welfare had to be my paramount goal even though, if all circumstances were known to the members of her family, I would be liable to the justified complaints of those who might be injured by the patient's premature death. I am fully aware that I might be censured by some members of the medical and juridical professions for such an opinion, but I do not see how a different decision can be made if the patient's welfare is made the physician's uppermost goal, which, after all, it should be.

However, after some time—it was two weeks before her demise—she did decide to change her will and seemed relieved after she had accomplished this. From a previous experience I knew that she was the victim of superstitions with regard to the making of a will, and that she had to go through a struggle before she found enough resolution to do anything active in testamentary matters.[2]

That resolved, Dr. Eissler had to decide how he would handle his patient as the disease accomplished its final end—a painful, slow, disfiguring death. He decided to "make use of the strong affectionate tie which the patient had formed and of the feeling of omnipotence she had projected upon me." This was "contrary to the usual technique applied in treatment of neurotics, when the growth of transference beyond the physiological optimum must be immediately reduced to combat the patient's illusionary belief in the therapist's omnipotence." The regimen worked, or so Dr. Eissler thought at the time:

The outbreaks of anger against her relative softened, and when she expressed the feeling that she seemed able now to forgive her, she seemed well on the way to achieving internal peace. She died in her sleep, without every having consciously doubted that she was on the way to recovery, and to the end she believed that I had saved her life by sending her to an internist and that she would soon embark upon an active life in the pursuit of long-cherished ambitions.

The patient "died without conscious knowledge of the fatal nature of her disease," he says, "but was convinced—in conformity with the content of my communicatio s and those of the other physicians who treater her—that she suffered from a minor disorder." He had seen this lady before he knew that her disease was fatal, under a normal professional relationship (e.g., he billed her for his services), but he changed this procedure when he knew she was dying; from that point on he did not mention fees to her:

[U]nder ordinary circumstances this would be a strange procedure, and logically the patient should have inquired about it. However, during this period she took for granted my not bothering her with financial obligations and did not draw any conclusions, although one might have expected that this circumstance alone would have aroused her suspicion that an essential change must have occurred in her condition.[3]

Not only did Dr. Eissler give this lady free psychiatric treatment, he also presented gifts to her; both actions were, he says, a way of conveying "the therapist's animistic conviction of the patient's immortality," and "helped the patient to maintain a strongly represented future."

Shortly after the patient's death, Dr. Eissler was informed by counsel that she had named him executor of her will and had left him "a considerable legacy." After some soul-searching, he decided to refuse the legacy; he specified to counsel that it be given to charity. He accepted the executorship, however, because he thought he could thereby avoid family strife. The patient's heir then filed suit, alleging that Dr. Eissler's legacy was the result of his undue influence over the testatrix. The suit was ultimately settled—with Dr. Eissler receiving no benefit from the estate—but not without an obviously unsettling experience for the physician.

Dr. Eissler writes both as an expert in the psychodynamics of confidential relationship and as one who wears the scars of legal battle. He notes first of all that the usual relationship of "positive transference" had developed between himself and the patient—that is, she had fastened upon him emotions that were out of place in the reality of the doctor's office; she was, to oversimplify, inappropriately affectionate toward him. This affection was exhibited in bizarre as well as in normal conduct. Because she was wealthy, she had supposed that her money and her position entitled her to be demanding toward him—a situation she felt she could maintain by the offer of gifts, that is to say, by bribery. This patient had, however, surprised Dr. Eissler and "graciously assented to the repeated explanation [that] the acceptance of gifts would lead to a detrimental psycho-therapeutic situation"; she did not react as he had expected she would, "with unfriendliness or hostility to the feeling of rejection which unavoidably occurs when a gift is refused." Dr. Eissler later concluded that the relative ease with which he resolved her impulse to bribe him may have concealed her determination to make him a beneficiary in her will.

Dr. Eissler did not, of course, consciously manipulate the patient toward making her will in his favor. But, he admitted, "the patient nevertheless . . . acted under my influence and may have been psychologically as unfree as the person who is [as he understood it] under undue influence in terms of the law." And this suggested a possibility in his own state of mind—"an unconscious utilization of a transference or . . . unconscious opportunism." In this situation, "some wish, quite unconscious in the therapist, may nevertheless be perceived by the patient—probably also unconsciously—and then be reacted upon by the patient out of an intensive transference relationship." The likelihood of this happening varies, he thinks, with the intensity of the transference:

> Thus it is quite feasible that a therapist, even when motivated by irreproachably honest *conscious* motives, inadvertently creates in a patient the disposition toward giving him a gift. I do not need to construct all the possibilities of how this may happen. The question of interest here is: how can one ascertain that unconscious strivings colored the physician's behavior in such a way as to create a disposition of that kind in a patient? Evidently the therapist's assertion that he did not behave in a reproachable way is not decisive since the behavior concerns his unconscious and he therefore must be ignorant of it, in case such a striving should become operative. The therapist is here in a difficult situation. He is accused of unethical conduct of which he is supposed to be unconscious; he has no witnesses since psychotherapy does not accept the presence of a third party; and the victim of his allegedly unethical conduct cannot be questioned because she is dead.

There is another possibility, beyond the possibility that the doctor might manipulate the patient unconsciously: The doctor need not be unethical and need not be incompetent; the patient might act out the transference without stimulation, conscious or unconscious:

> But another and even more important aspect imposes itself. This patient undoubtedly acted under the influence of a strong transference. Since transference per se, and a strong transference even more, is comparable under certain circumstances to hypnotic states, the question may be raised whether the mere acting out of the transference is tantamount to acting under the impact of undue influence.

The possibility poses a serious dilemma for those who treat mental disease and who routinely exploit transference situations for therapeutic purposes:

> Transference . . . whether interpreted or not, is the essential lever of psychotherapy, as it is of psychoanalysis. In psychotherapy I prefer to use transference as much as possible through the everyday channels of interpersonal communication. The whole inventory of stimuli with which one person acts on the other stands here at the therapist's disposal. It depends on his knowledge and skill whether, on the one hand, these stimuli are used in

such a way as to reduce the patient's anxiety or the other emotions which block his access to reality-adjusted action, or, whether, on the other hand, they are used to facilitate the patient's access to the sources of pleasure and enjoyment at his disposal. The intensity of the transference which is necessary to accomplish these two goals varies from patient to patient. It was evident in this patient, who had suffered for many years from a serious disorder, that the optimum of transference was a very high one. Only if she felt reliably protected would she dare to develop that degree of activity which the particular circumstances of her life situation required.

The question which is of interest here concerns the extent to which a therapist must or may make himself the protector of the patient. I believe that in such instances as the one under discussion, when the patient had gone through a long series of highly traumatizing disappointments, there was scarcely an upper limit if the patient's confidence in the world and in herself was to be restored.

The dilemma is exceptionally keen in Dr. Eissler's therapy for dying patients; they, unlike patients who may be expected to survive psychoanalysis, need not have the transference dissolved. Their demand is for comfort and growth during a relatively short period of time, a period expected to end with death:

During the terminal phase, of course, the necessity for maintaining a maximum positive transference—if it still can be called transference—was evident, and any consideration of the problem of the patient's dependency would have become incongruous in the exigencies of the clinical situation. I trust it is not necessary to emphasize that these opinions concern exclusively the technique of psychotherapy and even within this area only exceedingly sick patients and emergency situations. To raise this question regarding the psychoanalytic technique proper would betray a misunderstanding and lack of comprehension of the basic fundament and the goal of that technique.

Dr. Eissler recognized that his patient-testatrix had developed a very strong transference and that she did not, therefore, "from the psychoanalytic point of view . . . act as a free agent when she included me in her will; she was under an undue influence. . . ." Not only that, but sound medical technique, in his opinion, presented him no alternative to putting the patient in a situation where she was motivated to make what lawyers have for years called an "unnatural" will. This was true despite complete innocence—and even precaution—on the part of the doctor:

Transference reactions are outside the scope of the ego's will power. The ego is victimized here by impulses which are beyond the strength of its regulative apparatuses. The patient had evolved a very strong transference; I was the only person in her environment whom she trusted and by whom she felt protected, and the seeming—seeming only as we shall see later—generosity of looking at me as an "object of her bounty" does not require the assumption of any foul play on the side of the psychiatrist, but rather it becomes explainable by considering well-known clinical facts.

The alternative for the psychiatrist is an austere and self-denying attitude toward the generosity of his patients:

> The particular and unique prominence which the transference acquires in mental treatment in turn requires particular and unique professional ethics for the worker in the field. Since only in mental treatment does the handling of the transference coincide with essential professional activity, the psychiatrist (and all the more, of course, the psychoanalyst) must take a different attitude toward the result of the positive transference than is necessary in any other profession. If the patient's attorney or surgeon had helped her to the extent I had done, and she had left a legacy to either of them, there would have been no objection to their accepting the bequest, although positive feelings of the transference nature might have been as much at work as they were in the patient's relationship to me. But in surgery and law practice "positive transference" is taken for granted as an unknown and undetermined factor for which the person who becomes the subject of the patient's or the client's "transference" does not carry responsibility in the way in which the psychotherapist does. If surgeons and lawyers do not intuitively handle transference correctly, they will soon be out of business, though they may be excellent surgeons or lawyers. If a psychotherapist or psychoanalyst does not handle transference in a therapeutically correct way, he may nevertheless increase his clientele, but he will not cure his patients, and therefore he must be considered a poor therapist despite the success he may have in his social group. The austerity which the therapist must impose on the patient must be equally valid for himself, and he cannot enjoy some of the benefits which other professions are permitted to enjoy. Therefore, I made a mistake when I initially thought my bequest could be used for charitable purposes. Even if this could be done in strict anonymity, without any benefit to the therapist's prestige, it still would have been against a self-evident and therefore unwritten basic principle.

The only exception to this austerity is the exception demanded by the treatment itself. "For example, in psychotherapy the refusal of a gift might end the transference; then the acceptance of the gift is put into the therapeutic process and has become necessitated by therapeutic requirements. . . ."

Dr. Eissler concluded, after reading a book on psychiatry and law (Guttmacher and Weihoffen), that this situation probably does not constitute undue influence in the legal sense, but his account suggests that he may have doubted whether this legal result is desirable. First he noted that transference, particularly in psychotherapy, may rise to an inordinate intensity. "All the latent strivings of a positive nature, desirous of giving and of expressing affection might become mobilized and focus upon the therapist. The intensity of these strivings in its relationship to the strength of the ego can be compared to a hypnotic state." Second, the patient may act on this emotional framework without any conscious activity by the therapist—and even without any unconscious activity. "[T] he patient's transference wish still may find a symbolic and factual gratification in giving the therapist a gift. In the situation of the dying this may easily lead to the psychiatrist's inclusion in the will of the patient who looks at him as an object of his bounty." He concluded—but I think tentatively—that the law probably ought not to regard such a will as invalid, but that medicine should, as a matter of ethics, not permit the psychiatrist to accept the legacy.*

Dr. Eissler's experience was a product of the coincidence of the most common of all psychotherapeutic phenomena—transference—and of an ancient legal principle that a person subject to extraordinary influence ought to be protected by the law from his own impulses. Dr. Eissler's problem was the result of the fact that he did not see the legal implications of a familiar and even beneficent affective relationship with his patient. And it may be that the legal tradition has not yet seen the psychological implications of its familiar and even beneficent rule against undue influence. The affinities seem to be significant; I assume that exploration of them will be useful to lawyers in three ways. First, the exploration may criticize what appear to be the modern contours of

---

*"It would actually lead to an infringement upon the patient's freedom if he could make a valid will only by excluding his psychiatrist." Dr. Eissler concluded from this that the psychiatrist should renounce the legacy. However, a distortion in the testator's plan is not so easily avoided; renunciation will benefit either a residuary legatee or intestate heirs. He also thinks his situation is peculiar to psychotherapy. But he is wrong in supposing that lawyers do not have to be governed by the same considerations. See Magee v. State Bar of California, 58 Cal. 2d 423, 374 P.2d. 807, 24 Cal. Rptr. 839 (1962).

the undue influence principle, particularly in wills cases. Second, in a more positive analysis, the psychotherapeutic insights may appear to have been foreshadowed in the legal insights, so that the process may become one of comparison—more of a matter of illumination than of criticism. Finally, consideration of the affective relationship between helping persons and those they help—the atmosphere in which Sigmund Freud first identified transference—may be useful to lawyers in counseling their clients. A principal benefit in any exploration of law and psychology is the benefit that comes to the lawyer as a counselor of troubled people.

Observations on Transference from
the Literature of Psychotherapy

> The enormous importance that Freud attached to the transference phenomenon became clear to me at our first personal meeting in 1907. After a conversation lasting many hours there came a pause. Suddenly he asked me out of the blue, "And what do you think about the transference?" I replied with the deepest conviction that it was the alpha and omega of the analytical method, whereupon he said, "Then you have grasped the main thing."
>
> *—C.G. Jung*

Transference Is a Specialized
Instance of the Ego Defense of Projection

One way to live with myself is to blame all my troubles on other people. It is comforting to find you crabby when in fact I am crabby. Psychology regards the maneuver as defensive; what I am defending is my conscious self, my ego; and the ego defense in this case is *projection.*

David Riesman gives an example of projection that should be familiar to lawyers. "Lawyers," he says, "learn not to take the law too seriously"—this as a product of legal education in "the art of debunking legal rituals and debunking authority, especially the authority of upper-court judges." The layman who consults a lawyer, on the other hand, consciously regards "the law"—and this concept includes the people who administer law and who create it—with awe, even though, unconsciously, he is cynical about the fairness and honesty of the legal process. He is surprised and even resentful when he finds that his lawyer takes "the law" lightly.

> [T]he layman is not quite sure how he feels about such a person, whose usefulness he may need and whose knowledge may

fascinate him; the more he needs him, the more he may be apt to project on to him his own tendencies to cynicism about authority and procedure.

In other words, the layman resents his lawyer because his lawyer's matter-of-factness about legal authority reminds him of a cynicism and fear that he will not admit to himself. Riesman suggests that this projection may explain why some clients demand of their lawyers emotional support and economic identification, even at the expense of effective advocacy.

Displacement is a kind of projection in which feelings toward one person are refocused on another person, or even on an animal or inanimate object.* For example, a patient has feelings for his doctor that were originally (and are really) the feelings he has for his father. Displacement is also defensive, as all projections are; by displacing his feelings a person may avoid confronting in a realistic way his relationship toward significant people. Commentators universally regard transference as a projection. Freudians tend to regard it as displacement projection; Jungians tend to regard it as projection without displacement. Brussel and Cantzlaar, who are Freudians, define transference as "unconscious displacement of libido, whereby the patient shifts his antagonism and libidinal attachments from the disturbing 'characters' in his underlying emotional conflict to [in therapy] the psychiatrist." Even Carl Rogers, who is no Freudian, sees transference as involving "attitudes transferred to the therapist which were originally directed, with more justification, toward a parent or other person."

Ernest Jones, one of the greatest of the original Freudians, defined transference in alternative ways. Sometimes, he wrote, transference is "displacement of an affect, either positive or negative, from one person on to the psycho-analyst." At other times transference is "displacement of affect from one idea to another." Dr. Andrew Watson's recent book for lawyers defines transference as "the unreal attributes which the observer believes he sees or feels to be present in the observed, and

---

*Displacement is a "mechanism . . . whereby persons, objects, situations, and ideas disturbing to the ego are replaced by less offensive ones." Brussel and Cantzlaar. Projection is "[a] defense mechanism in which the subject unconsciously attributes his own unacceptable ideas or impulses to another." Peck defines the "transference situation" as:

. . . the emotional situation which develops between patient and physician; during the course of psychoanalysis, wherein the patient transfers now affection and again hostile feelings to the analyst which are based on transient unconscious identifications and have no relation to reality.

which are drawn from some superficial likeness to an important person from the past, such as a parent." He adds that "this tendency to make a whole from a part represents projection on the part of the observer."[4]

C. G. Jung analyzed transference as projection *without displacement*. This might mean that an unreal attachment to the physician represents an aspect of the patient's character from which he must defend himself. Under Jung's theory, as under the Freudian displacement theory, transference is a defensive process[5] which has its origins— or etiology as the doctors put it—deep in the transferring person's past, and which results in regarding the object of the transference in an unrealistic way in order that the patient may avoid the necessity of regarding himself (in Jung's theory), or some more significant person (in Freud's theory), in a realistic way.[6]

It may help to explore the transference-by-displacement idea in one of its earliest reported clinical manifestations, Freud's patient Dora.

Dora was an unmarried young lady who was brought to Freud with what were then thought to be "hysterical" physical symptoms for which her physician could find no pathological or systemic explanation. Freud treated her for three months, in the process discovering that she was in the midst of a romantic triangle involving her father and a married couple (Herr and Frau K) in whose home Dora had been an employee. Freud did not get to the bottom of all of the confusing relationships that caused Dora's illness, but he suspected they involved homosexual attachments to Frau K (who was her father's mistress) and a proposition from Herr K (Dora had repulsed the proposition though she was attracted by it).

When Dora suddenly announced to Freud that she was terminating treatment, Freud did not accept her conventional explanation that she found it too lengthy. (She had earlier agreed to treatment for a year or more; the value of even the three months she spent with Freud is evidenced by the fact that she later married and apparently led a relatively normal life.) Freud explained Dora's decision in terms of her emotional identification of him with her potential lover, Herr K. She had, Freud thought, severed her relationship with the physician in order to punish Herr K. This was apparently one of Freud's earliest experiences with transference. He explained the phenomenon this way:

[Patients] replace some earlier person by the person of the physician. To put it another way: a whole series of psychological experiences are revived, not as belonging to the past, but as applying to the person of the physician at the present moment.

Sometimes, he said, the transferences are exact reproductions of the earlier feelings—the only difference being that the object of the feelings is a new person, an object of transference. On other occasions, the transferences are disguised, "ingeniously constructed":

> [T]heir content has been subjected to a moderating influence—to *sublimation,* as I call it—and they may even become conscious, by cleverly taking advantage of some real peculiarity in the physician's person or circumstances and attaching themselves to that. These, then, will no longer be new impressions, but revised editions.[7]

Freud appears to have believed that Dora's feelings for Herr K were themselves transferred from someone else, probably her father. Dora, in other words, had projected onto Herr K her feelings for her father (who had rejected her in favor of a liaison with Frau K). She had then projected onto Freud her feelings for Herr K, and had acted as she did toward Freud in order to punish Herr K.[8] Freud went on to express his opinion that transference feelings for him as a doctor were almost inevitably present, and present throughout the course of therapy, and that cure depended on their being recognized by the patient and, through a process of awareness, dissolved. The problem in Dora's treatment was, Freud thought, that he had not recognized the transference soon enough; he did not treat it before Dora had an opportunity to act it out by rejecting him.

Freud explained that he could have taken an altogether different course. He could have retained Dora as a patient by encouraging the transference. He could have done what Dr. Eissler does with dying patients—ignoring the possibility that transference might prevent cure. Dr. Eissler's therapeutic goal, after all, is not cure but endurance until the patient dies. Freud elected not to encourage the transference:

> Might I perhaps have kept the girl under my treatment if I myself had acted a part, if I had exaggerated the importance to me of her staying on, and had shown a warm personal interest in her—a course which, even after allowing for my position as her physician, would have been tantamount to providing her with a substitute for the affection she longed for? I do not know. . . . [T]here must be some limits set to the extent to which psychological influence may be used, and I respect as one of these limits the patient's own will and understanding.

Clearly, Freud believed he could have maintained his relationship with Dora if he had been willing to respond to her emotion—either genuinely (a countertransference*) or falsely.[9] Dr. Eissler responds as Freud refused to respond. His practice of giving gifts, of not billing for his services, and of indicating for the patient what he refers to as "unambivalent love," is an encouragement of transference. Dr. Eissler's dying lady patients, often as a product of his skillful cultivation of their feelings, project onto him strong feelings of affection for someone else—probably for their fathers, or brothers, or husbands—and he encourages those feelings in order to make their dying days more psychologically comfortable. His embarrassment in the will case reported above occurred only because he did not foresee what must, to a lawyer, seem entirely predictable—that the patient would make him a generous legacy and turn over to him the post-mortem management of her affairs. Because the patient is soon to die, Dr. Eissler views his practice as defensible and even medically sound (I do not suggest that I disagree). Is it possible to imagine this same critical juncture in human relationships occurring outside the doctor's consulting room—a juncture at which an object of the transference is called upon to either encourage feelings or to reject them? Might not that same human relationship explain cases of extravagant inter vivos gifts and generous legacies in cases the courts later consider under the head of undue influence?

Transference Occurs Commonly in All Schools of Psychotherapy and is Fundamental in Freudian and Jungian Psychoanalysis

The first observation suggests the contours of transference theory as it has been developed in Freudian psychiatry, the school of psychotherapy most directly associated with the American medical profession. It may serve the purposes of the present observation, and some important tangential purposes, to look at the concept as it operates in Rogerian nonmedical psychotherapy and in Jungian analytical psychology.

Carl R. Rogers, in a system for talking to troubled people which has significance both in psychotherapy and in counseling, is defensive about transference—probably because he has been accused of exploiting it in

---

*"Countertransference   is the analyst's emotional involvement in the patient's psychic problem. It is due to arousal by the patient of repressed feelings in the analyst's unconscious." Brussel and Cantzlaar.

his relationships with, as he calls them, "clients." Rogers believes that transference in his "client-centered therapy" develops to some extent in almost all cases but to a troublesome extent in only a few. In each situation, he sees four indications that transference is present: (1) "a desire for dependence upon the counselor, accompanied by deep affect"; (2) "fear of the counselor, which is . . . related to fear of parents"; (3) "attitudes of hostility . . . beyond the attitudes . . . realistically related to the experience"; and (4) "expressions of affection, and a desire for a love relationship."

Rogers believes that the milder—and more common—transference disappears as the client is led to rely on his own judgment rather than that of his counselor. He reports the case of a young woman who wanted to drop her sessions with her therapist because of a dream:

> I was up for trial, and you were the judge. . . .
>
>   * * *
>
> I didn't see how I could come back into the situation. I mean the circumstances, you already judged me, and therefore I didn't really see how I could possibly talk any more.
>
>   * * *
>
> . . . I suppose in my own way I was judging myself.

In the process of talking the dream out, Rogers believes, this lady came to see that she was projecting a self-assessment and was capable of recognizing "that there are other sensory evidences which I have not admitted into consciousness, or have admitted but interpreted inaccurately." When this happens:

> the "transference attitudes" . . . simply disappear because experience has been reperceived in a way which makes them meaningless. It is analogous to the way in which one attitude drops out and another entirely different one takes its place when I turn to watch the large plane I have dimly glimpsed out of the corner of my eye, and find it to be a gnat flying by a few inches from my face.

In other cases, those involving "aggressive dependence" and those in which the patient "insists that the counselor must take over," Rogers feels that his system of "client-centered therapy" is relatively unsuccessful. He gives an example that also illustrates the intensity of some transference reactions. Another young lady has developed a strong negative transference toward her therapist; she is ravaged by guilt feelings that relate to possible incest with her father:

I want to be independent—but I want to show you I don't have to be dependent. . . . You feel I want to come, but I *don't!* I'm not coming anymore. It doesn't do any good. I don't like you. I hate you! . . . All I've had is pain, pain, pain. . . . You think I can't get well, but I can. You think I had hallucinations, but I didn't. I hate you. . . . You think I'm crazy, but I'm not.

Rogers believes that psychoanalysis develops transference more strongly than his system of psychotherapy does. The truth or falsity of this assertion is not of importance here, but the substance of Roger's explanation for his position is directly relevant to the lives we lawyers have with our clients; for that reason it might be useful to consider it briefly.

Rogers explains transference in terms of dependence. First, he says, evaluation by an authoritative person tends to create dependence—evaluation of a moral character ("It is perfectly normal to. . . ."), or evaluation of characteristics (as in psychological testing, or I suppose, an assessment of chances for success in litigation), or evaluation of causes or patterns in the client's life. Second, "dependency arises when it is expected," something which follows from "the analyst's stress upon the use of free association," and other devices in which "the patient is advised to avoid all feeling of responsibility," which in turn "would tend to imply that another will be responsible for him." (One might pause to ask if there is a resemblance between this assessment of analysis and the assessment Rogers might make of lawyers who tell clients, "Don't worry about a thing; I'll take care of it.") In summary:

When the client is evaluated to realize clearly in his own experience that this evaluation is more accurate than any he has made himself, then self-confidence crumbles, and a dependent relationship is built up. When the therapist is experienced as "knowing more about me than I know myself," then there appears to the client to be nothing to do but to hand over the reins of his life. . . .[10]

The example he gives, of a patient who became dependent on his doctor for every sort of practical, day-to-day advice, resembles examples given by Fromm-Reichmann as well as experiences most practicing lawyers could relate on the subject of client dependence.

Jung's treatment of transference is at the center of his view of man (and "the main problem of medical psychotherapy") and illustrates his use of the concept of collective unconscious to explain behavior. Jung regarded transference as a natural phenomenon rather than a manipulative device. While he admitted that the phenomenon was common, he thought psychotherapy would probably be better off without it. When it occurs, it poses a delicate and even insurmountable obstacle to the doctor:

> What seems to be so easily won by the transference always turns out in the end to be a loss; for a patient who gets rid of a symptom by transferring it to the analyst always makes the analyst the guarantor of this miracle and so binds himself to him more closely than ever.

This diffidence seems to be fundamentally at odds with Freud, who said that "the field of application of analytic therapy lies in the transference neurosis," and even suggested that any mental disorders "differing from these, narcissistic and psychotic conditions, is unsuitable to a greater or less extent" for psychoanalysis. This leads the Freudian and his patient to work for transference, a venture Jung believed to be futile. "[T] ransference is only another word for 'projection.' No one can voluntarily make projections, they just happen. They are illusions which merely make the treatment more difficult." When transference does occur it is delicate, time-consuming, and not so methodically broken as the Freudians implied. "Words like 'nonsense' only succeed in banishing little things—not the things that thrust themselves tyrannically upon you in the stillness and loneliness of the night."

Psychotherapeutic relations rest, in Jung's view, on rapport—and he apparently did not regard therapeutic rapport as coextensive with transference, although his discussion suggests that transference is often present along with rapport. Transference, when it occurs, is a projection; and projections are dissociative—they are unintegrated bits of the personality wrongly seen as belonging outside the self.[11] The cure for them is integration—individuation—and this involves two or three features that are noteworthy for present purposes. First, honest rapport minimizes transference:

> The transference is the patient's attempt to get into psychological rapport with the doctor. He needs this relationship if he is to overcome the dissociation. The feebler the rapport . . . the more intensely will the transference be fostered and the more sexual will be its form.

235

A concomitant feature of transference, according to Jung, is that it seems to answer an affective hunger that is often present in disturbed people; their mental weakness "is enough to set these instinctive urges and desires in motion and bring about a dissociation of personality." This accounts, at least in part, for the sexual element in transference. Another feature—and one that seems to bear potently on cases like Dr. Eissler describes—is that the doctor's personality is *unavoidably* involved in the transference. "[T]wo psychic systems interact . . . individuality is a fact not to be ignored, the relationship must be dialectical." The very survival of the patient may depend on "the doctor's knowledge, like a flickering lamp . . . the one dim light in the darkness." The doctor has an opportunity to lead his patient to the integration of personality—"[n]o longer a mere selection of suitable fictions, but a string of hard facts, which together make up the cross we all have to carry or the fate we ourselves are." This idea is central:

> So long as the patient can think that somebody else (his father or mother) is responsible for his difficulties, he can save some semblance of unity. . . . But once he realizes that he himself has a shadow, that his enemy is in his own heart, then the conflict begins and one becomes two. Since the "other" will eventually prove to be yet another duality, a compound of opposites, the ego soon becomes a shuttlecock tossed between a multitude of "velleities", with the result that there is an obfuscation of the light," i.e., consciousness is depotentiated and the patient is at a loss to know where his personality begins or ends.

But Jung is at some pains to make it clear that this therapeutic process is not a matter of manipulation. The transference relationship is most of all a link between the unconscious of the doctor and that of the patient; Jung believes they share in a collective unconscious. Without going so far, though, one can appreciate the relevance of his insight to any legal analysis of the confidential relationship a litigant in Dr. Eissler's position may have had with his patient:

> The transference . . . alters the psychological stature of the doctor, though this is at first imperceptible to him. He too becomes affected, and has as much difficulty in distinguishing between the patient and what has taken possession of him as has the patient himself.

Jung's conception of transference is that it is a third force which possesses both patient and analyst.

A final important insight of Jung's is that the sexual element in transference is archetypal rather than oedipal. Both Freud and Jung had to take account of the sexual element. Freud, linked it to the infantile Oedipus complex, the child's desire to replace his father in his mother's life. Transference to a female therapist by a male patient would therefore involve these sexual feelings, though not all modern Freudians would agree. Jung thought that the projection was fundamentally of the contrasexual element within the patient himself. A man tends to project the female within him—the *anima*. In childhood he has made this projection on his mother and sisters; he later projects it on other women, but it often retains a certain incestuous character.[12] (He also projects homo-erotic feelings from within himself on his father, his brothers, his male doctor.) This *anima* projection in its purest form involves the incest taboo; but it affords also the therapeutic opportunity for a "spiritual marriage" in which the projected and unprojected elements of the patient's personality are integrated into a new conscious self.[13] This process, insofar as it is therapeutic, is a process which needs some substitute for the biological unity of the family— "family" here in the sense of ancient, archetypal, "kinship" as well as in an etiological sense. The idea that integration takes place in a human association that is libidinal but not sexual is complex—almost mystical— but it is obviously central to what Jung says about transference in modern man:

> Everyone is now a stranger among strangers. Kinship libido . . .
> has long been deprived of its object. But, being an instinct, it is
> not to be satisfied by any mere substitute such as a creed, party,
> nation, or state. It wants the *human* connection. That is the core
> of the whole transference phenomenon, and it is impossible to
> argue it away, because relationship to the self is at once
> relationship to our fellow man, and no one can be related to the
> latter until he is related to himself.

Transference is Not Limited to Psychotherapeutic
Relationships. It May Occur in any Relationship
in Which the Transferring Person Feels Trust
Toward the Object of the Transference.

In his recent book, *Psychiatry for Lawyers,* Dr. Andrew S. Watson suggests that transference is an essential "tool" in the relationship between lawyer and client. Transference is, he says, an "ubiquitous phenomenon"; lawyers who bother to understand the phenomenon "can profit immensely." He quotes former Justice Abe Fortas and

Talcott Parsons in support of the proposition that transference and countertransference are commonplace in the law office. He directs most of his brief discussion of the subject toward legal counseling, but not without noticing in the process that a father-son transference relationship often develops between young lawyers and their senior partners. "The capacity to accept the possibility that one's feelings about another may be due to unconscious and unrealistic coloring rather than to the other's reality traits," he says, "is a major step toward understanding" in relations among lawyers and in lawyer-client encounters. "Without awareness of transference phenomena, people are over- or under-convinced by their own emotional responses and have no opportunity to work out any understanding of them." Jung had some important words to say to lawyers about that:

> So, if a patient [client] projects the saviour complex into you, for instance, you have to give back to him nothing less than a saviour. . . .
> . . . Each profession carries its respective difficulties, and the danger of analysis is that of becoming infected by transference projections. . . . So he begins to feel, "If there are saviours, well, perhaps it is just possible that I am one," and he will fall for it, at first hesitantly, and then it will become more and more plain to him that he really is a sort of extraordinary individual.

Dr. Watson applies, close to home, the insight that transference is a matter of everyday living. The point is rare and important. Personal observation by physicians gives them little opportunity to work out principles of "relatedness" in nonmedical contexts, but the relatedness is present everywhere. "[E]arly experiences in interpersonal relatedness," Fromm-Reichmann said, "affect . . . later relationships with [a] family doctor, dentist, minister, etc. Even the mere anticipation of consulting any kind of qualified helper . . . may pave the way for the development of transference reactions." She added that "[a]s a result, present-day persons and interpersonal situations will be misjudged, incorrectly evaluated, and parataxically distorted along the lines of the patients' unrevised, early, dissociated experiences." "The transference itself," Jung said, "is a perfectly natural phenomenon which does not by any means happen only in the consulting room—it can be seen everywhere and may lead to all sorts of nonsense. . . ."[14] Dr. Peck suggested that transference is likely to exist in any professional relationship in which good rapport has been established; one psychiatrist (Kahne) even attempted to gauge transference between students and their teacher in an engineering class.

Transference Often Crosses Sexual Lines and May Involve a Reversal of Generations

Jung used a medieval book on alchemy to explain transference. He built his explanation around woodcuts that illustrated the *coniunctio* between symbolic, mythical male and female figures. His theory was that transference involves the projection of contrasexual contents in the unconscious of the transferring person. Although he did not confine transference to this sort of projection—it was possible, he said, to transfer even onto inanimate objects—it is clear that the Jungian prototype of transference is contrasexual. Freud's view of transference was tied to his view of the Oedipus complex. Feelings transferred by the patient originated in competition between the patient and his father for the love of the patient's mother—a necessarily contrasexual relationship. It is possible to exaggerate the importance of the sexual element in transference—especially in a limited discussion, for nonmedical purposes. Fromm-Reichmann appears to disagree with Freud's view on the Oedipus complex in transference; she regards the affective content in the transference as a "wish for closeness and tenderness with the beloved parent . . . without recognizable sexual roots," and attributes the apparently contrasexual character of transference to the fact that people in our culture find it easier to talk about sex than about "friendly, tender, asexually loving aspects of . . . interpersonal relationships." However, the evidence for some contrasexual tendency in transference is at least strong enough to justify seeking a parallel between clinical experience with the phenomenon and the apparent incidence of contrasexual transference in undue influence wills cases.*

---

*Patrick E. Maloney, a third-year Notre Dame law student, undertook to check this impression and an impression on generation reversal against the appellate literature. He took random samples from all of the cases indexed under "undue influence" in the Indiana Digest and the California Digest. Based on a study of fourteen randomly selected Indiana cases and forty-three randomly selected California cases, he obtained the following results. In Indiana sixty-four percent of the cases involved contrasexual relationships and eighty-six percent involved what I have called generation reversal. In California, seventy-seven percent of the cases involved contrasexual relationships and sixty-three percent involved generation reversal. These figures indicate a significant level of transfers to younger people thought by plaintiffs or their counsel to justify an undue-influence

239

A more evasive aspect of transference is that it frequently appears to involve generation reversal. Ernest Jones, an early giant of psychiatry, noted that children tend, almost universally, to believe that people grow smaller as they grow older. "When I am a big girl and you are a little girl," a child says to her mother, "I shall whip you just as you whip me now." The fantasy extends, as in this example, to a general reversal of parent-child positions; Jones finds parallels in certain Eastern and Egyptian myths and even in Little Red Riding Hood. He attributes this phenomenon to an early, narcissistic conviction of immortality, to early impulses of love and hate for parents, and to a childish need to find, in fantasy, a position in which the child can both demand from and help his parents. The phenomenon has a number of important results, most notably in a parent's compulsion to compare his own child with his parent. "I have . . . noticed," Jones says, "how the parent's attitude toward quite minute specific traits . . . in his or her own parent is reproduced when dealing with his or her child." This has a significant cultural effect in the transfer of traditions, traditions which may be defied, as well as accepted, by the child on whom they are imposed.

This piece of clinical observation is relevant here because it may help to explain the fact that transference often appears to involve an object—contrasexual or not—who is younger than the patient or client making the transference. This was apparently true in Dr. Eissler's case.

---

contest. They further indicate that the level of contrasexual transfers was higher in both states than would occur by accident (assuming that chance occurrence would be approximately fifty percent).

In terms of what courts do with these situations, the study indicates that in California twenty-nine percent of all cases resulted in appellate holdings against the will; thirty-seven percent of all cases involving contrasexual relationships resulted in appellate holdings against the will; and twenty-six percent of all cases involving generation reversal resulted in appellate holdings against the will.

In Indiana, thirty percent of all appellate holdings were against the will; thirty-six percent of appellate holdings in contrasexual relationship cases were against the will; and thirty-one percent of all appellate holdings in generation reversal cases were against the will.

From all this I conclude that:

(1) A contrasexual will transfer is more likely to be subject to contest than a transfer where testator and legatee are of the same sex. And, when the suit is brought, it is more likely to be successful where the transfer is contrasexual than where it is not.

(2) A transfer which is cross-generational tempts contest in a great many cases (as much as four-fifths of all cases brought). But, when the suit is brought, the chances of winning or losing are about the same as if no generation reversal were involved. The first part of this second conclusion is not very useful, since there is no "normal" transfer situation with which it may be compared. One would expect that most testamentary transfers would go from older to younger persons.

It was often true in Jung's practice and may account in part for his conviction that the process of individuation, toward which the transference tends, occurs in the second half of life.

It may be that use of Jones' explanation is overly complex, and that the transference onto younger people is merely a species of regression.* Regression was sufficient to explain the transference noted by Bloch, Silber and Perry; they found that parents in the 1956 Vicksburg tornado disaster turned to their children for emotional support. Burton noted that an elderly, dying lady in a hospital tended to regress to a need for the sort of love she had as a child. However this contragenerational element in transference is explained, it is important to suggest some clinical parallel here because many undue influence wills cases involve testators influenced by younger, trusted legatees.

Transference Relationships May
Become Exceptionally Strong

Dr. Eissler's assessment was that transference can be virtually hypnotic. Examples from Freud and Jung may illustrate the point. Freud's case involved a Herr P who had developed a strong positive transference for Freud. Freud had decided he could not help Herr P and had told him so, but Herr P wanted to continue therapy for some few weeks until his duties at a university began. Freud agreed, although he recognized that his only link to the patient was that Herr P "felt comfortable in a well-tempered father-transference to me," and that this indefinite arrangement was "in disregard of the strict rules of medical practice." The relationship became so intense that the patient seemed to know facts—most notably the name of a foreign visitor to Freud's office— which were, objectively, hidden from him. Freud was tempted to believe that the relationship between him and Herr P caused a transfer of thought.

Jung's examples are even more candid; one of them involved Freud, with whom he had a strong father-son relationship, which Freud also

---

*Regression is a "[r]eversal of psychosexual development; a primary feature of schizophrenia. . . . The patient in extreme cases retraces his steps back to the protective shell of security of babyhood and there, beyond the reach of society's demands, constructs his own thoroughly satisfying world of fantasy. . . ." Brussel and Cantzlaar. In his *Analytical Psychology,* Jung notes that some ancient and medieval sexual practices were designed to prevent spouses from regressing all the way to attachment to parents. The theory was that the spouse would regress to interim feelings toward a temple prostitute or a feudal lord (prima nox).

experienced.† While they were still speaking to one another, Jung had a dream that signaled to him their forthcoming break and that represented both aspects of the ambivalent transference relationship:

> [H]e still meant to me a superior personality, upon whom I had projected the father, and at the time of the dream this projection was still far from eliminated. Where such a projection occurs, we are no longer objective; we persist in a state of divided judgment. On the one hand we are dependent, and on the other we have resistances. When the dream took place I still thought highly of Freud, but at the same time I was critical of him. This divided attitude is a sign that I was still unconscious of the situation and had not come to any resolution of it. This is characteristic of all projections.

Jung cited his other example in explanation of parapsychological phenomena. A patient, with whom Jung had formed a strong transference, was progressing toward cure when he discovered that his wife resented Jung. In the face of stress between wife and surrogate father, the patient relapsed into depression. One night Jung was awakened as if someone were in his room. While awake he felt a dull pain at the back of his skull. The next day he learned that his patient had shot himself in the head, at the time of Jung's experience. "The collective unconscious is common to all," Jung said of this experience. "[I] t is the foundation of what the ancients called the 'empathy of all things.' In this case the unconscious had knowledge of my patient's condition."

The Transference Relationship
in Undue Influence Cases

> . . . recollecting, that, in discussing whether it is an act of rational consideration, an act of pure volition, uninfluenced, that inquiry is so easily baffled in a Court of justice, that instead of the spontaneous act of a friend, uninfluenced, it may be the impulse of a mind misled by undue kindness, or forced by oppres-

---

†*Time* reports the discovery of correspondence between Freud and G. Stanley Hall in which Hall wrote to Freud that the split between Freud and Jung was a classical case of adolescent rebellion. Freud replied:

> If the real facts were more familiar to you, you would very likely not have thought that there was again a case where a father did not let his sons develop, but you would have seen that the sons wished to eliminate their father, as in ancient times.

sion. . . . And, therefore, if the Court does not watch these transactions, with a jealousy almost invincible, in a great majority of cases it will lend its assistance to fraud. . . .

—Lord Eldon[15]

Dr. Eissler's discussion of transference, coupled with reasonable conjecture from other clinical discussions, suggests four situations in which the subject of the transference might make gratuitous disposition of property in favor of the object of the transference—situations to which the law of undue influence has been applied.

First, the object of the transference consciously manipulates it to his own advantage. Second, the object of the transference is (a) aware of his power over the subject, (b) aware of the transfer, or plans for the transfer, in his favor, and (c) disinclined to do anything about the effect of the transference, which favors him. In this second situation, conscious manipulation of the transference cannot be shown. Third, the object of the transference is not aware of any of the facts noted in the second case, but *unconsciously* manipulates the person in his power ("unconscious opportunism," in Dr. Eissler's phrase). Fourth, there is no evidence of manipulation, conscious or unconscious, but there is evidence that a transference existed, and the evidence supports a conclusion that the gratuitous transfer was a result of the transference— i.e., it was an inappropriate gift, what the law terms "unnatural."[16] Each of these four examples can be found in the appellate and secondary literature on undue influence.

A Conscious Manipulation

In re Kaufmann's Will made two trips to the appellate division of the New York Supreme Court and was finally resolved, by a divided court, against legacies made by Robert Kaufmann to his friend Walter Weiss.[17] The majority held that the evidence supported a jury finding that the will had been obtained by undue influence. The relationship between Kaufmann and Weiss spanned eleven years. Kaufmann was a middle-aged bachelor, a millionaire, an amateur painter, and an inept businessman who had inherited all of his wealth; Weiss was a lawyer not in practice, a domineering personality, and a loyal companion to his well-heeled friend. The contestants were Robert's brothers and nephews. Both opinions in the appellate division are fervent; the majority seemed to absorb the emotional force of the contestants' argument and represented Weiss's conduct in such righteous hyperbole as "deceitful," "improper, and insidious," "deliberately false," and "unnatural . . . influence"; the brothers and nephews were subjects of such cordial phrases as "natural warm family" and "intimately and warmly associated." The dissenters saw the family as "disappointed relatives," noted "business differences" between Kaufmann and his brother, and said Kaufmann "rarely saw his relatives" even before he came to know Weiss. The majority opinion speaks of Kaufmann himself as weak and submissive; the dissenters describe him as sensitive, intelligent, and merely peculiar.

Kaufman and Weiss met in 1948 and entered into a business arrangement under which Weiss was to be Kaufmann's financial advisor. Within two years they were sharing Kaufmann's apparently palatial New York townhouse. Five wills were at issue. The first, which gave his property to brothers, nephews, friends and charities—and a small legacy to Weiss—was seen by the majority as a "natural testamentary disposition." The other four, dating from 1951 to 1958, progressively increased Weiss's share and ultimately eliminated all other legatees except the two nephews; these were characterized as the result of a calculated scheme:

> To overtly seize Robert's property would risk a challenge by his family. So long as Robert was under his control and influence, Weiss was assured of a life of ease and luxury. He, therefore, need only direct Robert toward making him his principal beneficiary in the event of his death. This he could do without the knowledge of the family. The result was to be substantiated by written declarations of Robert assigning reasons for the unnatural disposition.

This last sentence referred to Robert's handwritten letter, put with the first of the contested wills (executed in 1951); the letter explained to the family that Weiss had encouraged Robert's painting, had given him "a balanced, healthy sex life," and had been responsible for his peace of mind. The majority explained the letter with alternative theories—either it was dictated by Weiss, or it was so filled with errors as to indicate Robert's weakness of mind.[18]

The majority's view of the relationship was that it began in dependence, largely because Robert "sought help and direction to satisfy his drive for independence." Robert immediately made a bad bargain ($10,000 a year for Weiss's advice). He then began to take Weiss's advice in business and lost large amounts of money because Weiss was a bad advisor. Weiss then, in the majority view, began to use business quarrels within the family as a pretext for alienating Robert from his brothers; "Weiss exploited Robert, induced him to transfer to him the stewardship formerly exercised by [his brother, and] increased Robert's need for dependency, prevented and curtailed associations which threatened his absolute control of Robert and alienated him from his family." (The majority also thought that Weiss attempted without success to win the support of Robert's brothers.)

Once family control was eliminated, in the majority's view, Weiss intensified his own virtually parental control over Kaufmann. They travelled together (at Kaufmann's expense); Weiss wrote notes to Kaufmann that were sometimes curt and commanding, sometimes condescending. ("I think you are finally growing up and realize you are not playing with marbles.") Weiss dominated the household while Kaufmann "stood by mutely ... submitted silently ... complied." Once control was undisputed, Weiss built the system of gratuitous transfers at issue—legacies of corporate stock, of cash, of real estate; beneficiary designations on life insurance; and cash gifts.[19]

The majority believed that throughout this carefully constructed relationship Weiss practiced calculated, pervasive deception on Robert and his brothers and manipulated Robert's affections. The court called this eleven-year adventure a "skillfully executed plan," and carefully implied that Weiss exploited a homosexual relationship with Robert.[20] Robert was, the majority said, "a personality with pathological dependency; one unable to deal with reality, insecure, unstable and who tends to submit unreasonably to the will of another."[21] This was a case of the "insidious, subtle and impalpable kind which subverts the intent or will of the testator, internalizes within the mind of the testator the desire to do that which is not his intent but the intent and end of another."[22]

The dissenters thought the evidence was circumstantial and unconvincing; the verdict, they said, rested "upon surmise, suspicion, conjecture and moral indignation and resentment, not upon the legally required proof of undue influence. . . ." The two dissenting judges felt that Weiss was being tried for admitted discrepancies between pretrial testimony and facts in the record, and for the peculiar "intimate relationship," which neither set of judges was able to be candid about.[23] The dissenting view of the four wills at issue was that they were the result of close friendship and gratitude. The dissenters could not accept the notion that undue influence could be exercised progressively and consistently for eleven years: "It is not claimed that the

245

testator was hypnotized by Weiss during all this period, and certainly no evidence thereof has been presented."

Both sets of judges, for all their hyperbole, agreed on the existence of a confidential relationship. Dicta in the majority opinion puts the case within New York precedents that place the burden of proof on the proponent when it is shown there is "a marked departure from a prior, natural plan of testamentary disposition which excessively and unnaturally favors a nonrelative under circumstances establishing motive, opportunity, overreaching and persistent involvement in transfers and dispositions of property. . . ."[24] The dissenters admitted the influence, and even deplored it, but felt the majority encroached too far on freedom of testation. "Undoubtedly the testator was influenced but the evidence . . . is entirely consistent with the complete lack of undue influence," the dissenters said. "Yet, because of the suspicious circumstances involved, the majority . . . would deny him his legal right to dispose of his property as he has chosen to do."

Kaufman appears to be a clear case of manipulation. Evidentiary sophistication in dealing with it—most notably the sophistication of a presumption or shift in the burden of proof—is not necessary to the decision. The majority alluded to the New York rule on presumption of undue influence, but its holding does not rest on a presumption nor on an esoteric view of burden of proof; the case was decided solely on the record. Psychological sophistication is not necessary either, given the majority's view of the evidence. A transference clearly existed, and it was clearly contrasexual, even though both parties were male. It was a strong transference, an emotional level Weiss could have exploited in all of the ways the family pointed out. It probably gripped Weiss, too, but the majority could not discuss that because it was too intent on finding a villain. Moral judgments about Weiss and his power over Robert Kaufmann were doubtless made by the jury. They were made expressly by appellate judges on both sides of the issue; they were made by the majority in such a way as to resolve the evidence into both a finding and a righteous condemnation. Transference theory illuminates this sort of case; it would temper judicial rhetoric to have the theory out in the open—if only because the judges would see that we all manipulate and are manipulated—but it would probably not change the decision.

The "Let It Happen" Case

Transference may work its way without overt manipulation; the sagacious potential legatee simply lets matters take their course. This is the second category of undue influence case suggested by Dr. Eissler's experience. The object of the transference is aware that he has power over the subject; he is aware (or should be) that the subject plans some more or less inappropriate memorial of the relationship; and he does nothing about it. Dr. Eissler thought that the psychotherapist who allows this to happen is unethical, and that the psychotherapist who doesn't know it is happening is incompetent.

This case is harder to resolve than the overt manipulation case because the object of the transference let the testator's emotions do his work for him. What Jung saw as virtually a third personality—the shared unconscious of both parties—is at work. Even if Jung's analysis seems unduly mystical, it at least provides a useful metaphor. The unconscious interaction is like a third person: neither party controls it, but the testator is controlled by it.

In re Faulks' Will is an example.[25] Mrs. Mary Faulks was the testator; the litigation was between a will offered by her quasi-adopted son Will Jensen and a later will offered by her physician, Dr. L. G. Patterson. All of the relevant facts occurred during the last two years of Mrs. Faulks's six-year widowhood, while she was between the ages of 76 and 78 and Dr. Patterson was between 36 and 38. Her earlier wills (not at issue) had given her estate largely to Will Jensen. She and her husband had raised Will, saw him married to a neighbor's daughter, and then made the young couple their successors on the family farm. Mrs. Faulks was close to the Jensens' daughter, Lorraine.

Mrs. Faulks employed Dr. Patterson about two years before her death. She loaned him large sums of money for investment in real estate and in the doctor's airplane. A year before she died, in the fourth will she made after her husband's death, Mrs. Faulks forgave several thousand dollars of the doctor's indebtedness to her. In the following months she loaned him additional money, paid his debts, purchased real estate for him, and gave him cash—for a total value of more than $14,000 at the time of her death. During this period, according to a parade of witnesses:

> Her conversation was always about the Doctor and it gradually grew more and more that way. She expressed feelings of sympathy and sorrow for him.
>
> * * *
>
> We started a subject and then she would stop it and talk about Dr. Patterson. That was every time I went there. She did not carry on a conversation on the same subject very long. It would always turn to the doctor. She was always telling how

nice he was, how wonderful a doctor she had. . . . Her manner was different when she referred to him. . . . She was kind of happy and smiled. The last time I was there she sat on the studio couch . . . with her hands folded and . . . looked at the sky and just beamed about the doctor.

* * *

. . . She felt sorry for him. She said she guessed he was the son she never had. She requested him to come and see her every day . . . but not to put himself out if he was busy. At one time she made the remark to me, "I don't know why I've taken such a liking to Dr. Patterson." * * * She mentioned to me that she wished she had more money than she did have. She said to try and help Dr. Patterson build a hospital for the city. She said she would like to live another year at least to see Dr. Patterson become famous.

* * *

. . . She referred to him as Dear Pat, Dear Doctor. When she spoke about him she always seemed to be very happy. . . . She used to tell me how good he was. He would come up there every night when he was so tired.

* * *

I always like her as an old friend. . . . She kept up with current events up to two or three years ago. She had a radio and spent time with that. She talked with me about things she heard over the radio. The last couple of years she did not do this. . . . I don't think she was well. The last couple of years I visited her it wasn't much only Dr. Patterson.

When a cousin of the testatrix once appeared to disparage Dr. Patterson's professional competence, Mrs. Faulks drove her from the house and later disinherited her.

During that conversation the subject came up regarding a patient that Dr. Patterson had had. It was an old neighbor of ours, Mrs. Nickel. I said something to Mary respecting the condition of this patient. I said her hip had only partly knitted and she wasn't well. . . . She had been a patient of Dr. Patterson. I was just telling her what I had learned. When the visit ended she told me to get out of the house and stay out. I learned after that there had been a will by Mary cutting me off entirely.

Half of the last two years of Mrs. Faulks's life was spent in Dr. Patterson's private hospital. During her intermittent hospitalization, Dr. Patterson gave her flowers, took her out of the hospital for admittedly risky airplane rides, and took her (at her expense) for a vacation in Wyoming.

Will and Pearl Jensen eventually confronted Mrs. Faulks with their opinions about her beneficence to the physician. This proved an economically naive thing to do. Within a month Mrs. Faulks had ordered Will out of her presence and executed a new will in favor of Dr. Patterson. The will was not drawn by Mrs. Faulks's regular lawyer but by new counsel, who was summoned to Mrs. Faulks's hospital bed by one of Dr. Patterson's nurses. There was no significant evidence of lack of mental capacity at the time the will was executed.

The probate judge found against the will in favor of Dr. Patterson and admitted the earlier will that merely forgave his indebtedness to Mrs. Faulks. The Supreme Court of Wisconsin, three members dissenting, reversed. The appellate court's view of the relationship suggests the essential human fact it had to decide on the record:

> Here was an elderly woman with a serious heart ailment living alone, attended by a faithful and competent physician, as she believed an unusually competent one. . . . Under the circumstances there is nothing strange about her attachment. The extent of it is perhaps unusual but not infrequent. A doctor might well hesitate before accepting such gratuities from a patient. Such transactions are in the minds of the general public subject to the inference that something wrong has occurred. Offers from clients and patients to make gifts of considerable value are not at all uncommon in the experiences of lawyers and doctors. While a sensitive man might not accept such gifts, there is no rule of law which prohibits it.

This is the essence of the appellate majority's view of the case, and it significantly resembles Dr. Eissler's view as to what the law ought to be. To arrive at the conclusion, the court had to make several preliminary judgments. The first was the doctor had not *done* anything. "The [trial] court . . . found that . . . the proponent was disposed to influence the deceased," the court said. "We are unable to find a single shred of testimony in support of this finding." One of the dissenters, however, in reference to Dr. Patterson's suggestion to Mrs. Faulks that the Jensens were eager for inheritance, was moved to suggestive rhetorical quesitons:

> It, also, is evident that Jensen and others were not excluded from her consideration as objects of her bounty until after appellant's suggestion to her that Jensen was not cordial in his relations to him. Was that an innocent observation? Were other acts referred to in the opinions . . . unselfish, not colorable and prompted by design?

Secondly, the court observed that the bequest to Dr. Patterson was causally unrelated to his relationship with her. In the majority's view, the change in will was precipitated by the Jensens, who attacked Mrs. Faulks's beneficence to her physician and who deserted her after she drove Will Jensen from her hospital room:

> Death is a great leveler and a great solvent of human relations and however deep their resentment might have been . . . if there was nothing more between them than her request that they stay away, they would have attended her funeral [which they did not] and made some inquiry in regard to her. . . .

In the view of the dissenters, who insisted on similar moral fulminations in the other direction, this alienation was the product of Dr. Patterson's design:

> The quarrel with the Jensens . . . explains cutting them off . . . [but] does not apply to their daughter Lorraine. There was no quarrel with or misconduct by her. . . . Cutting off Lorraine in favor of one for whom only a foolish infatuation existed, was unnatural and indicates some mental abnormality or impairment. . . . It would also seem that something must have been done by the doctor between the making of the wills . . . whereby the doctor was given nothing and the will . . . wherein he was forgiven debts of $13,600. . . . The relation between the doctor and his patient was manifestly very close. The influence attributable to the confidential nature of that relation that the doctor might exert upon his patient in view of her age and physical condition is very great. But for that confidential relation the view of this court would be correct, but that relation existing I think that the conclusion of the county court that undue influence was exerted by Dr. Patterson is justified.

Ultimately, the dissenters make the object of all this affection the villain, as the majority had done in *Kaufmann:*

> [T]he bestowal of $14,700, to say nothing of $40,000 or more, can hardly be accounted for except by inference that such service was rendered with the purpose of securing benefactions as a result of it. The doctor . . . knew that she was an "easy mark." The conclusion that he took advantage of the confidential relation that exists between doctor and patient . . . can hardly be avoided. The doctor clearly did not take his patient up in an airplane for her health. That he did this for his own rather than her good, went with her to Yellowstone Park, gave her two hundred

forty-nine days hospitalization, paid for an eye operation which he himself was unable to perform and made countless unnecessary calls, all beyond the requirements of professional duty . . . and poisoned her mind against Mr. Jensen, all as means of influencing benefactions to himself, was not an unreasonable inference for the trial judge to draw.*

Most of the majority opinion in *Faulks* is given over to analysis of two legal questions: whether the burden of proof shifts, in an undue influence case, to the proponent of the will; and whether the existence of a confidential relationship raises a presumption of undue influence. But the essence of the decision, in the midst of an interminable exposition of precedent, is in the relationship between doctor and patient and, as a sort of counterpoint, the relationship between Mrs. Faulks and her sometime surrogate son, Will Jensen. The thrust of the majority's conclusion on the recondite legal questions is that *the existence of the relationship itself is not enough to invalidate the will,* however intense the relationship may be and however unusual its testamentary product. The majority stated the rule:

[T]he mere existence of a confidential relation between a testator and a beneficiary under his will such as attorney and client, physician and patient, priest and parishioner, confidential advisor and his advisee, etc. does not of itself constitute undue influence, nor cast upon the beneficiary the burden of disproving undue influence. However, the existence of such a relationship may cause a court to scrutinize the evidence more closely and weigh it more carefully. When coupled with other circumstances such as the activity of the beneficiary in procuring the drafting and execution of the will or a sudden and unexplained change in the attitude of the testator or some other somewhat persuasive circumstance, it gives rise to an inference of undue influence which the proponent has the burden of rebutting.

The dissenters in effect accepted this standard: their real disagreement was on the facts presented, facts that they felt were sufficient to show that Dr. Patterson was a man of evil heart.

Inferences, presumptions, and the burden of proof theories are of no assistance at all in resolving this sort of case. These are only means for disguising a decision that turns, despite the court's protestations to the

*This paragraph illustrates two of the "principles of the common law" that I find helpful to a wills teacher: (1) people are no damned good; and (2) it's not the principle of the thing, it's the money.

contrary, on a judicial view of human relationships. One cannot imagine that the evidence could have been presented more fully—from Dr. Patterson or anyone else concerned in the estate, nor from disinterested witnesses, medical or lay. Dr. Patterson might, had the votes gone the other way, have been said to have the burden of explaining what happened, but he could not have added anything to the record except clinical psychological terms (assuming, which is probably true, that he did not procure the will by overt manipulation). No amount of procedural sophistry was needed in the case. What the court had to decide, and what it necessarily decided, was that a gift so clearly the product of transference was allowable within the limits of freedom of testation. And what the dissenters would have had the court decide was that physicians should not be permitted to accept gifts which are so clearly the product of transference.

The "Unconscious Opportunism" Case

In *In re Pitt's Estate*, Julie H. Pitt, a strong-willed, frontier Arizona businesswoman, gave almost all of her estate to Guy Anderson, her lawyer.[26] She was a widow the last eleven years of her life; she depended on Anderson for legal assistance and companionship in time of stress. When she first suggested a will in Anderson's favor—and asked him to draft it for her—he expressed surprise at her choice. She told him that she was making the will because Anderson had been her husband's friend. Anderson saw to it that another lawyer drafted that will, but took care of later versions of it himself. There was no evidence of Anderson overtly manipulating Mrs. Pitt; in fact, there was a great deal of evidence that she was self-reliant and even stubborn in this and all other property transactions. The question, as the Arizona court saw it, was whether the coincidence of three facts—"[o]ne, that Anderson occupied a confidential relationship to Mrs. Pitt. . . . Two, that he was active in the preparation of the wills. Three, that he was the principal beneficiary"—was enough to require a presumption of undue influence that would survive Anderson's denial that he had influenced or attempted to influence the testatrix. The Arizona court decided that it was not and reversed a jury verdict against the will, a verdict the court saw as "supported by nothing beyond speculation, suspicion and bottomless inference." The same court made a similar analysis in a more recent case in which the confidentially related legatee was the testatrix's husband.[27]

In another case of this type, Mabel Banta was rescued from a lonely, grieving widowhood by her niece, Ila Green, and her niece's husband.[28] She left an apartment in Chicago and moved into the Greens' home in Rockford, Illinois. Within a month, with the help of the Greens' lawyer, Mrs. Banta executed trust documents and a will in favor of the Greens, these largely disinherited the contestant, a nephew. The Illinois appellate court affirmed a jury verdict finding the will to be the product of undue influence. The evidence included testimony that Mr. Green had peremptorily urged Mrs. Banta to make a will. The court spoke of the relationship as one involving a fiduciary:

> Under certain circumstances, a presumption will arise that the instrument is the result of undue influence. One such circumstance is: where a fiduciary relationship exists . . . where the testator is the dependent and the . . . legatee the dominant party; where the testator reposes trust and confidence in the . . . legatee, and where the will is prepared by or its preparation procured by such . . . legatee. Proof of these facts will establish a *prima facie* case that the execution of the will was the result of undue influence.

An interesting aspect of the case was a tendered instruction that would have charged the jury that "any degree of influence over another acquired by kindness and attention, can never constitute undue influence"; the court held that the instruction was properly refused. "[W]hether the influence is . . . undue depends not on the manner of influence, but on the degree of influence.

In another case, Dr. Ulrich A. Fritschi divorced his wife and made his receptionist a principal legatee in his will.[29] In a codicil, the only instrument contested, he rearranged the disposition so that his children, rather than the receptionist, bore death taxes. He died six days later. There was some evidence of mental deficiency, but not enough to establish incapacity. The California Supreme Court, sitting en banc, reversed a verdict for the contestants. The substantial inroads that death taxation has made on the freedom of testation, the court said, "have served to sharpen the court's vigilance in protecting the testator's right to be free of interference in the area which remains to him." According to the court, undue influence cannot be found unless the evidence shows: (1) a confidential relationship, (2) an "unnatural will," and (3) the legatee's activity in procuring the will. The third element was not met. "[T]he record does not show that . . . she ever or at all discussed the wills with the testator." Evidence that she was greedy or that she spent a great deal of time with the doctor would not suffice to meet the third requirement. "Plaintiffs have failed to show that the alleged ability and desire of Mrs. Teed unduly to influence the decedent were ever brought to bear upon the testamentary act." *Fritschi* is similar to a later California case, *In re Estate of Straisinger*, in which an elderly widow changed her principal beneficiaries from a missionary society to two close friends.[30] The testatrix, Maude Straisinger, often referred to one of the legatees, Gladys Uldene Cunningham, as her "foster" or "adopted" daughter—although Mrs. Cunningham was neither. The court thought this confusion made the will less "unnatural" than it would have been without the confusion and held—as in *Fritschi*—that opportunity to influence, and even motive, would not be enough to raise a presumption. "There must be activity on the part of a beneficiary in the matter of the actual preparation of the will."

In another case, Mary Smith, an eighty-two-year-old widow, was hospitalized in Liston Falls, Maine.[31] Marion M. Chambers, a trained and registered nurse, was hired to care for her. Mrs. Smith drew a check for $3,500 on her bank in Lewiston, handed it to Mrs. Chambers, and asked Mrs. Chambers to take the draft to the bank. Mrs. Chambers returned with a cashier's check, whereupon Mrs. Smith endorsed the check, handed it to Mrs. Chambers, and told her she was making a gift of the money—which represented about a third of Mrs. Smith's estate. The court of last resort in Maine held that the transfer was presumptively the product of undue influence:

> [The] rule is that, whenever a fiduciary or confidential relation exists between the parties to a deed, gift, contract or the like, the law implies a condition of superiority held by one of the parties over the other, so that in every transaction between them by which the superior party obtains a possible benefit equity presumes the existence of undue influence and the invalidity of the transaction, and casts upon that party the burden of proof of showing affirmatively by clear evidence that he or she acted with entire fairness and the other party acted independently, with full knowledge and of his own volition free from undue influence.

The court's opinion made it clear that the holding was based on the relationship between the two ladies and that the court did not expect that the nurse could conceivably explain away the judicial inference of undue influence:

> Mrs. Smith was entirely dependent upon her nurse for her every care and comfort, including the administration of the opiate when her cravings for the drug and the sufferings of her body

demanded relief. There can be no doubt that a confidential relation existed between Mrs. Smith and her nurse. Indeed, it would be difficult to visualize a more complete condition of dependence and trust between any patient and her caretaker. It is an entirely warranted conclusion that, even permitting Mrs. Smith, without impartial and disinterested advice, to make this transfer of this large sum of money to her, the defendant Marion M. Chambers took an unconscionable and unfair advantage of her patient. The presumption of fraud which the law casts upon transactions of this kind is not overcome by the evidence. It is confirmed.

In all of these cases some unconscious manipulation of the testator seems likely; in all of them the ability to manipulate unconsciously, the "unconscious opportunism," arises out of an apparent transference. The difference in them, which merits fuller discussion below, is that some of the cases (Mrs. Pitt, Mrs. Banta, Mrs. Smith) involve a socially useful professional relationship, while others (Dr. Fritschi, Mrs. Straisinger) involve personal relationships in which the isolation and judicial treatment of the transference are more difficult.

The No-Manipulation Case

Dr. Lunette Powers, a spinster and a physician, gave almost all of her half-million-dollar estate to her best friend, the wife of the lawyer who drew her will.[32] A jury verdict against the will was reversed in the will's third trip to the Supreme Court of Michigan. The holding turns on procedural error, but the opinion intimates, and a concurring opinion emphasizes, that the Michigan rule on undue influence was involved in the case. "The issue of the relationship of the attorney and his client, and the attorney and his wife as beneficiaries, is an . . . element in the broader concept of undue influence," the majority said. The evidence showed that Dr. Powers was very close to her lawyer's wife and that she had suffered progressive mental disability in the months before the will at issue was made. But for the procedural errors in the case, the verdict would have been affirmed on the theory that Dr. Powers lacked testamentary capacity; the concurring opinion was directed principally to the view that an additional theory, the law of undue influence, ought to reach this lawyer-client relationship:

> When the fiduciary so benefited directly or indirectly, happens to be a lawyer-scrivener of the challenged testament, the burden of overcoming the presumption quite obviously is substantially greater than had an independent and disinterested person pre-

pared the testamentary instruments. . . . [T]his Court . . . [has] blunty warned the profession against such conduct. . . .[33]

Even the majority suggested that the Michigan state bar procedure for unethical conduct was relevant in considering the lawyer's conduct, and noted that "[i]f any prizes were to be awarded for dismal professional judgment, the proponent here would be in a fair way to be signally recognized."

There is, in *Powers,* no evidence that the legatee's husband held any sway over Dr. Powers. There is little evidence that a transference relationship existed between Dr. Powers and the legatee. Dr. Powers gave her estate to friends, the evidence showed, because she had no close relatives. If the court in Michigan is willing to invalidate this kind of will, it is not because there was an emotional tie that produced the will, but because the court wishes to punish an errant lawyer.[34] It is important to note, though, that neither the concurring opinion nor the majority goes this far. Nothing these judges say justifies the conclusion that they would, on this professional ground, invalidate the will. What they do say is that the lawyer may have the burden of explaining how it came about. This use of the presumption is altogether different from the Wisconsin court's use of it in *Faulks* or the Maine court's use of it in Mrs. Smith's case. In those cases no explanation from the legatee was likely and none was expected. In *Powers,* on the other hand, the lawyer involved would probably have been able to show that no transference relationship existed between him and Dr. Powers.

Conclusion

A differentiation among these four classes of cases can be made both psychologically and on the basis of ancient, often neglected, common-law authority. It is helpful, first, to remove from consideration the case of conscious manipulation (*Kaufmann*).[35] Transference illuminates such cases, makes proof easier perhaps, explains something about the way people are, but is not essential to solution. Cases like *Kaufmann* may even be disposed of as involving fraud in the inducement. Fraud theory requires a showing of false representation, but the manipulation of a transference is false representation. Love is as much a fact as residence, age, or digestion. It is just as capable of being falsely represented. (Dr. Eissler, for instance, falsely represents "unambivalent love"—for benign ends; Freud refused to make that false representation to his Dora.) If the law can take cognizance of false representations

256

about the loyalty or honesty of third persons it can take cognizance of the falsity in a person who pretends love in order to gain property.[36] But even if the law of fraud won't do that, the law of undue influence has shown itself capable of dealing with cases like *Kaufmann.*

The other three cases—"let it happen," "unconscious opportunism," and "no manipulation," unconscious or otherwise—are more difficult for two reasons. First, they often seem to involve the results of human affection, which the law ought to honor, not frustrate.[37] Second, they are not often accessible to the judicial process. Although proof of transference is not unduly difficult—psychotherapists of all faiths seem able to detect it—proof of unconscious influence by the object of transference would often be very difficult.[38]

One possible approach would be to apply to all three kinds of cases an equitable version of the *Durham* test:* "If a will is the product of a transference (i.e., a displacement of feeling, or affect, which is inappropriate in the judgment of an informed fact finder), it is invalid." That would be a fairly workable test, since transference is not nearly as difficult to establish as the "mental defect" of the *Durham* rule. But this test perhaps limits freedom of testation more than our legal tradition will allow. Dr. Eissler says "it would actually lead to an infringement upon the patient's freedom if he could make a valid will only by excluding his psychiatrist." One might disagree with him; one might nobly disagree with the proposition that a man may make a will in favor of his lawyer.[39] But it is probably too restrictive to deny that one should be free to make a will in favor of his (ordinary) physician, his nurse, his housekeeper, his brother or sister, or his best friend.[40]

If my judgment as to the sentiment of those who mold the common law is correct, I am left where the *Faulks* court was left; I must suggest a plus factor: Transference *plus* something equals undue influence. What is the plus factor to be? Is it possible to formulate it more informatively than the cases and texts have done to date?[41] In the "let it happen" (*Faulks*) case, there is good common-law authority for holding the legacy invalid. The theory rests in cases where T is influenced by A to make a gift to B, or where T is influenced by A to make a gift to A and B.[42] In both situations B's legacy fails. The same result would obtain for "unconscious opportunism" if an unconscious, probably neurotic, third force could be equated, at least metaphorically, to a third person.

---

*"[A]n accused is not criminally responsible if his unlawful act was the product of mental disease or mental defect." Durham v. United States, 214 F.2d 862, 874-75 (D.C. Cir. 1954).

One might say that the only difference between the "let it happen" case and the "unconscious opportunism" case is that in the latter (*Pitt Swenson* [Mrs. Banta] *Fritschi*) the object of the transference was not sufficiently aware of what was going on to be negligent about it. The third force still produced the legacy. The object's innocence should be irrelevant, just as B's innocence is irrelevant when he receives a gift as the result of A's undue influence. This argument stumbles, though, when it reaches the "no manipulation" class of cases, where unconscious influences were projections from the testator. One distinction might be that in this fourth class of cases the force of transference is weaker. In Jungian terms the transference is probably not a third force at all. The transference is still purely projection at what Jung called the level of "personal unconscious." Even so, drawing the line here—allowing the transference-caused gift to stand—seems arbitrary and, more important, establishes a distinction that is likely to be impossible to make on specific conglomerations of evidence.

Transference is of more value to the law if it is used to support a line of distinction between the "let it happen" and "unconscious opportunism" cases. The object of the "let it happen" transference is aware of what is going on. He may not be able to diagnose the emotional climate precisely, but he comprehends it and allows the benefits of it to flow to him inappropriately.[43] He will often be what Rogers calls a "helping person" whose ideals are to accept emotions for professional ends: a medical person, therapist, teacher, or lawyer (e.g., Dr. Patterson in the *Faulks* case). The law can workably and fairly require that the results of influence from these professional "helping" relationships be confined to their appropriate compensatory ends; any "let it happen" gifts will thus be disallowed. There is some ancient authority for this proposition, in an opinion by Lord Langdale often cited as a leading case on undue influence in inter vivos transactions.

In that case, Dennis Chandler owed his solicitor more money than he had available.[44] The solicitor, Barsham, suggested that Chandler convey real estate to him and prepared the necessary deed. Chandler refused, argued with Barsham, consulted members of his (Chandler's) family, argued some more, and then finally—after Barsham unsuccessfully offered property for trade in addition to the debt—signed the deed. Members of the family sued to set the deed aside, arguing that it was obtained by fraud and undue influence. The jury found for Barsham on the fraud issue, but found for the family on the question of undue influence. Barsham moved for a new trial; the Master of the Rolls (Lord Langdale) granted the motion.

Langdale's opinion made a number of important distinctions about undue influence. The first was between undue influence and fraud; he said that the jury finding on that issue meant "there was no deception and no misrepresentation or suppression of truth." Undue influence, therefore, does not involve falsehood. This is a seminal distinction, which American courts, by use of rhetoric suggesting that undue influence is a species of fraud, have incorrectly ignored.

Langdale also distinguished between two species of undue influence. The first species turns on the existence of a relationship in which "there is . . . great . . . inequality between the transacting parties . . . habitual exercise of power on the one side, and habitual submission on the other . . . [for example] transactions between parent and child . . . [or] solicitor and client." The other species rests on circumstances—"on the nature of the transaction and the fact of habitual or occasional influence." The difference is in the proof necessary to make the case. In the habitual relationship situation the act complained of can be set aside "without any proof of the exercise of power beyond that which may be inferred from the nature of the transaction itself." According to Langdale the court could, in this first situation, "impute" undue influence. In the second situation, however, where the influence is occasional or circumstantial, "it is required to shew that some advantage was taken, or that there was some fear, some use of threat or of undue practice or persuasion." He felt that it was within the province of the court to decide which type of undue influence was involved, and that only the second type presents a question for a factual determination on the relationship itself.

Another distinction is subtle and important. Langdale's finding that Chandler's deed was not the product of undue influence turned on Chandler's susceptibility to a wide array of influences—especially from members of his family who opposed the transfer.* This fact, in addition to the fact that Chandler argued with Barsham and resisted signing the deed for some time, apparently suggested to the Master of the Rolls that Chandler acted out of considered self-interest rather than "by the undue influence of Barsham, as a solicitor." The case seems to hold that the solicitor-client relationship fell within the "imputed influence" category, but that the evidence was sufficient to prove that no controlling influence was exerted.

---

*Langdale even suggested that these plaintiffs knew more than they submitted in evidence. "[I]t seems singular that they should not have stated what were the motives which Barsham offered to induce the father to execute the deed against their objections."

An earlier English opinion, this by Lord Eldon, rested the distinction between the two kinds of influence on an affective relationship, not on a legal or formal association having a clear beginning and a clear end.[45] In this case, Ann Kerby, an octogenarian widow, had bought an annuity from her former attorney. The price of the annuity was arguably excessive. Lord Eldon set the transaction aside. The principal defense was that the attorney-client relationship had been dissolved before the transaction, but, Lord Eldon held, "it is the confidence [which] must be withdrawn." If the affective relationship remained, it was up to the attorney "to have acted with more providence and attention than are required even in the case of parent and child." It is asked, Lord Eldon continued, where is that rule to be found?

> I answer, in that great rule of the Court, that he, who bargains in a matter of advantage with a person placing confidence in him is bound to shew, that a reasonable use has been made of that confidence; a rule applying to trustees, attorneys, or any one else.

He secured the rule procedurally with a presumption—a procedural holding that is clearer here than Lord Langdale's imputation was in *Casborne v. Barsham:*

> It is necessary to say broadly, that those, who meddle with such transactions, take upon themselves the whole proof, that the thing is righteous. The circumstances, that pass upon such transactions, may be consistent with honest intentions: but they are so delicate in their nature, that parties must not complain of being called on to prove, they are so.

These are equitable principles that suggest a relatively ancient and philosophically sound rule for distinguishing cases involving a perceived relationship from those undoubtedly involving real psychic interchange but which are probably too subtle to be handled by the blunt instruments of the law. The rule suggests that the Wisconsin court was wrong in *Faulks* and the Arizona court wrong in *Pitt.* Both cases involved professional relationships and strong transference. On the other hand, the rule would support the Illinois court in Mrs. Banta's case, the California court in *Fritschi,* and the Maine court in Mrs. Smith's case. It would support also the Michigan court in *Powers,* but indications from that opinion imply that the relationship could be explained to exclude Lord Langdale's imputation of undue influence.

The operation of transference in undue influence cases suggests that the law should draw a distinction between the "let it happen" transfer and cases of unconscious manipulation. In "let it happen" cases the proponent or transferee ought to be required to show that the contested transfer was not the product of unreal psychological disturbances in the transferor or testator. Most relationships of the "let it happen" type are "helping" relationships, professional associations that the law ought to protect. In these cases the helping person involved ought to be required to demonstrate that the transfer of property to him by patient or client is consistent with the positive value the law seeks to protect in the relationship.[46] If retention of the transferred property is not consistent with the ideals expressed in the relationship the transfer ought to be set aside. This is simply a vindication of the professional trust involved—something the law protects through evidentiary privileges and legally sanctioned status symbols, and which it ought to protect in the field of gratuitous transfers.

In a few other cases (Mrs. Banta's case is an example), the "let it happen" transfer has not been made in a professional relationship, but the relationship is so much like professional trust, so strongly *fiduciary*, that it deserves the same protection. The test, as Lord Eldon said in *Gibson*, is whether the facts indicate human confidence justifiably reposed.

There are some few "let it happen" cases—*Fritschi* for example—in which the transfer ought not be set aside because the relationship is unimportant.[47] Such results can be categorized as exceptions to a general rule on "let it happen" transfers, or they can be regarded as not included in a rule that purports to reach only professional relationship "let it happen" cases. Even if the abstract rule fails to reach them, it is probable that the proponent can show, on the evidence, that transference, if any, was not strong enough to come within the evidentiary boundaries of the rule I am suggesting. (My suggestion is that the proponent be required to justify the transfer; in cases like *Fritschi* and *Powers* the evidentiary requirement can probably be met by the proponent.)

It is too much to hope that future generalizations about undue influence in appellate literature will turn only on the value of helping-person relationships and that the courts will abandon their traditional reliance on gimmicks such as presumptions and burden of proof.[48] But there is solid scientific ground for some improvement in the expression of rules governing gratuitous transfers within intimate human relationships, at least in those relationships that the law ought to protect from the penury of its society's "helping persons."[49] The ancient English opinions in *Casborne* and *Gibson* pointed in that direction long ago and that the psychological revelations of this century support those early judicial insights.[50]

I am suggesting a substantial departure from both the American majority and minority rules as they are usually stated. The majority rule—represented starkly by the court's opinion in *Faulks*—refuses to require explanations from transferees *unless* some overt activity procuring the transfer can be shown. The majority rule was formed and is maintained in psychological ignorance. It rests on the tenuous assumption—illustrated by the Wisconsin court's treatment of Mrs. Faulks's will—that the transferee must *do* something (with his hands?) in order to influence the transferor. We have known for a long time that the influences that radiate from one man to another are far too strong and far too subtle to be reduced to the flimsy test of overt activity.

The minority rule, as it was announced by the Michigan court recently, rests too heavily on illusive mechanical doctrines of evidence and, even when those doctrines operate clearly, infringes too far on the traditional American respect for freedom of testation. The Michigan court would raise a presumption of undue influence (or shift the burden of proof to the transferee) in *every* case where a confidential relationship (transference) is shown.[51] That rule is, I think, too broad and mechanical. It departs too far from the distinction put by Lord Langdale, who would have required an explanation from the transferee only in cases where there is "habitual exercise of power on the one side, and habitual submission on the other." The Michigan court's rule would be better were it confined to (1) cases of overt manipulation, (2) cases where a professional relationship is involved, and (3) cases where circumstances indicate a de facto fiduciary relationship.

The Transference Relationship
in Legal Counseling

At several points this paper has made the tangential observation that transference theory has something of value to say about legal counseling. This impression of mine was encouragingly supported by Dr. Andrew Watson in his recent book on psychiatry for lawyers. There he develops the idea that transference is a common phenomenon in the law office. If Dr. Watson is correct, as I believe he is, a few paragraphs to suggest an analogy from the practice of psychotherapy may be useful.

262

The analogy is found in a paper by the Jungian analyst J. Marvin Spiegelman. His theory is built on an observation made by Professor C.A. Meier, which he paraphrases as follows:

> [I]n the subject-object relation, A, the analyst, in investigating his patient, B, ever more intimately and deeply, soon finds that the 'cut'—that is, the distinction between subject and object, between himself and his patient—becomes blurred. As he moves more and more into the object, the analyst eventually finds that he cannot distinguish between what belongs to him, as his own complexes, and what belongs to the patient.

This means, Spiegelman says, that the analyst "cannot really go deeply into the psyche of his partner without discovering his own unresolved complexes and confusions as to what is patient and what is himself. Should he stubbornly resist this realization about himself and the situation, he will . . . *require that the patient carry the whole burden of the contents activated.*" In the process "the analyst . . . protects [both] his patient and himself from anything not quite right in his own condition."

Annoyance or impatience or anxiety in the lawyer—to extract the analogy—affects his clients far more than he realizes.[52] It would be better to "acknowledge one's fatigue, boredom, or anger . . . where it occurs, and analyze it, jointly." Spiegelman believes that analysts learn from patients, and most good lawyers would agree that lawyers learn from their clients. "To learn, one must be ready to submit to the other and expose one's ignorance."

Spiegelman believes that members of his profession have too often let themselves fall into one of two unsatisfactory models—the doctor-patient model or the teacher-pupil model. Neither of these takes account of the fact that "the relationship itself is central and . . . the desired objectivity, individuality, and understanding come out of the actual experience, rather than out of some presumed . . . objectivity" in the helping person. The doctor-patient model does not produce this human interaction because doctors tend to be "technique-oriented, impersonal, often mechanical, cut off from or not aware of . . . the spiritual factor." The doctor does not, even when sensitive, enter into the process as an equal. Nor does the teacher-pupil model satisfy him. "However wise a guru," he says, "[the teacher] is never quite human." It takes too long "to simply react to the situation and the person with some naturalness and not out of a theory."

Lawyers are not analysts and clients are not in the law office for analysis. But people who come to law offices are troubled, and the lawyers who talk to them—whether they admit it or not—are also troubled. The best guidance and support probably come from lawyers who intuitively appreciate and enter into what Dr. Watson identifies as a transference relationship. Not all of Spiegelman's personal experience is applicable to lawyers—partly because it is so personal that not all of it is applicable to anybody but Spiegelman—but there is much that is important and instructive for lawyers: "I found," he says, "that I, too, was shown to be human, limited, have complexes, and not be responding. . . . I find that the best interpretations come out of what is actually transpiring in the relationship. . . ."

Notes

(Complete references are in the Table of References at end of book)

1. K. Eissler, "The Psychiatrist and the Dying Patient" 144-47, 200-40 (1955). Copyright 1955 by International Universities Press, Inc. Quotations used by permission of the publisher.

2. The ego activity changes as death approaches and the patient becomes more capable of acts of forgiveness, kindness, and personal growth. *See also* Zinker and Fink.

3. Dr. Eissler believes that his personal generosity toward the patient must demonstrate "unambivalent love" toward two general emotional objectives in the patient—a (false) feeling of personal immortality and a more vague conviction that the environment will survive even if he does not. *See generally* Lifton, *Psychological Effect of the Atomic Bomb in Hiroshima—The Theme of Death;* Lifton, *On Death and Death Symbolism: The Hiroshima Disaster;* and Anthony.

4. Anna Freud referred to transference as "the most powerful instrument in the analyst's hand" and defined it to include "all those impulses experienced by the patient in his relationship with the analyst which are not newly created by the objective analytic situation but have their source in the early—indeed, the very earliest—object relations." Because of this infantile origin, transference reactions are valuable "as a means of information about the patient's past affective experiences." She analyzes transference reactions as: (1) those involving libidinal impulses ("The patient finds himself disturbed in his relation to the analyst by passionate emotions. . . . which do not seem to be justified by the facts of the actual situation.") and (2) transference of defense, which differs in that it is attributable to the ego rather than to the id ("[I]n the most instructive cases [the transference of defense is attributable] to the ego of the same infantile period in which the id impulse first arose."). The peculiar value of transference of defense is

that it contains information on the patient's ego development, "the history of the transformation through which his instincts have passed."

5. Etiology includes (according to Brussel and Cantzlaar):

[t]he facts concerning the origin and development of a patient's illness. Often used loosely to mean "cause," the term is actually more comprehensive, embracing predisposition, environmental influences, and other phenomena directly or indirectly involved in the development of the illness.

6. Freud said:

By transference is meant a striking pecunarity of neurotics. They develop toward their physician the emotional relations, both of an affectionate and hostile character which is not based upon the actual situation but are derived from their relations to their parents (the Oedipus complex). Transference is a proof of the fact that adults have not overcome their former childish dependence; it coincides with the force which has been named "suggestion"; and it is only by learning to make use of it that the physician is enabled to induce the patient to overcome his internal resistances and do away with his repressions. Thus psychoanalytic treatment acts as a second education of the adult, as a corrective to his education as a child.

7. Sublimation is "[a] defense mechanism whereby consciously unacceptable instinctual demands are channeled into acceptable forms for gratification." Brussel and Cantzlaar.

8. Gill refers to this process as a "regressive transference neurosis" and enumerates the "trappings of analysis" that both encourage and flow from it:

the recumbancy and inability to see the analyst . . . with the inevitable accompanying sense of being inferior; the frustration by silence and through other techniques; the awakening of strong needs without gratification; the absence of reality cues from the analyst; the general atmosphere of timelessness, with the relative disregard of symptoms . . . free association, bringing into the field of consciousness the thoughts and feelings ordinarily excluded from the usual interpersonal relationship; the emphasis on fantasy; and . . . the frequency of visits which, metaphorically speaking, we may regard as the constant irritation necessary to keep open the wounds into the unconscious, and indeed as a general strong invitation to become dependent, to regress, and to feel safe enough to do so because there is time enough and stability and frequency.

Fromm-Reichmann gives examples.

9. Gill discusses "transference cure":

> I think there is little doubt that . . . by overt behavior toward the patient one can more quickly get him to change some aspects of his behavior. But what is the meaning of such a change? It is an adaptation to this particular interpersonal relationship—as it exists between patient and analyst. But this is not the goal of analysis. The goal of analysis is an intrapsychic modification in the patient, so that for example his dependent behavior is given up not because he has learned that if he acts too independent he will be punished . . . but because despite the invitation to regress . . . he has come to feel and understand his dependency in such a way that he no longer needs it or wants it—and that is a conclusion valid not simply for this particular interpersonal relationship but has more general applicability, in short has the status of an intrapsychic change.

And Karl Menninger finds it common in psychiatric practice:

> Every psychiatrist has had scores of patients who have been sick for a long time with a nervous illness and who are miraculously cured after a few interviews with him. . . . The patient is cured if he or she happens to develop a strong transference and feels that the physician's attitude is reciprocal. This does not mean that the physician must love him or her in the ordinary sense, but that he must be loving in the same way that the original person of the transference—that is, the mother or father—was loving.
>
> The only trouble about these cures is that they last only so long as the transference lasts. . . . That is why some people are well as long as they keep running to the doctor. . . .

Menninger mentions, as Freud's experience with Dora illustrates, that the transference feelings can often be discovered only through dream analysis or through the disguised expression of feelings.

10. Two comments should be made on this assessment of psychoanalysis. First, Rogers does not discuss the use of transference to discover etiology—to find out about the patient's past experiences. Second, he does not emphasize (at least not as much as the psychiatrists who write on transference) the important effects of dissolution of the transference as a last step in treatment. The early stage of transference is positive in that it leads to discussion of "trains of thought ordinarily automatically repressed," and leads the patient to feel that "he may not be so different from other people . . . he feels hope, and his attitude . . . is that at last he has found . . . someone to understand him." It is difficult but essential that this attitude be ultimately made realistic.

"The analysis is not complete . . . until he has given up the analyst as an object of very special significance in his own emotional life." Peck sees a technique of dissolution as important to avoid "the difficulty of a permanent transference bondage." He suggests that one problem with nonmedical psychotherapy is that it may develop and depend on a permanent transference. Peck, ironically, ends up accusing "client-centered therapy" of the same sins Rogers finds in psychoanalysis.

11. [T] he essential factor is the dissociation of the psyche and not the existence of a highly charged affect and, consequently . . . the main therapeutic problem is not abreaction but how to integrate the dissociation. This argument advances our discussion and entirely agrees with our experience that a traumatic complex brings about dissociation of the psyche. The complex is not under the control of the will and for this reason it possesses the quality of psychic autonomy.

12. "Whenever this drive for wholeness appears, it begins by disguising itself under the symbolism of incest, for, unless he seeks it in himself, a man's nearest feminine counterpart is to be found in his mother, sister or daughter."

13. Jung goes beyond the therapeutic; he describes the process as virtually political.

14. Jung:

All activated contents of the unconscious have the tendency to appear in projection. It is even the rule that an unconscious content which is constellated shows itself first as a projection. Any activated archetype can appear in projection, either into an external situation, or into people, or into circumstances—in short, into all sorts of objects. There are even transferences to animals and to things.

15. Hatch v. Hatch, 9 Ves. Jr. 292, 297, 32 Eng. Rep. 615, 617 (Ch. 1804).

16. *See* 3 W. Bowe and D. Parker, Page on Wills § 29.124, at 669 (1961).

17. 20 App. Div. 2d 464, 247 N.Y.S.2d 664 (1964), *aff'd,* 15 N.Y.2d 825, 205 N.E.2d 864, 257 N.Y.S.2d 941 (1965).

18. "The emotional base reflected in the letter . . . is gratitude utterly unreal, highly exaggerated and pitched to a state of fervor and ecstasy." The court suggested that Weiss had a hand in writing it.

19. These transfers were summarized by the dissenters. The majority regarded the inter vivos transfers as circumstantial evidence of undue influence in the execution of the will.

20. The majority, in referring to Kaufmann's ambiguous allusion to Weiss's effect on his sex life, saw an "implication . . . that Weiss in some fashion was identified with Robert's sex life," but noted Weiss's denial of such involvement. The dissenters spoke of "love and affection" and "the intimate relationship which existed between the two men" but insisted that "the morals of these men" were irrelevant. The dissenters later admitted, rather more bluntly, that "the relationship may be likened to that of one who has a mistress."

21. 247 N.Y.S.2d at 682 (paraphrasing medical testimony from the record). The majority saw the manipulation as a shift in affection from Robert's brothers to Weiss, rather than as a creation of affection *ab initio*. That is, of course, similar to Freud's description of his experience with Dora.

22. This was, the majority said, not overcome by "[t]he fact that the instrument . . . was prepared by reputable, competent attorneys. . . ." It is clear—although the point is well hidden—that the holding does not rest upon a presumption of undue influence, but upon a finding that the evidence supported the judgment of the trial court.

23. "Of course, the court does not condone the relationship, but the moral law may not be substituted for the law of wills; and it should be overlooked that difficult cases tend to make bad law." Ibid. at 492, N.Y.S.2d at 691.

24. See 1 W. Bowe and D. Parker, Page on Wills § 154 (1960); 3 W. Bowe and D. Parker, Page on Wills § § 29,124, 29,131, at 669, 685 (1961); 1 R. Jennings, Jarman on Wills 28-29 (8th ed., 1951).

25. 246 Wis. 319, 17 N.W.2d 423 (1945).

26. 88 Ariz. 312, 356 P.2d 408 (1960).

27. *In re* Estate of Harber, 102 Ariz. 285, 428 P.2d 662 (1967).

28. Swenson v. Wintercorn, 92 Ill. App. 2d 88, 234 N.E.2d 91 (1968).

29. *In re* Estate of Fritschi, 60 Cal. 2d 367, 384 P.2d 656, 33 Cal. Rptr. 264 (1963).

30. 247 Cal. App. 2d 574, 55 Cal. Rptr. 750 (Ct. App. 1967).

31. Garrish v. Chambers, 135 Me. 70, 189 A. 187 (1937).

32. *In re* Powers' Estate, 375 Mich. 150, 134 N.W.2d 148 (1965).

33. *See In re* Wood's Estate, 374 Mich. 278, 132 N.W.2d 35 (1965).

34. Estate of Karabatian, 170 N.W.2d 166 (Mich. 1969) is a recent confirmation of this determination. *See also* Matter of Casey (Sur. Ct. 1969), N.Y.L.J., Nov. 25, 1969, at 16; 1 J. Story, *Equity Jurisprudence* 301 (12th ed., 1877); Annot., 19 A.L.R. 3d 575 (1968); Comment 38 Miss. L.J. 156, 159 (1966).

35. *See* Grondziak v. Grondziak, 12 Mich. App. 61, 162 N.W.2d 354 (1968); Lipson v. Lipson, 183 S.2d 900 (Miss., 1966), *noted in* 38 Miss. L.J. 156 (1966).

36. 1 W. Bowe and D. Parker, Page on Wills § 15.4, at 721-22 (1960).

37. For example, *In re* Estate of Harber, 102 Ariz. 428 P.2d 662 (1967); Galvan v. Miller, 79 N.M. 540, 445 P.2d 961 (1968).

38. 1 W. Bowe and D. Parker, Page on Wills § 15.1 (1960); *see* Richardson v. Bly, 181 Mass. 97, 63 N.E.3 (1902).

39. *See In re* Estate of Taylor, 423 Pa. 276, 223 A.2d 708 (1966); Stapleton, *The Presumption of Undue Influence,* 17, *University of New Brunswick Law Journal* 46, 53 (1967); Annot., 19 A.L.R.3d 575, 585-87 (1968).

40. Galvan v. Miller, 79 N.M. 540, 445 P.2d 961 (1968); *see* Vantrease v. Carl, 410 S.W.2d 629 (Tenn. App. 1966).

41. *See* 3 W. Bowe and D. Parker, Page on Wills § 29.81, at 591-97 (1961). Bowe and Parker attempt to enumerate the "plus factors," at Ibid. § 29, 81, at 602-7.

42. 1 W. Bowe and D. Parker, Page on Wills § 15.9 (1960).

43. "The question in such cases does not turn upon the point whether there is any intention to cheat or not; but upon the obligation from the fiduciary relation of the parties to make a frank and full disclosure." Story. *See* O'Rourke v. O'Rourke, 167 N.W.2d 733 (Minn. 1969); Comment, 38, *Mississippi Law Journal,* 156, 158-59 (1966).

44. Casborne v. Barsham, 2 Beav. 76, 48 Eng. Rep. 1108 (Exch., 1839). There is some authority both ways for the proposition that the rules on confidential relationship do not apply in wills cases as they do in inter vivos transfer cases. 3 W. Bowe and D. Parker, Page on Wills § 29.84, at 600 (1961). Story discusses the subject in great detail without affirming the distinction.

45. Gibson v. Jeyes, 6 Ves. Jr. 266, 31 Eng. Rep. 1044 (Ch. 1801).

46. "If the means of personal control are given, they must be always restrained to purposes of good faith and personal good."

47. S. Bailey, Wills 76, 80 (6th ed., 1967). *See* 1 W. Bowe and D. Parker, Page on Wills §§ 15.2-3, 15.5-6 (1960); Annot. 25 A.L.R.2d 1429 (1952).

48. *See In re* Wood's Estate, 374 Mich. 278, 132 N.W.2d 35 (1965); 3 W. Bowe and D. Parker, Page on Wills §§ 29.77-.134 (1961); Comment 65, *Michigan Law Review,* 223 (1966).

49. *See* Brown v. Commercial Nat'l Bank, 42 Ill. 2d 365, 247 N.E.2d 894 (1969); Richardson v. Bly, 181 Mass. 97, 63 N.E. 3 (1902); Zipkin v. Freeman, 436 S.W.2d 753 (Mo. 1968); 3 W. Bowe and D. Parker, Page on Wills §§ 29.84-106 (1961); Story and Stapleton.

50. Opinions too often begin by badly confusing undue influence with fraud or mental incapacity, as in Hatch v. Hatch 9 Ves. Jr. 292, 297, 32 Eng. Rep. 615, 617 (Ch. 1804). Story is an ancient textbook source of the confusion ("constructive fraud"); a more modern English textbook example is D. Parry, Law of Succession 10 (5th ed., 1966). *See* Logan v. Washington, 408 F.2d 1303 (D.C. Cir. 1969).

51. *See Comment,* 65, *Michigan Law Review,* 223, 230-31 (1966); Comment, 38, *Mississippi Law Journal* 156, 160-61 (1966). *See also* Stapleton, Annot., 19 A.L.R.3d 575 594-98 (1968).

52. See Redmount, *Attorney Personalities and Some Psychological Aspects of Legal Consultation;* Redmount, *Humanistic Law Through Legal Counseling.*

Table of
References

Table of References

(Omitted from this table are reports of judicial opinions; these are contained in footnotes at the end of the chapters.)

Books

Allport, *Becoming* (1955).

Anthony, *The Child's Discovery of Death* (1940).

Ardrey, *The Territorial Imperative* (1966).

Auchincloss, *The Ambassador From Wall Street* (1963).

Auchincloss, *Powers of Attorney* (1963).

Bailey, *Wills* (6th ed., 1967).

Baldwin, *Tell Me How Long the Train's Been Gone* (1968).

Barrett, *Irrational Man* (1958).

Berne, *Games People Play* (Grove ed., 1967).

Berne, *Transactional Analysis in Psychotherapy* (1961).

Bowe and Parker, *Page on Wills* (1960).

Bromley, *The Psychology of Human Aging* (1966).

Brussel and Cantzlaar, *The Layman's Dictionary of Psychiatry* (1967).

Burton and Harris, *Clinical Studies of Personality* (2 vol., Torchbook ed., 1966).

Campbell and Stanley, *Experimental and Quasi-Experimental Designs for Research* (1963).

Dunne, *The City of the Gods* (1966).

Eissler, *The Psychiatrist and the Dying Patient* (1955).

Farberow, *Taboo Topics* (1963).

Feifel, *The Meaning of Death* (1959) (paperback ed., 1965).

Ferenczi, *Sex in Psycho-Analysis* (1958).

Festschrift von C.A. Meier (1965).

Forster, *Howard's End* (1943).

Fox, *Experiment Perilous: Physicians and Patients Facing the Unknown* (1959).

Frank, *Persuasion and Healing* (Schocken ed., 1963).

Frankl, *Man's Search for Meaning* (1963).

Freeman, *Legal Interviewing and Counseling* (1964).

Freud, A., *The Ego and the Mechanisms of Defense* (1936).

Freud, S., *Beyond the Pleasure Principle* (Strachey tr., Bantam ed., 1959).

Freud, S., *Dora: Analysis of a Case of Hysteria* (Collier ed., 1963).

Freud, S., *The Ego and the Id.* (Riviere tr., Norton ed., 1960).

Freud, S., *The Future of An Illusion* (Strachey tr., Anchor ed., 1964).

Freud, S., *New Introductory Lectures on Psycho-Analysis* (Strachey tr., Norton ed., 1965).

Freud, S., *On Creativity and the Unconscious* (Nelson-Harper ed., 1958).

Freud, S., *Psychoanalysis* (1926).

Freud, S., *The Psychopathology of Everyday Life* (Mentor ed., Brill tr., 1951).

Freud, S., *Totem and Taboo* (Norton ed., Strachey tr., 1950).

Freud, S., Ferenczi, Abraham, Simmel, and Jones, *Psychoanalysis and the War Neuroses* (1921).

Fromm, *Sigmund Freud's Mission* (1959).

Fromm-Reichmann, *Principles of Intensive Psychotherapy* (Phoenix ed., 1960).

Fulton, *Death and Identity* (1965).

Fulton, *The Sacred and the Secular: Attitudes of the American Public Toward Death, Funerals and Funeral Directors* (1963).

Ginzburg, *Journey Into A Whirlwind* (1967).

Glaser and Strauss, *Awareness of Dying* (1965).

Goffman, *Asylums* (1961).

Goody, *Death, Property and the Ancestors* (1962).

Green, *Judge and Jury* (1930).

Green, *The Rationale of Proximate Cause* (1927).

Guttmacher and Weihoffen, *Psychiatry and the Law* (1952).

Hazard, *Law in a Changing America* (1968).

Heidegger, *An Introduction to Metaphysics* (Manheim tr., Anchor ed., 1961).

Hertz, *Death and the Right Hand* (Needham tr., Free Press ed., 1960).

Hocking, *The Meaning of Immortality in Human Experience* (1957).

Jennings, *Jarman on Wills* (8th ed., 1951).

Jones, *Papers on Psycho-Analysis* (Beacon ed., 1961).

Jung, *Analytical Psychology, Its Theory and Practice* (1968).

Jung, *Freud and Psychoanalysis* (Hull tr., 1961) (including The Significance of the Father in the Destiny of the Individual).

Jung, *Memories, Dreams, Reflections* (R. and C. Winston tr., 1963).

Jung, *Modern Man in Search of a Soul* (Dell and Baynes tr., Harvest ed., 1933).

Jung, *Psychological Reflections* (Harper ed., 1961).

Jung, *The Collected Works* (Bollingen, 2d ed., 1966) (including in Vol. 16, "The Psychology of the Transference and The Practice of Psychotherapy").

Katz, Goldstein, and Dershowitz, *Psychoanalysis, Psychiatry and the Law* (1967).

Kierkegaard, *Fear and Trembling; and The Sickness Unto Death* (Lowrie tr., Anchor ed., 1954).

Kubler-Ross, *On Death and Dying* (1969).

Lambert and Lambert, *Social Psychology* (1964).

Lifton, *Death in Life* (1968).

Lorenz, *On Aggression* (Bantam ed., 1967).

Lowndes and Kramer, *Federal Estate and Gift Taxes* (1962).

Mauss, *The Gift* (Cunnison tr., Free Press ed., 1954).

Menninger, *Man Against Himself* (1938).

Menninger, *The Human Mind* (1930).

Montagu, *Immortality* (1955).

Murdoch, *The Red and the Green* (1965).

Parry, *Law of Succession* (5th ed., 1966).

Peck, *The Meaning of Psychoanalysis* (Permabooks ed., 1950).

Porter, *An Introduction to Therapeutic Counseling* (1950).

Post, *The Personality of a House* (rev. ed., 1933).

Rahner, *On The Theology of Death* (1961).

Reik, *Masochism in Modern Man* (Beigel and Kurth tr., 1941).

Reik, *The Inner Experience of a Psychoanalyst* (1949), (also published as Listening With the Third Ear).

Rogers, *Client-Centered Therapy* (Houghton-Mifflin ed., 1965).

Sartre, *Being and Nothingness* (Barnes tr., 1956).

Sartre, *Existential Psychoanalysis* (Barnes tr., 1953).

Shneidman and Farberow, *Clues to Suicide* (1957).

Simon, *The Sociology of Law* (1968).

Singer, *The Magician of Lublin* (Gottleib and Singer tr., 1960).

Skinner, *Science and Human Behavior* (Free Press ed., 1965).

Snow, *The Conscience of the Rich* (1960).

Southard, *Shell-Shock and Other Neuropsychiatric Problems* (1919).

Story, *Equity Jurisprudence* (12th ed., 1877).

Stouffer, *Communism, Conformity and Civil Liberties* (1963).

Sykes, *The Society of Captives* (1958).

Tinbergen, *Social Behaviour in Animals* (2d ed., 1965).

Tolstoy, *The Death of Ivan Ilyitch and Other Stories* (1923).

Trachtman, *Estate Planning* (1965).

Tyler, *The Work of the Counselor* (3d ed., 1969).

Van Den Berg, *The Psychology of the Sickbed* (1966).

Vincent, *Melville and Hawthorne in the Berkshires* (1966).

Watson, *Psychiatry for Lawyers* (1968).

Wigmore, *Evidence* (3d ed., 1940).

Anthologies

(These works collect periodical articles, parts of books, and unpublished papers. Included at the end of each reference is a shorthand phrase, which is used in referring to these collections in the "Articles" portion of this table of references.)

Farberow, *Taboo Topics* (1963). (*Taboo*)

Feifel, *The Meaning of Death* (1959) (paperback ed., 1965). (*Meaning*)

Fulton, *Death and Identity* (1965). (*Identity*)

Hollins, *Peace is Possible* (1966). (*Peace*)

Katz, Goldstein, and Dershowitz, *Psychoanalysis, Psychiatry and the Law* (1967). (*Psychoanalysis*)

The Study of Lives (1963). (*Lives*)

Shneidman and Farberow, *Clues to Suicide* (1957). (*Clues*)

Articles and Papers

Akers, "Fraud and Undue Influence—Confidential Relationships and the Assumption of Undue Influence," 38, *Mississippi Law Journal*, 156 (1966).

Alexander and Alberstein, "Affective Responses to the Concept of Death in a Population of Children and Early Adolescents," 93, *Journal of Genetic Psychology,* 167 (1958); also in *Identity*.

Alexander and Alderstein, "Death and Religion," in *Meaning*.

Alexander, Colley, and Alderstein, "Is Death a Matter of Indifference," 43, *Journal of Psychology*, 277 (1957); also in *Identity*.

Armstrong, "West African Inquest," 56, *American Anthropologist*, 1051 (1954).

Barry, "Significance of Maternal Bereavement Before Age of Eight in Psychiatric Patients," 62, *Archives of Neurology and Psychiatry*, 630 (1940); also in *Identity*.

Becker, "Problems of Inference and Proof in Participant Observation," 23, *American Sociological Review*, 652 (1958).

Belli, "Demonstrative Evidence," 10, *Wyoming Law Journal*, 15 (1955).

Blauner, "Death and Social Structure," 29, *Psychiatry*, 378 (1966).

Bloch, Silber, and Perry, "Some Factors in the Emotional Reaction of Children to Disaster," 113, *American Journal of Psychiatry*, 416 (1956).

Brewster, "Separation Reaction in Psychosomatic Disease and Neurosis," 3, *Psychosomatic Medicine*, 154 (1952); also in *Identity*.

Briggs, "The Psychology of Successful Persuasion," *Chartered Life Underwriter Journal* (April, 1967), p. 49 (July, 1967), p. 59 (April, 1968), p. 51.

Burton, "Death as Countertransference," 49, *Psychoanalysis and the Psychoanalytic Review*, 3 (1962).

Christ, "Attitudes Toward Death Among a Group of Acute Geriatric Psychiatric Patients," 16, *Journal of Gerontology*, 56 (1961); also in *Identity*.

Cohen, Motto, and Seiden, "An Instrument for Evaluating Suicide Potential," 122, *American Journal of Psychiatry*, 886 (1966).

Corcoran, "The Contingent Insurance Trust—A Hidden Bonanza for Minor Children," 55, *Illinois Bar Journal*, 596 (1967).

Crocker, "New Fields for Demonstrative Evidence," 26, *Insurance Counsel Journal*, 562 (1959).

Crown, O'Donovan, and Thompson, "Attitudes Toward Attitudes Toward Death," 20, *Psychological Reports*, 1181 (1967).

Coulson, "Notes Toward the Basic Encounter Group as a Research Tool" (Unpublished, 1967).

Diggory and Rothman, "Values Destroyed by Death," 63, *Journal of Abnormal and Social Psychology*, 205 (1961); also in *Identity*.

277

Dooley, "Demonstrative Evidence—Nothing New," 42, *Illinois Bar Journal*, 136 (1953).

Dunham, "The Method, Process, and Frequency of Wealth Transmission at Death," 30, *University of Chicago Law Review*, 241 (1963).

Farberow and Shneidman, "Suicide and Age," in *Clues.*

Faxon, "Demonstrative Evidence and Handwriting Testimony," *Trial Lawyers Guide* (February, 1957), p. 1.

Feifel, "Attitudes of Mentally Ill Patients Toward Death," 122, *Journal of Nervous and Mental Disease*, 375 (1955); also in *Identity.*

Feifel, "Attitudes Toward Death: A Psychological Perspective"(Unpublished, 1967).

Feifel, "Attitudes Toward Death in Some Normal and Mentally Ill Populations," in *Meaning.*

Feifel, "Death," in *Taboo.*

Feifel, "Physicians Consider Death," *Proceedings of the 75th Annual Convention, American Psychological Association*, p. 201 (1967).

Feifel, "Some Aspects of the Meaning of Death," in *Clues.*

Feifel and Jones, "Perception of Death as Related to Nearness to Death," *Proceedings of the 76th Annual Convention, American Psychological Association (1968).*

Feldman and Hersen, "Attitudes Toward Death in Nightmare Subjects," 72, *Journal of Abnormal Psychology*, 421 (1967).

Ferracuti, "Suicide in a Catholic Country," in *Clues.*

Friedman, "The Dynastic Trust," 73, *Yale Law Journal*, 547 (1964).

Freud, A., "The Ego and the Mechanisms of Defense" (1936), in *Psychoanalysis.*

Fulton, "Death and the Self," 3, *Journal of Religion and Health*, 359 (1964).

Fulton, "The Sacred and the Secular: Attitudes of the American Public Toward Death, Funerals and Funeral Directors," in *Identity.*

Fulton and Geis, "Death and Social Values," 3, *Indian Journal of Social Research*, 7 (1962); also in *Identity.*

Gerhart, "A New Look at Estate Planning: The General Practitioner and Mr. Average," 50, *American Bar Association Journal*, 1043 (1964).

Gibbs, "The Kpelle Moots: A Therapeutic Model For the Informal Study of Disputes," 33, *Africa*, 1 (1963).

Gill, "Psychoanalysis and Exploratory Psychotherapy," 2, *Journal of the American Psychoanalytic Association*, 771 (1954); also in *Psychoanalysis*.

Gill, B., "The Theatre, Aren't We Lucky," *The New Yorker* (February 10, 1968), p. 86.

Golding, Atwood, and Goodman, "Anxiety and Two Cognitive Forms of Resistance to the Idea of Death," 18, *Psychological Reports*, 359 (1966).

Goldner and Mrovka, "Demonstrative Evidence and Audiovisual Aids at Trial," 8, *University of Florida Law Review*, 185 (1955).

Gordon, "Demonstrative Evidence Past, Present, and Future," 32, *Wisconsin Bar Bulletin*, 11 (1959).

Grismer and Shaffer, "Experience-Based Teaching Methods in Legal Counseling" (Unpublished, 1969).

Halbach, "Stare Decisis and Rules of Construction in Wills and Trusts," 52, *California Law Review*, 921 (1964).

Hale, "A Good Light," *The New Yorker* (September 28, 1968), p. 100.

Hale, "The World, The Flesh, and the Devil," *The New Yorker* (April 27, 1968), p. 38.

Halleck, "The Psychiatrist and the Legal Process," *Psychology Today* (February, 1969), p. 24.

Henry and Short, "The Sociology of Suicide," in Henry and Short, *Suicide and Homicide, Some Economic, Sociological, and Psychological Aspects of Aggression* (1951); also in *Clues*.

Hilgard, Newman, and Fisk, "Strength of Adult Ego Following Childhood Bereavement," 30, *American Journal of Psychiatry*, 788 (1959); also in *Identity*.

Hug-Hellmuth, "The Child's Concept of Death," 34, *Psychoanalytic Quarterly*, 499 (1965).

Hutschnecker, "Personality Factors in Dying Patients," in *Meaning*.

Hochman and Lindsay, "Taxation, Interest and the Timing of Intergeneration Wealth Transfers," 20, *National Tax Journal*, 219 (1967).

Jackson, D., "Theories of Suicide," in *Clues*.

Jackson, E., "Grief and Religion," in *Meaning*.

Jeffers, Nichols, and Eisdorfer, "Attitudes of Older Persons Toward Death: A Preliminary Survey," 16, *Journal of Gerontology*, 53 (1961); also in *Identity*.

279

Joseph, "Transference and Countertransference in the Case of a Dying Patient," 49, *Psychoanalysis and the Psychoanalytic Review*, 21 (1962).

Jung, "The Soul and Death," from *Wirklichkeit der Seele* (1934), in *Meaning* (tr. by R. F. C. Hull).

Kahne, "Psychiatrist Observer in the Classroom," 15, *Medical Trial Techniques Quarterly*, 81 (1969).

Kalish, "Some Variables in Death Attitudes," 59, *Journal of Social Psychology*, 137 (1963); also in *Identity*.

Kalven, "The Quest for a Middle Range; Empirical Inquiry and Legal Policy," in Kasper, *Law In a Changing America*, 56 (1968).

Kapser, "The Doctor and Death," in *Meaning*.

Kastenbaum, "Time and Death in Adolescence," in *Meaning*.

Kimbrell, "Planning Insurance Transactions to Avoid Transfers in Contemplation of Death," 36, *University of Missouri at Kansas City Law Review*, 1 (1968).

Ladner, "Demonstrations and Experiments," *Trial Lawyer's Guide* (August, 1959), p. 1.

Lester, "Fear of Death of Suicidal Persons," 20, *Psychological Reports*, 1077 (1966).

Lester, "Attempted Suicide and Body Image," 66, *Journal of Psychology*, 287 (1967).

Lifton, "On Death and Death Symbolism: The Hiroshima Disaster," 27, *Psychiatry*, 191 (1964); also in *Peace*.

Lifton, "Psychological Effects of the Atomic Bomb in Hiroshima: The Theme of Death," 92, *Daedalus*, 462 (1963); also in *Identity*.

Lindemann, "Symptomatology and Management of Acute Grief," 101, *American Journal of Psychiatry*, 141 (1944); also in *Identity*.

Litman, "Some Aspects of the Treatment of the Potentially Suicidal Patient," in *Clues*.

Lowndes and Stephens, "Identification of Property Subject to the Federal Estate Tax," 65, *Michigan Law Review*, 105 (1966).

Lydgate, "Where Is Thy Sting?" 206, *Spectator*, 308 (1961).

McClelland, "The Harlequin Complex," in *Lives*.

Mandelbaum, "Social Uses of Funeral Rites," in *Meaning;* also in *Identity*.

Meier, "Projection, Transference, and the Subject-Object Relation in Psychology," 4, *Journal of Analytical Psychology*, 21 (1959).

Mills, "Medicolegal Ramifications of Current Practices and Suggested Changes in Certifying Modes of Death," 13, *Journal of Forensic Sciences,* 70 (1968).

Milwid, "The Misuse of Demonstrative Evidence," 28, *Insurance Counsel Journal,* 435 (1961).

Moss, Hamilton, and English, "Psychotherapy of the Suicidal Patient," 112, *American Journal of Psychiatry,* 112 (1956); also in *Clues.*

Murphy, "Discussion," in *Meaning.*

Nader, "The Anthropological Study of Law," 67, *American Anthropologist,* 3 (1965).

Nagy, "The Child's View of Death," 73, *Journal of Genetic Psychology,* 3 (1948); also in *Meaning.*

Natterson, "Observations Concerning Fear of Death in Fatally Ill Children and Their Mothers," *Medicine,* 456 (1960); also in *Identity.*

O'Connor, "Bring in the Whiskey Now, Mary," *The New Yorker,* (August 12, 1967), p. 36.

Pollack, "Suicide in a General Hospital," in *Clues.*

Redmount, "Attorney Personalities and Some Psychological Aspects of Legal Consultation," 109, *University of Pennsylvania Law Review,* 972 (1961).

Redmount, "Humanistic Law Through Legal Counseling," 2, *Connecticut Law Review,* 98 (1969).

Redmount, "Humanistic Law Through Legal Education," 1, *Connecticut Law Review,* 201 (1968).

Rhudick and Dibner, "Age, Personality, and Health Correlates of Death Concerns in Normal Aged Individuals," 16, *Journal of Gerontology,* 44 (1961); also in *Identity.*

Richter, "The Phenomenon of Unexplained Sudden Death in Animals and Man," in Gantt, *Physiological Bases of Psychiatry,* (1958); also in *Meaning.*

Riecker, "A Pragmatic View of Transfers" in *Contemplation of Death,* 53, *Minnesota Law Review,* 265 (1968).

Riesman, "Some Observations on Law and Psychology," 19, *University of Chicago Law Review,* 30 (1951).

Rogers, "The Group Comes of Age," *Psychology Today,* (December, 1969), p. 27.

Schuyler, "The Art of Interpretation in Future Interests Cases," 17, *Vanderbilt Law Review,* 1407 (1964).

Shaffer, "A Classroom Will Form for Wealthy Clients" (Unpublished, 1970).

Shaffer, "Appellate Courts and Prejudiced Verdicts," 26, *University of Pittsburgh Law Review,* 1 (1964), in Frumer and Friedman, *Personal Injury Annual,* 751 (1965).

Shaffer, "Bullets, Bad Florins, and Old Boots: A report of the Indiana Trial Judges Seminar on The Judges' Control Over Demonstrative Evidence," 39, *Notre Dame Lawyer,* 20 (1963), in Frumer and Friedman, *Personal Injury Annual* (1969), p. 553.

Shaffer, "Undue Influence, Confidential Relationship, and the Psychology of Transference," 45, *Notre Dame Lawyer,* 197 (1970).

Shaffer, "A Conversation on Death" (Unpublished, 1968).

Shaffer, "Empirical Research in Trusts and Estate" (Unpublished, 1969).

Shaffer, "Fifty Estates in Elkhart County," *Res Gestae* (September, 1969), p. 22.

Shaffer, "Judges, Repulsive Evidence, and the Ability to Respond," 43, *Notre Dame Lawyer,* 503 (1968), in Frumer and Friedman, *Personal Injury Annual* (1969), pp. 553, 578.

Shaffer, "The Law and Order Game" (Unpublished, 1969).

Shaffer, "Nonestate Planning," 42, *Notre Dame Lawyer,* 153 (1966), 106, *Trusts and Estates,* 319 (1967), 11, *Tax Counselor's Quarterly,* 161 (1967).

Shaffer, "The Estate Planning Counselor and Values Destroyed by Death," 55, *Iowa Law Review,* 376 (1970).

Shaffer, "The Psychological Autopsy in Judicial Opinions Under Section 2035," 3, *Loyola University of Los Angeles Law Review,* 1, (1970).

Shaffer, "The Psychology of Testation, 108 Trusts and Estates," 11 (1969).

Shaffer, "Will Interviews, Young Family Clients, and the Psychology of Testation," 44, *Notre Dame Lawyer,* 345 (1969).

Sheridan, "Power to Appoint for a Non-Charitable Purpose: A Duologue or Endacott's Ghost," 13, *DePaul Law Review,* 210 (1964).

Shneidman, "Orientation Toward Cessation: A Reexamination of Current Modes of Death," 13, *Journal of Forensic Sciences,* 33 (1968).

Shneidman, "Orientations Toward Death: A Vital Aspect of the Study of Lives," 2, *International Journal of Psychiatry,* 167 (1966).

Shneidman, "Suicide," in *Taboo.*

Shneidman, "Suicide, Sleep and Death," 28, *Journal of Consulting Psychology,* 95 (1964).

Shneidman, "The Deaths of Herman Melville," in Vincent, *Melville and Hawthorne in The Berkshires* (1966).

Shneidman and Farberow, "Genuine and Simulated Suicide Notes," in *Clues.*

Shneidman and Farberow, "Clues to Suicide," 71, *Public Health Reports,* 100 (1956); also in *Clues.*

Shneidman and Farberow, "Suicide and Death," in *Meaning.*

Shneidman and Farberow, "The Logic of Suicide," in *Clues.*

Shneidman and Lane, "Psychologic and Social Work Clues to Suicide in a Schizophrenic Patient," in *Clues.*

Shoor and Speed, "Death, Delinquency, and the Mourning Process," 37, *Psychiatric Quarterly,* 540 (1963); also in *Identity.*

Shrut, "Attitudes Toward Old Age and Death," 42, *Mental Hygiene,* 259 (1958); also in *Identity.*

Silving, "Suicide and Law," in *Clues.*

Spangenberg, "The Use of Demonstrative Evidence," 21, *Ohio State Law Journal,* 178 (1960).

Spiegelman, "Some Implications of the Transference," in *Festschrift von C.A. Meier* (1965).

Spock, "Helping Your Children to Learn About Money," *Redbook,* (December, 1967), p. 29.

Stapleton, "The Presumption of Undue Influence," 17, *University of New Brunswick Law Journal,* 46 (1967).

Stern, Williams, and Prados, "Grief Reactions in Later Life," 58, *American Journal of Psychiatry,* 289 (1951); also in *Identity.*

Swenson, "Attitudes Toward Death Among the Aged," 42, *Minnesota Medicine* 399 (1959); also in *Identity.*

Szasz, "The Concept of Transference," 44, *International Journal of Psychoanalysis* (1963).

Szasz, "The Myth Of Mental Illness," 15, *American Psychologist,* 113 (1960).

Tabachnick, "Observations on Attempted Suicide," in *Clues.*

Teicher, " 'Combat Fatigue' or Death Anxiety Neurosis," 117, *Journal of Nervous and Mental Disease,* 234 (1953); also in *Identity.*

Thomas, "Dealing with Approaching Death: Changes in Attitudes in the Past One Hundred Years" (Unpublished, 1967).

Tolor and Reznikoff, "Relation Between Insight, Repression-Sensitization, Internal-External Control, and Death Anxiety," 72, *Journal of Abnormal Psychology*, 426 (1967).

Trachtman, *Maxims For Estate Planners*, The Practical Lawyer, (February, 1965), p. 77.

Volkart and Michael, "Bereavement and Mental Health," in *Explorations in Social Psychiatry* (1957); also in *Identity*.

Wahl, "Suicide as a Magical Act," in *Clues*.

Wahl, "The Fear of Death," 22, *Bulletin of the Menninger Clinic*, 214 (1958), expanded version in *Meaning*; also in *Identity*.

Weisman and Hackett, "Predilection to Death," 23, *Psychosomatic Medicine*, 232 (1961); also in *Identity*.

Westie, "Toward Closer Relations Between Theory and Research: A Procedure and an Example," 22, *American Sociological Review*, 144 (1957).

"When Death Comes," *Newsweek* (December 9, 1968), p. 54.

Wills, "Undue Influence in Gifts to Testator's Attorney," 19, *American Law Reports*, 3d Series, 575 (1968).

Wunder, "My Most Unforgettable Character," *The Reader's Digest* (June, 1962), p. 83.

Yegge, "How Much 'Blood' May a Jury See?" *Insurance Law Journal*, 215 (1959).

Zinker and Fink, "The Possibility for Psychological Growth in a Dying Patient," 74, *Journal of General Psychology*, 185 (1966).

Index

Index

GLASSBORO STATE COLLEGE